Explore the World Using Protozoa

NSTA Web
Tim Weber, Webmaster
Printing and Production
Catherine Lorrain-Hale, Director
sciLINKS
Tyson Brown, Manager

National Science Teachers Association
Gerald F. Wheeler, Executive Director
David Beacom, Publisher

NSTA Press, NSTA Journals, and the NSTA Web site deliver high-quality resources for science educators.

Shirley Watt Ireton, Director
Beth Daniels, Managing Editor
Erin Miller, Associate Editor
Jessica Green, Assistant Editor
Anne Early, Editorial Assistant

Explore the World Using Protozoa
NSTA Stock Number: PB137X
ISBN 0-87355-159-1
Library of Congress Control Number: 96-71589
Copyright © 1997, 2000 by the National Science Teachers Association. All rights reserved.
07   06   05   5   4   3

For more information on the Society of Protozoologists, visit www.uga.edu/~protozoa/. Or contact: Society of Protozoologists, Lawrence, KS 66044-8897.

Explore the World Using Protozoa

Edited by
O. Roger Anderson
and
Marvin Druger

A joint publication of
National Science Teachers Association
and
Society of Protozoologists

Explore the World Using Protozoa

TABLE OF CONTENTS

Explore the World Using Protozoa brings you *sci*LINKS, a new project that blends the two main delivery systems for curriculum—books and telecommunications—into a dynamic new educational tool for children, their parents, and their teachers. *sci*LINKS links specific science content with instructionally-rich Internet resources. *sci*LINKS represents an enormous opportunity to create new pathways for learners, new opportunities for professional growth among teachers, and new modes of engagement for parents.

In this *sci*LINKed text, you will find an icon near several of the concepts you are studying. Under it, you will find the *sci*LINKS URL (http://www.scilinks.org/) and a code. Go to the *sci*LINKS Web site, sign in, type the code from your text, and you will receive a list of URLs that are selected by science educators. Sites are chosen for accurate and age-appropriate content and good pedagogy. The underlying database changes constantly, eliminating dead or revised sites or simply replacing them with better selections. The ink may dry on the page, but the science it describes will always be fresh. *sci*LINKS also ensures that the online content teachers count on remains available for the life of this text. The *sci*LINKS search team regularly reviews the materials to which this text points—revising the URLs as needed or replacing

Topic: biotic/abiotic factors
Go to: www.scilinks.org
Code: PROT01

Web pages that have disappeared with new pages. When you send your students to *sci*LINKS to use a code from this text, you can always count on good content being available.

The selection process involves four review stages:

1. First, a cadre of undergraduate science education majors searches the World Wide Web for interesting science resources. The undergraduates submit about 500 sites a week for consideration.

2. Next, packets of these Web pages are organized and sent to teacher-Webwatchers with expertise in given fields and grade levels. The teacher-Webwatchers can also submit Web pages that they have found on their own. The teachers pick the jewels from this selection and correlate them to the National Science Education Standards. These pages are submitted to the *sci*LINKS database.

3. Scientists review these correlated sites for accuracy.

4. Finally, NSTA staff approve the Web pages and edit the information provided for accuracy and consistent style.

Who pays for *sci*LINKS? *sci*LINKS is a free service for textbook and supplemental resource users, but obviously someone must pay for it. Participating publishers pay a fee to the National Science Teachers Association for each book that contains *sci*LINKS. The program is also supported by a grant from the National Aeronautics and Space Administration (NASA).

Acknowledgments

Explore the World Using Protozoa is a first-of-its-kind publication produced jointly by the National Science Teachers Association and the Society of Protozoologists. While O. Roger Anderson was president of the Society of Protozoologists in 1994, he wanted to find a way in which protozoa research could be used to help teach biology. At the same time, National Science Teachers Association President Marvin Druger wanted to find ways of getting leading-edge science into the hands of teachers in ways that would energize classes.

Their ideas bore fruit when the two long-time colleagues met at a professional gathering, where they decided that a book of hands-on protozoa investigations would combine their two societies' strengths. A call for contributions was issued in the Society of Protozoologists newsletter, and responses poured in from around the world.

While many people have contributed both directly and indirectly to *Explore the World Using Protozoa*, it is more than anything the product of that initial collaboration. The investigations presented here have undergone many revisions as a result of suggestions provided by science teachers at the secondary and undergraduate levels, as well as by protozoologists, project consultants, and NSTA staff. Special thanks must be given to the reviewers for their creativity and unceasing attention to the needs of students and teachers in the classroom: Tom Allen, Randolph High School, Randolph, New Jersey; Dr. James L. Wee, Department of Biological Sciences, Loyola University, New Orleans, Louisiana; Mary Hebrank, Duke Middle School, Durham, North Carolina; Frances Garvert, Bishop O'Connell High School, Arlington, Virginia; Dr. Mark Farmer, Center for Ultra Structural Research, University of Georgia, Athens, Georgia; Mary Coffin, East Syracuse-Minoa Central High School, Syracuse, New York; and Thomas B. Allen, A. Philip Randolph Campus High School, City University, New York, New York.

Many of the book's illustrations were drawn by David Hagen, Sergey Ivanov, and Alan Stonebraker. Brian Marquis designed the cover.

Introduction

Life is everywhere on Earth. Inside our homes we keep pets and grow plants on our window sills. Insects and other small animals often keep us company, whether we want them or not. Outside our "built environment," forests and fields are teeming with life, with a remarkable variety of small and large plants and animals. Some are easily visible; others we need a magnifying glass to see.

Microscopic life forms are everywhere on Earth as well. These small forms of life are usually single-celled organisms: protozoa and bacteria. Though both protozoa and bacteria are single-celled organisms, bacteria do not have some of the internal structures found in protozoa, such as nuclei and vacuoles.

There are nearly as many kinds of protozoa as there are plants and animals in the visible world that surrounds us. The evolutionary tree of life (Figure 1) shows where protozoa occur in relation to other forms of life. They occurred relatively early in evolution, soon after the bacteria. Though protozoa consist of only one cell, they are remarkably diverse in form and activity.

How can these remarkable protozoa carry out all the functions of life within the single cell that forms their body? If we think about our own bodies, we can identify activities that are characteristic of life. For example, we need to get food. Our food provides the energy for moving, growing, and maintaining our health. We digest our food to break it down into smaller particles, the products of the digested food distribute throughout our bodies to provide for our cells' energy. Through excretion we

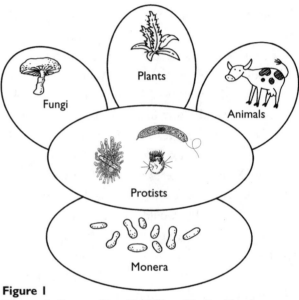

Figure 1
The evolutionary "tree" of life, with the kingdom Protista occupying a central position.

release indigestible matter from our bodies. Our nervous system and muscles allow us to respond to our environment and move about in our world. We reproduce, as must all forms of life.

Protozoa perform all of these activities within the small space of the single cell that forms their body. They have no nervous system or muscles, yet they respond and move in very complex ways. They also get food and energy, adjust to one another and survive in their environment.

There are three main groupings of these versatile protozoa, based largely on how they move. Some protozoa move by the beating action of very small hair-like projections on the surface of their body. These hair-like projections are called cilia, and we call these protozoa ciliates (Figure 2). Other

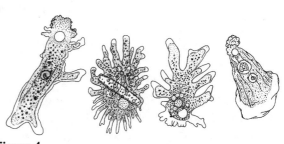

**Figure 4
Amoebae**

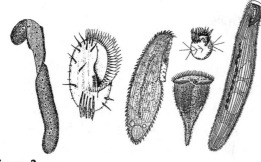

**Figure 2
Ciliates**

protozoa have one or more long whip-like projections, called flagella, that resemble tails. The beating motion of the flagella moves these protozoa—called flagellates—through water, much like the action of a fish's tail (Figure 3). Finally, some protozoa creep or crawl along surfaces in their environments. These are flattened protozoa that move by bulging outward along their edges and are called amoebae (Figure 4).

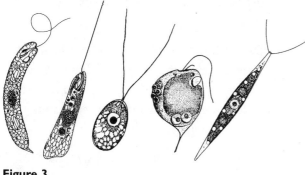

**Figure 3
Flagellates**

Why are protozoa important to us? The study of protozoa provides new ideas on how single cells live, reproduce, and adjust to their environment. Since all life is made up of cells, this information helps us understand how larger forms of life survive and maintain their health. Protozoa live in almost every environment—in soils, streams, ponds, and oceans. As they feed on other microscopic forms of life, they release nutrients into the environment needed by other living things. Therefore, protozoa are important in maintaining our world's food webs. They help maintain a healthy environment for other forms of life, including humans. Some protozoa are parasites—they invade other living things and cause diseases. A few disease-producing protozoa attack humans; others attack plants and animals we may use as food. It is important to know how to keep these protozoa from infecting humans and our food sources.

This book provides ideas for experiments with protozoa: how they eat, how they digest, how they jump, leap, creep, crawl, or swim. You will discover ways to study how protozoa react to their environment and how they reproduce. You'll explore their ecological contributions as you collect protozoa from soils, ponds, and streams near where you live. Once you begin exploring protozoa, you will probably think of more ways to study them beyond this book. These open avenues for our questions, our imagination, and our inventions lead us all into the excitement of science. We hope that you enjoy exploring the world of protozoa.

O. Roger Anderson and Marvin Druger

How to Use this Book

Explore the World Using Protozoa is designed to be easily used by educators on a number of different levels. Most importantly, its design lets you photocopy the sections you want students to benefit from, especially each investigation's student section. You can also photocopy the guidelines in the appendices for performing various laboratory procedures. This ability allows you to set up work stations in the laboratory for use by individuals or groups while attending to needs and questions as they arise at particular work stations. Students benefit not only by being able to work at various paces but also because science is fun, and therefore interesting, when it's done in groups. As you conduct several or all of the investigations offered here, you will no doubt want to experiment with different classroom and group dynamics, and *Explore the World Using Protozoa* is designed to afford you the greatest possible latitude.

Another important design element is found in the margins of both the student sections and teacher sections. Notes and guidelines pertain to each investigation's objective, materials and time management requirements, and preparation considerations—all in easy-to-understand, non-technical language. One primary purpose of this book is to use microscopic organisms to model macroscopic processes and systems, so each teacher section comes equipped with a "Micro-Macro Link" that suggests ways for you to extrapolate what students view through the microscope into their everyday field of vision. Finally, because the point of studying microscopic organisms isn't always readily

apparent to many, each student section comes furnished with a ready-made response to every student's most burning question: "So what?"

Organizationally, the book's investigations are grouped according to the broad scientific concepts and organizing principles they address. There are 28 investigations grouped among five sections, as outlined below.

- Section I, Protozoology Laboratory Skills, provides investigations that help students hone existing laboratory and microscope skills as well as acquire new ones.

- Section II, Comparative Physiology, enables you to model the fundamental life processes of many organisms, including humans, by using microorganisms.

- Section III, Interacting with Other Organisms, uses microorganisms to help teach about the interdependence of life on Earth, and how that interdependence is essential for maintaining healthy ecosystems.

- Section IV, Comparative Ecology, enables students to explore not only the varied habitats of protozoa—how they form communities and how they are distributed within those communities—but also how the ecology of microscopic communities compares and contrasts with the ecology of macroscopic communities.

- Section V, Adaptive Strategies, uses microorganisms as a tool for teaching how life on Earth adapts to changes in the environment.

- An extensive appendix section provides further details about making labware; caring for microscopes; and collecting, culturing, and maintaining microorganisms. The appendices also contain ready-to-photocopy student evaluation forms. Students can fill them out after they've completed an investigation, thus contributing to the evolution of your teaching dynamic. A bibliography of reference and resource materials is also provided.

Each of the 28 investigations has two distinct sections: a student section and a teacher section. As mentioned, the student sections are designed to be photocopied and handed out to individual students or to groups of students working together. Each student section begins with an easy-to-understand summation of the investigation's important concepts and objectives, and each ends with investigation-specific discussion and inquiry questions that help students think about the procedure they've just completed and what it means in terms of both scientific study and their own daily lives.

An important contribution to science education is found in each student section's procedures guidelines. Doing science in the laboratory means paying attention to details and doing things in order. It also means recording observations and compiling data for future analysis. All of the investigations in

Explore the World Using Protozoa were designed and tested by protozoologists and educators. Because of this, the procedures are much more than simple guidelines for doing lab work with high school or undergraduate students. They are state-of-the-art experiments made accessible for use not only in your science classroom or laboratory, but in the "outdoor classroom" as well. They use easily obtainable materials, and they provide step-by-step procedural guidelines that students can follow on their own. They also provide instructions for the proper use and care of laboratory instruments, for maintaining a safe and productive scientific environment, and for using microorganisms to explore our world.

Teacher sections provide more in-depth information about what is occurring in each investigation. Resources—such as further readings, points of departure for student research, and sources for biological supplies—are specified for each investigation. Adaptations and variations sections suggest methods for enhancing student interest, and provide extensions suitable for more advanced study, science fairs, and other competitions.

Each teacher section provides extensive recommendations for assessing and evaluating student performance. These recommendations take into consideration the *National Science Education Standards*, and are tailored to address the concepts of each investigation.

Explore the World Using Protozoa
and the National Science Education Standards

The *National Science Education Standards* identify specific areas of classroom activity that encourage and enable students to integrate skills and abilities with understanding.

To facilitate this understanding, an organizational matrix for *Explore the World Using Protozoa* appears on pages vii-x. The categories listed along the X-axis of the matrix (listed below) correspond to the categories of performing and understanding scientific activity identified as appropriate by the *Standards*.

• Subject Matter and Content—Specifies the scientific topics covered by each investigation.

• Scientific Inquiry—Identifies the primary processes of science employed by each investigation.

• Technology—Establishes a connection between the natural and designed worlds.

• Personal/Social Perspectives—Locates the topic covered by each investigation within an accessible framework.

• Historical Context—Portrays scientific activity as an ongoing human enterprise.

By encouraging students to organize and locate science content within an accessible framework, *Explore the World Using Protozoa* addresses the *National Science Education Standards'* call for making science something students do, not something that is done to students. The organizational matrix on the following pages provides a tool for helping teachers achieve this goal.

Investigation	Subject Matter and Content	Scientific Inquiry	Unifying Concepts and Processes
1.1	Developing and honing lab skills	Observing and comparing	Organisms share common attributes
1.2	Influences on ecological communities	Distinguishing and counting	Abundance and diversity
1.3	Preventing disease/monitoring health	Testing and analyzing	Organisms respond to chemicals
2.1	Organisms adapt to environments	Observing, identifying, comparing	Evolutionary adaptation
2.2	Ciliary action	Examining, comparing, discussing	All organisms exhibit motility
2.3	Flagellar action	Examining, comparing, discussing	Undulatory propulsion
2.4	Amoebic action	Examining, comparing, discussing	Motility and life stages
2.5	Avoiding predators	Observing, comparing, contrasting	Movement enhances survival
2.6	Ingestion, digestion, excretion	Identifying differences and similarities	All organisms require energy
2.7	Digestive diversity	Making connections	Specialization among diverse species
2.8	Ionic stimulation causes movement	Observing, comparing, contrasting	All life is made of protoplasm
3.1	Symbiotic relationships	Identifying, analyzing, comparing	Adaptation can be mutually beneficial
3.2	Parasitic relationships	Identifying advantages/disadvantages	Parasites derive nutrients from hosts
3.3	Adaptation through competition	Using math to analyze data	Adaptive species survive better

Investigation	Technology	Personal/Social Perspectives	Historical Context
1.1	Laboratory science	People have many similar life activities	
1.2		People impact a community's ecology	Human population growth
1.3	Medical science	Microbes can cause diseases	History of disease prevention
2.1	Form follows function	Humans' shape suits their environment	Forms of now-extinct species
2.2		Humans have cilia too	
2.3	Mechanical flagella enhance stability	Undulation can help swimmers	
2.4			Primordial organisms
2.5	Technology helps us survive in the wild	Humans avoid predation	
2.6			Single- to multicellular evolution
2.7		Humans ingest, digest, and excrete	
2.8		Ionic stimulation enables us to move	
3.1	Non-chemical pest control		
3.2	Combating microbe-borne diseases	Most societies no longer fear malaria	Disease prevention through medicine
3.3	Technology makes humans a top predator	Humans outcompete most species	Human evolution and adaptation

Investigation	Subject Matter and Content	Scientific Inquiry	Unifying Concepts and Processes
3.4	Responding to predation	Examining change	Adaptation enhances survival
4.1	Colonizing new and disrupted habitats	Analyzing change	Colonization results from disturbance
4.2	Succession of species	Identifying variables	Species gradually replace other species
4.3	Distribution patterns	Identifying and analyzing patterns	Nutrients affect population distribution
4.4	Net respiration and carbon budgets	Estimating	Biota contribute to global cycling
4.5	Community and population dynamics	Hypothesizing and extrapolating	Predation limits population growth
4.6	Natural gradients and species distribution	Analyzing, hypothesizing, discussing	Gradient means change over distance
4.7	Trophic levels and food webs	Testing, analyzing, hypothesizing	Contamination affects food webs
5.1	Sexual and asexual reproduction	Observing, comparing and contrasting	Reproduction strategies affect survival
5.2	Behavioral adaptations	Designing, observing, hypothesizing	Adaptation can be short-term
5.3	Physiological adaptations	Observing, analyzing, hypothesizing	Competition can lead to adaptation
5.4	Mixotrophism	Observing, analyzing, discussing	Feeding strategies affect survival
5.5	Life cycles and responding to stimuli	Describing, interpreting, discussing	Life strategies are adaptive responses
5.6	Locating nutrient sources	Observing, describing, contrasting	All life responds to external stimuli

Investigation	Technology	Personal/Social Perspectives	Historical Context
3.4			
4.1	Technology aided colonialism	Immigration and emigration	Colonialism affected native cultures
4.2	Hybridization and genetic engineering		Old-growth forests
4.3			
4.4		All life is interrelated	Environmental legislation
4.5	Technology aids the physically challenged		
4.6			
4.7	DDT and chemical pesticides	Biodiversity promotes ecological health	Rachel Carson's *Silent Spring*
5.1			
5.2	Helps meet environmental challenges		
5.3		Self defense	Societies rely on their food supply
5.4		Many humans are omnivores	
5.5		Growth and development	
5.6	Sensory mechanisms, like radar and sonar	Compensating for disabilities	Military history

1
Protozoology Lab Skills

There's an old saying about computer analysis: "Garbage in, garbage out." In other words, if the data used are bad then so are the results. The same also applies to working in a laboratory. If you can use a microscope properly, the chances are you'll obtain good results.

This section uses protozoa to help students either review lab skills they've already acquired or learn entirely new ones. As you lead students through these investigations, encourage them to observe and compare biological processes among the organisms. They will compare and contrast microorganisms, measure abundance and diversity, and acquire a technique for testing the susceptibility of microorganisms to chemicals. By acquiring these skills, students will feel comfortable with laboratory procedures. They will thus find their work more interesting, and develop confidence in their scientific abilities.

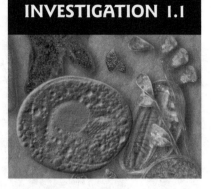
Observing and Comparing Microorganisms

So What?

You've got a lot in common with organisms you can't even see. You eat, move around, and interact with other organisms, such as your classmates. You also play a role in the ecology of your environment. As you conduct this investigation, keep a list of activities—like eating and moving—you share with the microorganisms you observe. You'll be surprised how alike you are!

We observe the life activities of plants and animals—how they eat, move around, and interact—all the time. But how do microorganisms that we can't see perform these same activities? Do all microorganisms perform these same kinds of activities? Do they perform them the same way? If there are differences, what do those differences tell us about an organism's role in an ecosystem?

To understand the different life activities among microorganisms, it helps to compare them with those of larger organisms you're familiar with, such as those shown in Figure 1. This comparison will also show the similarity between the ecological roles played by microscopic and macroscopic organisms. In this investigation you will first examine various microscopic protozoa, and then compare their activities and ecological roles with those of larger, macroscopic organisms.

Figure 1
The organisms in this woodland ecosystem play diverse, yet interactive, roles. Microorganisms play similar roles in their own microscopic ecosystems. As you conduct this investigation, compare the ecological roles of the protozoa you observe with those of the organisms in this figure. What similarities can you identify? What differences?

Procedure

1. Obtain the student worksheets for this investigation from your teacher: the Guide for Discovering Protists, the letter from the Micro-Macro Corporation, and a Protist Diversity Data Report. Write your group's name and the date on top of each.

2. Read the letter from the Micro-Macro Corporation. It will give you an idea of what you will be doing in this investigation. You will work in research groups, and prepare and examine wet mount slides of living protists. Before you begin, write down three things you should do to care for and properly use the lenses, mirrors, and diaphragms of your team's microscope in the space below.

   Lenses   Mirrors   Diaphragms

   1.

   2.

   3.

   Now prepare your microscope for use. *As you proceed, be careful not to leave your microscope unattended near the edge of the table. Clean the lens using lens paper only.*

3. Look at the fish tanks or culture jars in your classroom. Samples of protists have been taken, using long eye droppers, from different locations in them. The samples were scraped from the inner glass walls, taken off the bottom, withdrawn from the water column, and pulled out of the clear box filter. Now look at the collection of holding dishes. Each holding dish is labeled to show where the sample came from.

4. Bring a clean slide and cover slip to the holding dishes to make your slides. Place the clean slide, flat on the table, on a clean paper towel. Place a drop from each of the four different holding dishes onto the middle of your slide. Release each drop just above the slide and let it fall onto the slide. *Don't let the tip of the dropper touch the liquid on the slide.* Use a separate eyedropper for each holding dish, so that mixing occurs only on your slide and not in the holding dishes. Your slide will now contain a variety of protists.

   Place a drop of protozoan slowing agent on one side of the little pool of water you have created from the four drops. *Do not mix.* Gently lower a coverslip over the water and the slowing agent.

✔ Materials

- ❏ Compound microscope
- ❏ Slides, coverslips
- ❏ Small dishes
- ❏ Eyedroppers, 1 ml graduated pipets, or micropipets
- ❏ Electric light source
- ❏ Protozoan slowing agent
- ❏ Lens paper
- ❏ Colored markers or pencils
- ❏ Blank paper, pencil
- ❏ Scissors
- ❏ Student Worksheets
- ❏ Protists

1.1
INVESTIGATION

5. Keeping the slide flat, carefully carry it back to your group's research station and place it on the stage of your microscope. Position the little pool of mixed protozoans in the center of the stage so light passes up from the microscope's light source through the middle of your sample. Before you begin viewing, record the following:

What is the magnification of the ocular, or eyepiece?

How many objective lenses does your microscope have?

What magnification does each objective lens have? (low, med., high)

6. Locate a **field of view** with a variety of protists. Choose those protists that have been slowed down by the protozoan slowing agent. (The slowing agent contains methyl cellulose, which slows the protozoans down because it is thick like molasses and hard for them to swim through.) You may have to go to high power to see some of them clearly enough to draw them. As you observe, answer each of the following questions:

Did you find microscopic protists? Describe their colors. If they move, describe how. Look for hair-like appendages or other organelles you think might help a protist move.

What is the **total magnification** you are viewing with (total magnification = ocular x objective)?

low power _____ x   medium power _____ x   high power _____ x

7. Fill out the Protist Diversity Data Report handout. Using either 100x or 400x, draw and color at least two or more of the different types of protists you see in your sample. Draw a circle about the size of a silver dollar to represent your field of view. Draw the protozoa you see inside this circle, as shown in Figure 2. As you draw, try to include all of the internal parts, or organelles. You may want to try to duplicate the protists' color using the colored markers or pencils. Be sure to make a note of the magnification you used for each of your drawings.

8. At your research station, you have blank white paper and scissors. Draw larger versions of the two protists you find the most interesting. (The larger version should be drawn about the size of your microscope slide.) Color them, cut them out, and paste them onto the ecosystem chart your teacher has placed on the wall.

It is important for your group to decide ahead of time where to place your drawings on the ecosystem chart. Ask your classmates or

100x

400x

Figure 2
Draw a circle about the size of silver dollar under each of the Protist Drawing sections of the Protist Diversity Data Report to represent your field of view. Make sure to record the magnification you are using in the space provided. As you draw the protozoa you observe inside each circle, try to draw them to the same scale.

your teacher for suggestions if you are not clear. They should be placed to best represent the role or niche of the protist in comparison to the larger organism that appears on the chart. To decide where to place the cut-outs on the chart, compare the way the large and small organisms get food, what color they are, how or if they move, and any other criteria you think may be relevant. Try to place your drawing next to the macro-organism that has a similar ecological role in its own environment. For example, is it a producer or a primary consumer? Is it an herbivore or a carnivore?

Discussion and Inquiry

Protists belong to the Kingdom Protista. Most protists, including the Protozoa and Algae, are very small and many must be seen with a microscope. They are often found in bodies of water that receive direct sunlight. Some are autotrophic, which means they produce their own food through photosynthesis. Others are heterotrophic, which means they obtain their food by consuming organisms or organic matter. Here are some points for you to think about and discuss as your group conducts this investigation:

1. Appearance

   • What color are most autotrophic protists? How big are they in relation to your field of view?

   • What does a typical protist that obtains its nutrition by photosynthesis look like? What color would a protist be that functions like a plant? Why is the protist's color important in helping it produce its own food? What chemical is found in photosynthetic protists that helps them absorb or capture sunlight energy?

2. Movement

   • Why do different kinds of protists need to move? How do they move?

   • How does their size and color relate to how and why they move?

3. Nutrition

   • How do the protists obtain energy for their life processes?

   • How does the size and color of the protists you observed relate to how they obtain energy for their life processes?

   • Does their method of obtaining energy relate to where they were found in the tank? Considering their method of obtaining energy, where might these organisms be found in a pond or another natural body of water?

4. Environmental Factors

- What types of abiotic environmental factors are the protists you observed dependent on for their survival? What might happen to the entire protist community if they were deprived of their source of light?

5. Ecological Comparisons

- Do photosynthetic or autotrophic protists have any similarities with plants in an ecosystem you are familiar with?

- How do you think the more animal-like protists feed or obtain nutrition? Are the animal-like, or heterotrophic, protists dependant on the photosynthetic protists? How do the feeding relationships of the microscopic protists you observed relate to the feeding relationships you see on the macroscopic ecosystem wall poster? What might happen to the heterotrophic protists in your fish tank if the photosynthetic protists disappeared? What would happen to both the autotrophic and heterotrophic protists if the fish tank never received sunlight again?

- What life activities do macroscopic organisms have in common with microscopic protists? Are there any macroscopic organisms in the ecosystem that do the same thing? Do you think the two protists that your group is going to paste onto the chart are autotrophic or heterotrophic? Be ready to explain why you placed the two protists next to the different macroorganisms in the ecosystem.

6. Scientific Methodology

- Look at one of the protists you drew on the Protist Diversity Data Report. How long does this particular protist measure in length under low power? Even though the same exact protist appears much bigger under high power, does its actual size change when you switch from low to high power? How many millimeters in diameter is your low power field of vision? Medium power? High power?

- How many micrometers are there in a millimeter? How many microns in diameter is your low-power field of vision? Medium power? High power? How can you estimate the length in micrometers of the protists you observed? Does knowing the diameter of your field of vision provide an indication?

- Did anyone find Dr. Cabrera? Based on your observations, which type of protist might have posed a significant threat to Dr. Cabrera if she really were microscopic? Autotrophic or heterotrophic? Explain why?

MICRO-MACRO CORP. LTD.

FROM: Dr. Ver E. Small,
TO: The Biology Research Students
RE: Our records indicate that our model 2TNY2C microtizer is currently emitting a distress signal from your classroom.

Dear Biology Researchers,

Several months ago, our team of specialists developed the 2TNY2C. You may have seen some of our other microtizers at work in the movies *Innerspace* and *Fantastic Voyage*. Through an embarrassing mishap in our laboratory, our only 2TNY2C prototype disappeared with our lead biophysicist Dr. Joyce Cabrera. We would like her and the 2TNY2C back. For this reason, we are offering a reward for any information that leads to her recovery and the recovery of the 2TNY2C.

We think that the 2TNY2C may be in one of the fish tanks in your classroom. The 2TNY2C is often ingested by heterotrophic or autotrophic protists that can be found as part of the microscopic world of living things. These protozoa and algae, as they are sometimes called, are found throughout the world in all natural environments, especially in bodies of water that are exposed to sunlight and have an available source of atmospheric gases and minerals from the soil. Many protozoa depend on light to produce their own food through photosynthesis, while others eat such producers.

We have sent your teacher another microtizer and a protozoan identification booklet in advance. We suggest that one or more of you become microscopic and locate the 2TNY2C in person. *Warning: this procedure can be extremely dangerous.* Also, many protozoa are able to quickly reproduce by asexual reproduction and can be found in very high numbers in a very small area. Our last transmission from Dr. Cabrera reads: "See you soon! If all goes well, I'll be home in time for dinner."

The rest of the class can look for Dr. Cabrera, and get an idea of the diversity of microscopic living things by using their compound and high power binocular microscopes.

We feel we are very fortunate to have your class searching for the 2TNY2C because our information indicates you are exceptionally skilled at using the compound microscope, making wet mount slides, and measuring the size of microorganisms.

Good Luck,
Dr. Ver. E. Small, CEO
Education Director for Protozoa and Algae Divisions

*"At Micro-Macro we know a healthy and diverse macroworld
depends on a healthy and diverse microworld."*

1.1
INVESTIGATION

Protist Diversity Data Report

Name:
Date:
Class:
Period:

Provide a drawing and a description of any protozoa you observe. Be sure to indicate its color, its shape, how it moves, whether you think it is an autotroph, a heterotroph, or both, and approximately how many microns long it is. Also indicate the degree of magnification you used.

Protist Drawing: _____ x   Description:

Protist Drawing: _____ x   Description:

Protist Drawing: _____ x   Description:

Protist Drawing: _____ x   Description:

1.1
INVESTIGATION

Student Home Quiz

Name:
Date:
Class:
Period:

1. You've just landed on a barren, rocky planet and you need to radio back to Earth whether or not there is any life there. Name six or more life characteristics that the tiny, green, protist-appearing organisms at your feet must have to qualify as living.

2. After running exhaustive tests, you have determined that the little green things are indeed alive. But you also must inform Earth if they are cellular eukaryotes or not. Draw a typical cell with its organelles (internal structures), and label the organelles. Then list three basic organelles that you should be able to see with your space pocket-compound microscope, assuming they resemble single-celled protists you're familiar with back home. Remember to provide a description of how each organelle functions.

Observing and Comparing Microorganisms

Micro-Macro Link

What does a Paramecium's life process have in common with that of a butterfly? How does a Euglena's ecological role compare with that of a cat o' nine tails? What attributes do a Blepharisma and a student share? This investigation shows students how to address these and many other questions.

A variety of methods may be used to spark student interest. Science fiction is particularly effective because students like to have fun. You may want to initiate this investigation with a brief motivational tale.

Have a student read aloud the letter from Micro-Macro Corp. (page 7), or have several students read different portions of the letter. Next, ask for a volunteer from the class. This routine works best if you have planted a volunteer, providing instructions prior to class. The "volunteer" can raise their hand, jump out of their seat, and come to the front of the class to be shrunk down to microscopic size. Show the rest of the class the second microtizer, placed in a small petri dish—of course, it's 2TNY2C. The volunteer then leaves the room with both teacher and microtizer for a minute. Out of eyesight of the class, place a small ball bearing or a similar item in the petrie dish. Upon returning to the front of the class, ask for another volunteer to gently pour the first volunteer—who has been shrunken to microscopic size—into the fish tank from about a meter high. As the ball bearing falls into the tank, it will make a splashing noise, amusing even the most stoic student. Then proceed with the investigation, maintaining the fiction that the class is searching for the missing student—who is searching for the missing Dr. Cabrera.

This investigation enables students to discover and examine the diversity of microscopic organisms and their biological activities by comparing them with larger organisms they are already familiar with. Students will see the similarities between organisms large and small, but they will pick out differences as well. Many topics of biology become clearer when these kinds of comparisons are made.

To prepare the wall chart or poster, use an ecosystem with which students are familiar. (The woodland ecosystem depicted in Figure 1 is reproduced on page 11, and may be photocopied and enlarged for convenience.) Regardless of the ecosystem you choose to use, it should contain a variety of macroscopic plants and animals. You may want to add pictures cut from magazines or articles. Place the poster in full view of the class and put some glue or tape near it. After each student locates, identifies, and draws protozoans, the research groups may cut

To prepare the wall chart or poster illustration, use a recognizable ecosystem such as this woodland ecosystem. Your ecosystem should contain a variety of macroscopic plants and animals with which students are more or less familiar. Alternatively, enlarge this figure with a photocopy machine.

1.1
TEACHER SECTION

Time Management

This investigation works best if students familiarize themselves with their microscopes and observe and draw protist life processes one day, and then make comparisons between micro- and macro-organisms using the ecosystem poster the next.

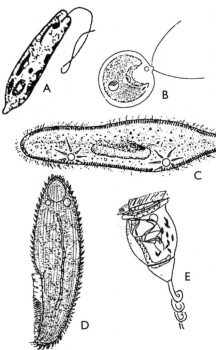

Figure 3
(A) *Euglena*, **(B)** *Chlamydomonas*,
(C) *Paramecium*, **(D)** *Blepharisma*,
and **(E)** *Vorticella*.

and paste the protist drawings onto the ecosystem poster in relation to the macroscopic organisms.

Living protists may be obtained directly from pond water, a pH balanced aquarium, or a biological supply company. The protists used for this investigation should include different types of autotrophic protists, such as large filamentous forms of green algae; flagellate cultures of *Euglena, Volvox,* and *Chlamydomonas;* photosynthetic protists, such as *Chlorella* and various diatoms; and heterotrophic protists, such as *Paramecium, Amoeba, Blepharisma, Didinium,* and *Vorticella.* Some of these protist species are depicted in Figure 3.

Students should be able to complete this investigation using only one prepared slide. Placing a wide variety and high density of protists on one slide gives students more time for viewing, scanning, focusing, describing, and drawing. It also reduces vibrations by decreasing movement around the classroom.

Adaptations and Variations

This investigation may be tailored to a variety of student group sizes. You may want to adapt student seating and materials placement accordingly. Larger student groups may need you to familiarize them with how to work cooperatively, both within their own groups and with other groups. Student groups that are able to perfect their observational, questioning, comparative, and data-collection skills are working together effectively.

◆

If time and resources allow, you may wish to have the students collect their own protozoa samples from different areas of a classroom aquarium, or from a nearby pond or lake. Have the students place their samples into beakers or flasks in a central classroom location. On each jar, students should clearly and accurately mark where the sample was taken from, or the location within the aquarium from which the sample was drawn.

◆

Chlorella (light green), diatoms (dark yellowish/brown spots), and other species may be found from scrapings on the inner glass surfaces. Amoebae, paramecia and other ciliates may be found in the upper 1–2 cm of the gravel. A variety of filamentous algae can be found floating among the other plankton. The aquarium's filter, if exposed to at least partial light, will accumulate higher levels of organic material and nitrates that will encourage rich colonies of blue-green algae and bacteria.

Assessment and Evaluation

Students should be made aware that how they work as members of a group will contribute to their evaluations. In this way, students may receive ongoing assessment throughout the duration of the investigation. Students may receive an individual as well as a group assessment, depending on how you organize them for this investigation.

Students should be able to estimate the actual size of the microscopic organisms they observe. If they know that the diameter of their field of vision under high power is 1.2 mm, for example, and it appears that about three protists stretched end-to-end would cross that entire diameter, then students should be able to work out an estimate of actual protist size in micrometers.

Another assessment and evaluation mechanism is provided by the Protist Diversity Data Report, on which students are required to draw and describe the protists they observe. The various portions of this investigation, such as how students work together and individually, the Protist Diversity Data Report, the Home Quiz, and the macro-ecosystem wall poster, may be weighted according to the needs of your particular learning environment.

About the Author

Thomas B. Allen teaches natural sciences at A. Philip Randolph Campus High School at the City University of New York. He designed this investigation to encourage students to discuss the ubiquitous nature of protozoans, to examine protozoan life processes, and to have students integrate their understanding of the "visible" living world into their observations of unknown microorganisms. Allen's use of this investigation shows that students enjoy participating in groups because it allows them to experience the support of their peers while generating questions and answers that expand their knowledge.

Resources

For distributors of protozoan slowing solutions and other biological supplies, see Appendix VI (pages 219–221).

Determining Abundance and Diversity

So What?

To understand the ecology of a community—how and why different organisms interact—you have to be able to count how many (abundance) and how many different kinds (diversity) of organisms live there. You can easily count the students in your community just by looking around. But how do you count the micro-organisms that live there as well?

SCiLINKS.
THE WORLD'S A CLICK AWAY
▼

Topic: biotic/abiotic factors
Go to: www.scilinks.org
Code: PROT01

The structure of an ecological community is influenced by abiotic and biotic factors. Abiotic means an ecosystem's non-biological elements, like temperature, light, and rainfall. Biotic means an ecosystem's biological elements, the organisms that live there. When scientists want to know what a food web looks like, and how its biotic elements influence the way that web is structured, they first consider the abundance and diversity of its biotic elements.

Abundance and diversity are terms used to quantify, or measure, an ecological community's biotic elements. Abundance refers to the number of individuals that live in a community, like how many trees or frogs or butterflies there are. Diversity refers to the number of species that inhabit a community, like how many different kinds of trees or frogs or butterflies there are.

Can you think of reasons why abundance and diversity might be important in a community made up of many different species? One reason abundance is important is that ecological communities can be heavily influenced by a single species. Such species are called dominant species, and they are dominant usually because they are the most abundant. Diversity is important because it improves an ecosystem's ability to regenerate after a disturbance.

In this investigation, you will use a standard method of separating protozoa from their environment. You will observe protozoan abundance and diversity, and acquire some basic skills for distinguishing between different protozoa species.

Procedure for Protozoa

1. Place 10–50 g of soil, at least 1 cm deep, in a petri dish.

2. Saturate the soils with distilled water, but don't flood them. Add water until 5–20 ml drain off when you gently press the soil with your finger. The run-off contains the protozoa.

3. To examine the protozoa, allow the run-off to settle in a container. Make a wet mount by pipetting a drop of the suspension on a glass slide and covering it with a coverslip. Samples of water taken from the suspension will contain many swimming protozoa.

4. If you have a centrifuge, concentrate the protozoa by gently sedimenting them in a conical centrifuge tube (centrifuge tube with a tapered end). The centrifuged sediment will be enriched in protozoa. Samples of this sediment can be observed as a wet mount.

   For larger protozoa, use a concave depression slide. Add enough protozoa suspension to fill the depression before adding a coverslip. Examine slides first with low power and then high power.

5. Examination schedule and usual succession of protozoa:

Days 2–3	Small flagellates and some ciliates
Days 5–6	Small ciliates and those with walking cilia on the under surface (hypotrich ciliates)
Days 8–10	Hypotrich ciliates, testacea (shelled amoebae)
Days 15–20	Mainly testacea

6. Make some simple sketches of the protozoa you see in each dish. Try to identify as many species as you can. Be sure to label your drawing with the date the dish culture was begun and to indicate the degree of magnification you used.

7. Display your drawings in the classroom. Do they show the succession of organisms you observed over the time interval?

Procedure for Amoebae

1. Pour melted 2 percent agar into petri dish. Allow it to cool.

2. Using a flamed (sterilized) scalpel, cut a 1×4 cm rectangular trough out of the agar in the lower half of the dish. Make three circular wells, about 1 cm in diameter each, in a row in the upper half of the dish using a cork borer or piece of glass tubing (Figure 1). *Follow normal safety procedures when using the bunsen burners.*

3. Transfer several colonies of bacteria (using a transfer needle) from the agar slant into a small beaker containing about 10 ml of water.

1.2 Objective

To acquire tools for determining abundance and diversity, and to understand how abundance and diversity affect the structure of an ecological community.

✔ Materials

- ❏ Compound microscope
- ❏ Slides, coverslips
- ❏ Petri dishes, non-nutrient agar
- ❏ Lab glassware
- ❏ Cork borer, or short piece of glass tubing (about 1 cm diameter)
- ❏ Balance
- ❏ Bunsen burner
- ❏ "Hockey stick" spreader
- ❏ Bacterial transfer needle, or inoculation loop
- ❏ Soil collected from top 3–5 cm from different sites
- ❏ Culture: *Klebsiella*, or a soil bacterium, on agar slant in capped test tube

Stir to make a suspension.

4. Transfer a drop of the suspension onto the agar and spread it evenly with the "hockey stick" spreader. (An inoculation loop may be used if used gently. Follow your teacher's instructions for preparing a "hockey stick" spreader or an inoculation loop.)

5. Add soil to wells and moisten with water. *Do not overflow.*

6. On days 4–6, use low-power objective *without* an added coverslip to examine for amoebae migrating out of wells. Add a drop of water to areas where there are amoebae, and gently stir with the tip of the "hockey stick" spreader. Draw the amoebae into a pipette and make a wet mount as described in Procedure for Protozoa Step 3, above.

7. Follow the same examination schedule as described in Procedure for Protozoa Step 5, and sketch amoeba species for display as described in Procedure for Protozoa Step 6.

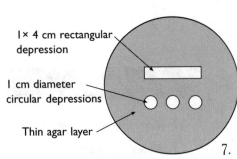

1 × 4 cm rectangular depression

1 cm diameter circular depressions

Thin agar layer

Figure 1
Agar surface in petri dish with depressions for adding soil to cultivate amoebae.

Discussion and Inquiry

- Based on the time required for your samples to peak in abundance, which species has the most rapid reproductive cycle?

- Which groups would be most likely to dominate when the environment has sudden spurts of food and favorable conditions?

- Which groups would be able to persist when food and resources are minimal, requiring lower growth rates?

- Estimate the abundance (average number of protozoa counted) in your microscopic field from each dish. Also estimate the diversity (number of different species of protozoa) you observe in the samples from each dish.

- What role does species abundance and diversity play in a food web?

- You probably noticed that some protozoa and amoeba species are able to breed faster than others, as well as exploit sudden bursts of nutrient resources. What macroorganisms in larger ecosystems are able to do the same thing? For example, what macroorganisms are fast breeding and exploit sudden bursts of resources in a grassland or forest ecosystem? What macroorganisms are more adapted to conserving resources and breeding more slowly?

Determining Abundance and Diversity

This investigation is designed to introduce students to two fundamental ecological tools—abundance and diversity. Abundance and diversity are described as tools because they are quantification mechanisms used by scientists as starting points for defining and measuring ecological concepts, especially dominance, succession, competition, and food web interactions. Abundance and diversity are two of the basic influences on the structure and dynamics of ecological communities.

The protozoa species in the first portion of this investigation have adapted to rapidly utilize resources. On average, they have higher metabolic rates and rapidly exploit sudden food abundances. They do not, however, have the capacity to survive long periods of diminished resources, tending to decline in abundance as resources wane. Figures 2 and 3 depict some of these early-appearing protozoans. Later-appearing species usually reproduce less rapidly, have lower metabolic rates, and conserve resources by growing slowly and storing food as carbohydrates or lipids in their cytoplasm. Such species can survive under less-than-perfect conditions, and tend to live longer. Among these latter species are the larger ciliates and the testate amoebae. Figures 4 and 5 depict some of these later-appearing protozoans.

During the first portion of this investigation, amoebae will sometimes be observed in the soil extraction procedure. To maintain an enriched sample of amoebae for the second portion, grow the amoebae on an agar surface in a petri dish. This will yield different results when students identify the succession of organisms.

Encourage students to estimate the abundance (average number of protozoa counted) in their microscopic field from each dish, and also the diversity (number of different kinds of protozoa) they observe in the samples from each dish. If time is too limited for individual students to

Micro-Macro Link

Abundance and diversity are two basic influences on the structure of an ecological community, and on the way the community functions. Abundance determines the total food and energy stored in living organisms; diversity may promote ecosystem stability.

SCILINKS.
THE WORLD'S A CLICK AWAY

Topic: protozoa
Go to: www.scilinks.org
Code: PROT02

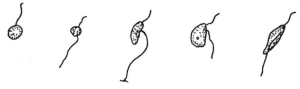

Figure 2
Flagellates: Distinguished by one or more flagella, usually one or more times their body length.

Figure 3
Amoebae: Triangulate to trapezoidal in shape, amoebae live mostly in soil and aquatic environments.

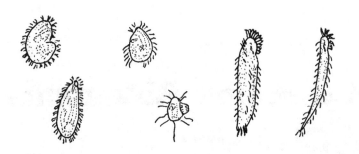

Figure 4
Ciliates: Distinguished by numerous, usually short cilia in longitudinal rows along the body, or grouped near the mouth.

Figure 5
Testacea: Oval to oblong in shape, testate amoebae can survive in less-than-perfect conditions.

Time Management

The preparation for this investigation may be completed in about 45 minutes. About 30 minutes per class will be required for observation and note-taking every 3–7 days over a 20-day period, as outlined in Procedure Step 5.

examine each dish, you may want to establish working groups, with each group responsible for a different dish. Compile the groups' drawings into a composite diagram for display. The groups may also share their prepared slides with other groups.

Adaptations and Variations

To adapt this investigation for use in a single class period, begin moistening soil-containing petri dishes in advance. Prepare dishes at regular intervals before the class period: 15–20 days, 8–10 days, 5–6 days, and 2–3 days, respectively. Seal the dishes with plastic wrap to prevent excessive evaporation. Mark the starting date on the side of each dish with a permanent marker. Do not mark the lids, since they tend to become mixed up during observation. This preparation will provide dishes that have been cultivating for different lengths of time preceeding the class period. Students can sample each of the dishes and note the kinds of organisms in each dish in relation to time cultivated.

◆

A second set of cultures using litter (e.g., decomposed leaf and detrital litter from a woodland floor) will show more species than the soils. This is because there is more decomposition activity in the former.

◆

For more extended projects, students may suggest different ways of preparing the dishes, such as adding pollutants to some, or adding small amounts of nutrient powder (only the amount on the tip of a spatula to 100 ml water) before moistening the soil.

Assessment and Evaluation

The first organisms to appear will be tiny flagellates, which are distinguished from each other by their manner of locomotion—fast, slow, straightforward, in circles, wobbly, and so forth. Next will appear *Colpoda*, oval-shaped ciliates with an indented mouth on one side. Many subsequently appearing ciliates will be hypotrichs, distinguishable by their darting movement and characteristic of sometimes walking on surfaces. These hypotrichs display a large band of cilia (cirri) on their bottom surface and around their mouths at their anterior end.

The smaller flagellates and *Colpoda* are simpler in structure and spend much of their energy on reproduction, hence they may be compared to some insects and rodents, which reproduce prolifically and grow rapidly. Hypotrichs, on the other hand, are the most complex single-celled organisms, and spend much of their energy just maintaining their physiological functions. Because hypotrichs reproduce less frequently, they may be compared to elephants or antelopes, which produce only one offspring per year. Soil protozoa, like other soil microorganisms, may spend much of their lives in a dormant (encysted) state waiting for favorable conditions in order to become active.

Student abilities at drawing connections between what they are observing through the microscope and these kinds of larger, macroscopic processes provide an appropriate assessment mechanism. Equally appropriate is evaluating students' comprehension of how abundance and diversity inform ecological structure, and how both concepts underlie much ecological theory.

About the Author

Stuart Bamforth teaches biology at Tulane University in New Orleans, Louisiana. He designed this investigation to help students understand that protozoa promote nutrient recycling out of proportion to their numbers, and must be included in all studies of soils and waters. Protozoa also serve as bio-indicators of soil and water quality.

Resources

For distributors of biological supplies, see Appendix VI (pages 219–221).

Preparation Note

Procedures for preparing the "hockey stick" spreader appear in Appendix IV (pages 215–216).

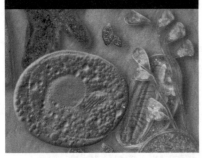

Testing for Chemical Susceptibility

So What?

Without methods for controlling microorganisms, our lives and the lives of other organisms are in jeopardy. This procedure will help you understand how scientists can determine the effectiveness of various chemicals for controlling microorganisms.

Figure 1
Naegleria fowleri **is a small species of amoeba that causes a fatal disease in humans called amoebic meningitis. It invades the brain by way of nasal mucosa and the olfactory nerve. (Shown here in flagellate stage.)**

Certain species of free-living amoebae, such as *Acanthamoeba* and *Naegleria* (Figure 1), live in large numbers in soil and water. Some cause disease, especially fatal meningoencephalitis, an infection of the meninges or linings of the brain, and amoebic ulcerative keratitis, an infection of the cornea of the eye suffered by contact lens wearers. Free-living amoebae generally are not harmful. Indeed, they are very beneficial in providing nutrients for other organisms and in helping to keep the environment healthy. They occur in ponds, lakes, streams, soil and the ocean. They are categorized as free-living since they are typically found dwelling in the natural environment. Parasitic amoebae must spend most of their active life living in the tissue of other organisms. It is important to develop ways to combat protozoa that are dangerous, disease-causing microbes. One way to control these pathogenic microbes is through chemicals. First, however, it is necessary to learn which microbes are susceptible to which chemicals.

Scientists have developed a simple test to determine how various drugs and chemicals combat free-living amoebae *in vitro*. The test gives vital clues about the amoebae's metabolism, which in turn provide a method for halting their growth and preventing disease. In this investigation you will learn how to perform this test and how to identify various chemicals' ability to halt the spread of microbe-borne diseases.

Procedure

1. Prepare a tissue culture flask that contains a medium of plate count broth. Inoculate amoebae into the medium. Add the amoebae using a sterilized pipette, as shown in Figure 2. Grow amoebae for 2–4 days, until they cover the bottom of the flask.

Figure 2
A tissue culture flask containing plate count broth. Add and remove the amoebae using a sterilized pipette as shown.

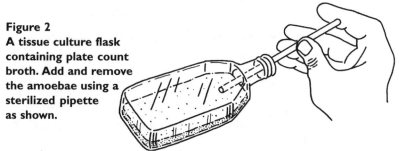

2. Remove the amoebae with pipette and make a wet mount. Use a compound microscope to observe their motility and state of health. Record your observations.

3. Make at least six different drug concentrations by adding different amounts of the growth medium to the drug. *Each concentration should be contained in a separate, labeled test tube!* Start with a dilution of 1:1, equal parts drug and growth medium. Then create a 1:2 solution by taking a portion out of the tube containing the diluted drug into a second test tube and adding an equal volume of the growth medium. This will dilute the drug by half again. Keep repeating this procedure until six dilutions have been produced.

4. Dispense 1 ml of each dilution into a separate well of your 24-well tissue culture plate.

5. Fill one of the wells with growth medium only. This will be your control. If you do not have tissue culture plates, dispense the drug-containing growth medium into small culture containers or even clean test tubes that can be closed with a cotton plug.

6. Take a suspension of the amoebae from the culture flask and use a hemacytometer to determine its concentration. Based on the concentration of amoebae in the culture medium, dilute to obtain a concentration of 1×10^5 amoebae/ml. For example, if you find there are 1×10^6 amoebae per ml, you would dilute it tenfold to get 1×10^5 amoebae per ml. Take 1 ml and add 9 ml of growth medium; this is a tenfold dilution.

7. Add 100 µl amoebae to each well in the culture plates, giving 1×10^4 amoeba per well.

8. Incubate the plate or culture container at 25°–30°C for seven days. Observe growth, morphology, and cell death at specific intervals—

✔ Materials

- ❑ Inverted microscope
- ❑ Slides, coverslips
- ❑ Eyepiece or whipple grid
- ❑ Aspirator
- ❑ 24-well tissue culture plates, or polystyrene tissue culture tubes (16×25 mm)
- ❑ Growth medium for amoebae
- ❑ Hemacytometer
- ❑ Pasteur pipets, or eyedroppers with narrow tips
- ❑ Sterile 1 ml, 5 ml, and 10 ml pipets
- ❑ Test drugs
- ❑ Incubators at 25°C, 30°C, and/or 35°C
- ❑ Test tubes
- ❑ Tissue culture dish or flasks
- ❑ Vacuum apparatus
- ❑ Student Data Sheet
- ❑ Cultures:
  Acanthamoeba polyphaga
  Naegleria gruberi
  Other non-pathogenic amoebae

9. To count the number of amoebae per well, use the whipple grid in the microscope ocular. If you do not have a whipple grid, take a small drop of the suspension from the well (culture container), make a wet mount and count the number of amoebae as viewed in at least 10–20 fields of the microscope. This will permit a relative count of the amoebae. The mean number of amoebae per field is determined. Carefully scan the wet mount to prevent overlap of the fields during counting.

10. The purpose of the remaining steps is to remove all the medium containing the drugs and replace it with fresh growth medium to see if the amoebae recover. Remove medium from the culture dishes using an aspirator.

11. Immediately add growth medium to all wells, and incubate at the same temperature used in Step 6.

12. Observe growth at specific intervals for seven days, as before. Look for recovery of growth and improved morphology. Make a cell count using the whipple grid or based on the number of amoebae per field of the microscope as described above.

Discussion and Inquiry

How strong is the evidence for a particular additive being anti-amoebic? For example, you have a control preparation. This is used as a comparison to validate that the drug in experimental treatments is indeed causing a certain effect. If the control cells are normal and the drug-treated cultures show debilitating effects, then we can conclude that there is evidence of anti-amoebal activity of the drug.

You should understand this design's logic, and the need for a control. If your data are sufficiently clear-cut, you should be able to rank the various drugs according to potency. The drug that caused the most destructive effect in the lowest concentration would be listed first, followed by the next most effective one, and so forth. What might the drug be doing physiologically to the cell? For example, it may inhibit respiration and deprive the cell of energy. Or some other major physiological process may be suppressed, perhaps by acting on an essential enzyme. In some cases, a drug may destroy essential membranous structures in the cell.

On a separate sheet of paper, use your observations from Step 2 and the data sheets to describe healthy ameoboid mobility. Use your observations from Step 8 and the data sheets to describe growth, morphology, and cell death over specific intervals. Lastly, describe any patterns you saw emerge from your two data sheets.

Note

Look for healthy amoebae, and describe them on the data sheet. Also look for amoebistatic (immobilizing) or amoebicidal (complete killing) activity, and describe this as well. Your description should include the amoebae's movement and appearance.

Name:
Date:
Class:

Dilution	Day 1	Day 3 or 4	Day 7
Control (growth medium only)			
1:1			
1:2			
1:3			
1:4			
1:5			
1:6			

Testing for Chemical Susceptibility

Micro-Macro Link

Testing the ways that living things, from micro to macro, respond to chemicals is a method for many sciences, especially in medicine and health. Ecology, for example, uses environmental monitoring to test for pollutants and toxic substances.

Time Management

This investigation may be completed in one class period, with 20-minute follow-up periods every two to three days over two weeks.

Teaching Note

Each student should receive two copies of the Student Data Sheet that appears on page 23. They should label one "Amoebae Activity Caused by Contaminants" and the other "Amoebae Activity After Contaminant Removal."

Most drugs or chemicals will only be amoebistatic, that is, the amoebae will recover when the chemical is removed and the new growth medium is added. Some chemicals will be amoebicidal, that is, they will kill the amoebae. A variety of chemicals can be tested, including some nonprescription drugs from the pharmacy, although they should be water-soluble. Some examples include: chlorhexidine, tincture of iodine, household bleach (sodium hypochlorite), and swimming-pool disinfectant (polyhexamethylene biquanine). These are all amoebicidal when tested in relatively low concentrations.

This investigation can be used to test pool disinfectant chemicals, clinical drugs, contact lens cleaners and solutions, eye drops, bactericidal soaps, disinfectants, and so forth. Take adequate precautions to protect students from excessive exposure to all microbial cultures. The students should not eat in the laboratory and a good disinfectant should be supplied, such as 70 percent ethanol, to wipe the work area. They should wash their hands after manipulating the amoeba cultures.

Adaptations and Variations

If you cannot use potentially pathogenic species in your teaching laboratory due to school restrictions, substitute any other small amoebae available from commercial supply companies. Or you can easily culture amoebae in the classroom following the procedure in Appendix II (pages 210–211).

Assessment and Evaluation

If students fully understand the logic of the experiment, they should be able to judge how good the evidence is to support a conclusion that a drug is active against amoebae. For example if given a chart showing the drug added as a row entry and with two columns labelled "1. Experimental Treatment" and "2. Control," students should be able to assess which drugs were effective. If a control and experimental treatment have the same effects (e.g., cells shriveled and not moving), then students should conclude there is no evidence that the drug was effective. Also, if the concentration of the drug is cited in the row label, students should be able to describe which of the drugs was most potent.

It is important for students to understand that drugs against amoebae and other parasites must be effective against the pathogen and not cause significant harm to the patient. Students should be able to discuss why certain drugs might be effective in killing a microbe while not harming the patient. This includes drugs that specifically inhibit physiological processes of the parasite, but that have little or no effect on the human host. In some cases, this can be explained as a specific effect of the drug on an enzyme or enzymes of the parasite that are unique to it. Since these enzymes are not present in the human host, the drug may cause little or no harm to the host.

About the Authors

Deborah Place is a microbiologist who has worked with free-living amoebae for nearly a decade. Dr. Stephen Allen teaches Pathology and Laboratory Medicine, and is the Director of the Division of Clinical Microbiology, at the Indiana University School of Medicine. Although pathogenic amoebae were discovered in 1958, no satisfactory treatment exists for the diseases they cause, nor any standard assay for testing amoebal susceptibility to various chemicals or drugs. The assay in this investigation provides a simple, reproducible method for determining amoebal response to chemicals or antimicrobials in a broth system.

Resources

For distributors of amoebae growth mediums, such as Plate Count Broth (PCB), and other biological supplies, see Appendix VI (pages 219–221).

Small plastic transfer pipettes can be purchased that have markings in 100 µl divisions (100 µl = 0.1 ml).

Teaching Note

Healthy ameobae are surrounded by a thin, smooth cell membrane and move by a crawling motion either flowing forward in a gliding motion, or by protruding a bulge or finger-like pseudopodium that extends from the anterior margin of the amoeba.

The amoebae will cease to move, perhaps become rounded when immobilized, and when killed may be shriveled and granular in appearance.

2
Comparative Physiology

When studying microscopic organisms, a common reaction among students is to ask, "What has this got to do with me?" It's a good question because, at first glance, protozoa have little to do with human beings.

But all the fundamental life processes we observe in macroscopic organisms, including humans, also occur in microorganisms. These processes include movement, ingestion and digestion of nutrients, excretion of waste matter, respiration, the maintenance of internal chemical concentrations, growth, and reproduction. This section explores some of the operating principles of cellular physiology and organismic biology using protozoa as model systems. The models provided by these investigations can easily be extrapolated to encompass the life processes of more complex organisms, and they can also be used to explore broader domains of both biology and physiology.

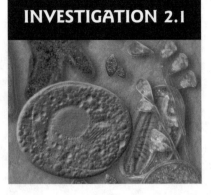

Morphology and Natural Habitats

So What?

There is a direct connection between how an organism is physically shaped and how its natural habitat is physically shaped. Why are giraffes so tall? Why is a mouse so small? Why do some insects crawl? Can you think of a reason at all?

All organisms have physically adapted to their natural habitats. This means that there is a relationship between an organism's morphology—its physical shape—and the structure of its natural habitat. Adaptation doesn't happen overnight, but can take thousands, even millions, of years. Can you think of any examples of the relationship between how an organism is shaped and where it lives?

Without the physical adaptation of organisms to their natural habitats, many places in the world might be altogether lifeless. But hardly any place on Earth is completely without some form of life. In fact, many habitats where you might not think any organism could live are teeming with life. Some protozoa, as well as other single-celled microorganisms, live in thick mud and fine sand, habitats where multicellular plants and animals are relatively rare. In fact, though, these two habitats support an abundance of biologically diverse microorganisms.

In this investigation, you will examine how certain microorganisms have physically adapted to the habitats of thick mud and fine sand.

Procedure

1. Look at the mud and sand samples with a hand lens. Is there variation between the species you observe between the grains or particles?

2. Using an eyedropper, place a drop of the water from one of the trays onto a microscope slide.

3. Using forceps, lift a coverslip from the lens paper and place it face down on the drop of water to make a wet mount slide.

4. Carefully place your wet mount slide onto the microscope's viewing stage. Using the contrast enhancement—ideally phase contrast, otherwise close condenser iris or lower condenser—adjust the focus knob until you are able to view microscopic organisms.

5. Using the Protozoa Identification Sheet, identify as many different kinds of protozoa as you can. How many different species of protozoa do you recognize?

Discussion and Inquiry

The protozoa you examined in this investigation provide an interesting example of the way organisms physically adapt to their natural habitats. Address the following questions:

- How does the morphology of the protozoa you've observed help them survive in thick mud and fine sand?

- Considering how various protozoa species are shaped, can you guess what the likely shape and size might be of the spaces found in the mud and sand samples in this investigation? Which of the organisms observed in those samples are most likely to be adapted to small-diameter spaces? Which organisms would be likely to live in very narrow, tunnel-like spaces with microscopic dimensions?

- What might be a highly adaptive shape for an organism occupying such a habitat? Can you think of any possible adaptations that might make the organisms you've observed even more suitable to their habitats?

2.1 Objective

To understand how protozoan morphology relates to habitat structure.

✔ Materials

- ❏ Compound microscope, phase contrast optics desirable
- ❏ Hand lens
- ❏ Slides, No. 2 coverslips
- ❏ Shallow plastic trays, about 30×20×5 cm
- ❏ Plastic wrap
- ❏ Tissues, eyedroppers, and forceps
- ❏ Thick mud or fine sand
- ❏ Protozoa Identification Sheet

Protozoa Identification Sheet

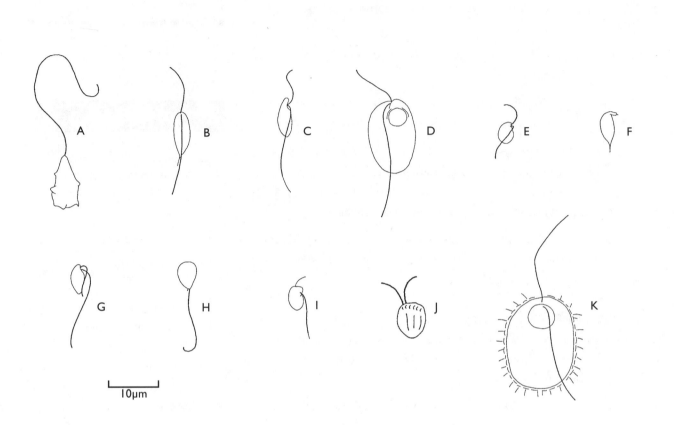

10μm

(A) *Mastigamoeba*, from organically enriched and oxygen-depleted sites. They have a very long flagellum that beats slowly, moving its amoeboid body through aquatic habitats; marine, and freshwater.

(B) *Cercomonas*, two flagella. The anterior one beats side to side, with a pliable body to facilitate movement through aquatic habitats.

(C) *Bodo designis*, two flagella with trailing flagellum; freshwater and marine habitats.

(D) *Protaspis*, a gliding flagellate with two, subapic flagella; its body may be ventrally grooved, and it may produce pseudopodia to ingest food from its aquatic habitats.

(E) *Heteromita*, gliding flagellate with anterior flagellum having a to-and-fro motion, body may be plastic, almost amoeboid at the front end; freshwater.

(F) *Amastigomonas*, a gliding flagellate with short anterior flagellum largely covered by a sheath; recurrent flagellum usually hidden under cell, sometimes with trailing strands of cytoplasm; marine and freshwater.

(G) *Bodo saltans*, attached by posterior flagellum to the substrate, anterior flagellum also flexed backwards and used to propel water toward the cell, with characteristic jumping or kicking motion, freshwater.

(H) *Metromonas*, attached or gliding flagellate, body tapered posteriorly, usually with one flagellum but very short second flagellum sometimes present, usually found attached and moving in a swinging motion; marine only.

(I) *Ancyromonas*, gliding flagellate, body inflexible, anterior flagellum very thin and may not be seen; freshwater and marine.

(J) *Goniomonas*, small flattened cells swimming along the surface of the substrate, two flagella emerge near one anterior corner of the cell, marine and freshwater.

(K) *Thaumatomastix*, gliding flagellate with two flagella inserting ventrally and slightly subapically, cell with scales and spines; marine and freshwater.

National Science Teachers Association

Protozoa Identification Sheet

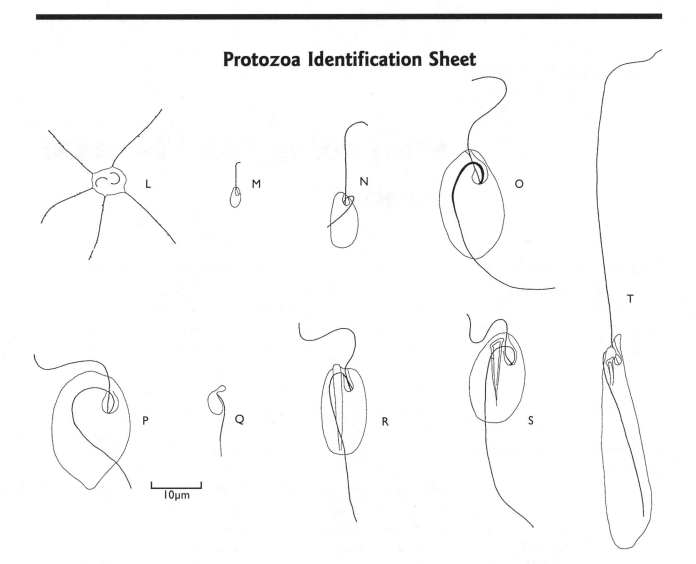

(L) *Massisteria*, sessile form with two short flagella and several pseudopodia; marine only.

(M) *Petalomonas*, small rigid gliding euglenid, with one (anterior) emergent flagellum arising from a flagellar pocket, flagellum usually not undulating and pointing in direction of motion; marine and freshwater.

(N) *Notosolenus*, a rigid gliding euglenid with two flagella inserting into a flagellar pocket; anterior flagellum doesn't usually beat but projects directly in front of cell; aquatic habitats.

(O) *Anisonema*, gliding euglenid, two flagella arise from a flagellar pocket, the trailing flagellum is very thick and follows a long curve after emerging from the flagellar pocket, the posterior flagellum can bend rapidly causing the cell to jump backwards, body rigid and may be grooved, no visible ingestion apparatus; marine and freshwater.

(P) *Metanema*, gliding and swimming metabolic (squirming) euglenids, two flagella emerging from a flaggelar pocket, typically with spiral markings, no ingestion apparatus; mostly marine habitats.

(Q) *Rhynchomonas*, gliding cell with bulbous snout and acronematic trailing flagellum; marine and freshwater.

(R) *Entosiphon*, gliding euglenid, with two flagella arising from a flagellar pocket, rigid body with longitudinal grooves, large protrusible ingestion apparatus; freshwater.

(S) *Ploeotia*, gliding euglenid with two flagella arising from a flagellar pocket, rigid body often flattened, and may be sculpted with ridges and grooves, non-protrusible ingestion apparatus; marine.

(T) *Peranema*, gliding euglenid, with two flagella emerging from a flagellar pocket, anterior flagellum very obvious extending in front of the cell, recurrent flagellum may be very hard to see and may adhere to cell surface, with ingestion apparatus and spirally-marked cell surface, metabolic; marine and freshwater.

Morphology and Natural Habitats

Micro-Macro Link

Over time, all organisms have physically adapted to their natural habitats, a major reason for Earth's biological diversity.

Time Management

If samples are prepared in advance, this investigation may be completed in a single class period.

Topic: autotrophic/heterotrophic
Go to: www.scilinks.org
Code: PROT03

A casual human observer might consider some habitats, such as the thick muds and fine sands used in this investigation, as being inhospitable to sustaining any forms of life. But thick muds and fine sands literally teem with a diversity of organisms. This is because protozoa, like all organisms, have physically adapted to their habitats. This investigation uses microorganisms to model a primary theme of evolutionary biology, that there is a direct relationship between an organism's morphology and the physical structure of its habitat (Figure 1).

Protozoa occupy an important ecological niche. The phrase "ecological niche" refers to the functional role of a species in an ecological community, including its activities and relationships to other species. Although individual protozoa are microscopic in size, the role of entire protozoan communities is significant to how an ecosystem functions. Autotrophic and heterotrophic protozoa, for example, provide a source of energy for other organisms, and protozoan inter-actions with communities of bacteria release chemical compounds into soils that help sustain plant life. In this way, microscopic aquatic and

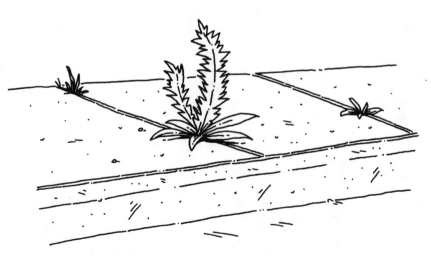

Figure 1
All organisms have evolved to suit their natural habitats, a fundamental reason for Earth's teeming biological diversity.

terrestrial protozoa contribute to the flow of energy throughout entire food webs. The procedure used here can provide a wide array of organisms. Students will identify algae, bacteria, and protozoa. By highlighting the diversity of microorganisms found in these two habitats, this investigation helps students appreciate the ecological contribution of microbial communities in those environments.

If you are collecting and preparing samples before class, you may find the most suitable muds and sands among intertidal and submerged sites. You may want to prepare and view a slide from your samples beforehand to ensure that students have something to see during the investigation. If possible, allow students to collect the mud and sand themselves. Photos or video of the collection sites will give students a better sense of the living conditions of the protozoa they are investigating.

Procedural steps for sample collection and preparation are as follows:

1. Two to three days before the investigation, collect samples of thick mud or fine sand that is wet at all times—usually with less than 30 cm of overlying water. Place the samples in a bucket and return to laboratory.

2. Sieve the samples through a flour or other kitchen sieve onto the shallow trays.

3. Leave for six hours and remove any overlying water until the samples are moist on the surface, and water is present only at their margins. Retain the overlying water for use during the investigation.

4. Place lens tissue directly upon the samples, and place coverslips directly upon the lens tissue, as shown in Figure 2. Communities of microorganisms will move upward toward the surface as their oxygen becomes depleted. After approximately 48 hours, the coverslips will be ready for harvesting. If a sample turns black beneath the lens tissue, it has been left too long.

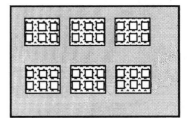

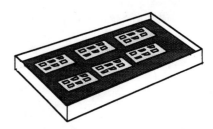

Figure 2
The rectangular tray is filled with mud, lens tissue is placed on top of the mud, and glass coverslips placed on top of the tissue. Protozoa will migrate up from the mud, through the tissue, and onto the under-surface of the coverslips as their oxygen becomes depleted.

Some sample collection sites will yield more organisms than others, and experience will guarantee a good yield of diverse microorganisms, providing students with examples of many types of microbes. You may want to view samples collected from a site beforehand to ensure that student energies will be productive once the investigation begins. If appropriate, share this preparation procedure with students.

Adaptations and Variations

If time and resources allow, you may want to organize a field trip so students can collect their own samples for observation and study.

Identify several potential sites for collecting thick mud and fine sand beforehand. By involving them in sample collection, you will provide your students with a more complete picture of scientific activity by linking field and lab skills. However, while it can also be fun for students to play in mud and sand, check with school authorities to identify any potential restrictions before engaging in such an activity. If a field trip is desirable and possible, incorporate the procedural steps listed in the Teacher section with those in the Student section.

Assessment and Evaluation

Students should understand that there is a relationship between an organism's physical form and that of its natural habitat. They should be able to respond to Discussion and Inquiry questions about the likely shape and size of the sediment spaces, for example, by comparing the protozoa's shape to that of its habitat, which is a series of inter-connected channels and dead-ends of varying widths and lengths. They should also note that this particular habitat's shape often changes from such forces as wind and rain, and the protozoa's physical structure must enable it to adapt.

Regarding highly adaptive shapes in soil habitats, students might respond that organisms must be able to move freely in tight spaces, and so would likely have small and highly flexible bodies. But, since moving through such spaces could require displacing particles, organisms would have to have enough mass to do so. Movement through soil substrates would require some form of adhesion, so locomotor organelles would reflect this. The organisms most likely to be adapted to spaces with microscopic dimensions would include hypotrich ciliates, euglenids, and both shelled and naked amoebae.

About the Author

D.J. Patterson is Head of the School of Biological Sciences at the University of Sydney in Australia. He carries out research on the evolution and taxonomy of protozoa, and is currently researching areas involving biogeography.

Resources

Patterson, D. J. 1992. *Free-living Freshwater Protozoa. A Colour Guide*. Wolfe Publishing, Ltd. (Illustrated by S. Hedley).

How Ciliates Move

Cilia are small hair-like structures extending from the cell body. They provide the main means for movement for many types of protozoa. Protozoa can also use cilia to collect food. Protozoa with cilia are grouped, or classified, as ciliates. Most ciliated protozoa, such as those in Figure 1, use cilia for swimming. Other ciliated protozoa, such as the *Vorticella* in Figure 2, use cilia to create a current in the water around it, which washes food particles towards the *Vorticella* so it can feed.

So What?

Most animal species, including humans, have cilia. You have cilia around your eyes, in your esophagus, and inside your lungs, among other places. As you conduct this investigation, think of similarities between how your cilia help you and how the protozoans you observe are helped by their own cilia.

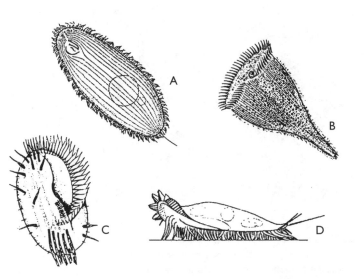

Figure 1
(A) *Tetrahymena,* **(B)** *Stentor,* **(C)** *Euplotes,* **(D)** *Stylonichia,* and **(E)** *Spirostomum.* These ciliated protozoa use their cilia for swimming through aquatic environments.

Figure 2
Vorticella in its extended position. It has no body cilia, but the cilia around its mouth are used to create a current in the water that washes food particles toward it so it can feed.

2.2 Objective

To understand how ciliated protozoa move, and how that movement helps them survive.

Ciliary action is fundamental to most multicellular animals as well. Cilia on the surface of flatworms, for example, help them move through their environments. Flatworms also have cilia in their excretory systems, where ciliary beating action helps them expel wastes. Cilia are known to occur on the specialized tissues of more complex organisms, such as those in Figure 3, where movement of fluids is required. The respiratory tract of multi-celled organisms, including humans, contain cilia. Can you think of ways that cilia in your esophagus might benefit you?

In this investigation you will examine the action of cilia among a variety of protozoan species that exhibit varying forms of gliding and darting motion. You will compare the function of cilia in these protozoans to the function of cilia in more slow-moving protozoans like *Vorticella*. You will also compare the ciliary action among microorganisms with ciliary action among macroscopic organisms.

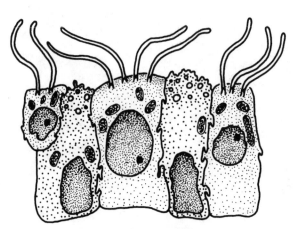

Figure 3
Cilia occur on the specialized tissues of more complex organisms where movement of fluids is required, such as the esophagus of multi-celled organisms like humans.

Procedure

1. Place a drop of a ciliate culture on a glass slide—begin with *Blepharisma*—and add a drop of protozoan slowing solution. Apply a coverslip and observe the ciliate, first with low- and then high-power lenses. Watch out also for smaller ciliates that may be darting about among the larger ciliates in the culture.

2. Use high power to examine the cilia, the many fine, hair-like projections on the surface of their bodies. Notice the cilia aren't all equal in length. *Blepharisma* will have a row of longer cilia near the front. These cilia are called membranelles since their coordinated action resembles a thin membrane.

3. Carefully watch the motion of the cilia. Reduce the size of the diaphragm in the substage condenser of your microscope to see them clearly. Do they move independently from one another, or is there coordination to their motion? How would you describe the pattern of movement you see them making?

4. Prepare another slide with a drop of the ciliate, and add some carmine powder suspension using the tip of a microspatula. Alternatively, add a small drop of India ink using an eyedropper. These additions will provide small particles that are moved by the beating action of the cilia. You should be able to see the motion of the water near the cilia.

5. Add a coverslip and observe under low power. Watch the flow of the suspended particles carefully to deduce the patterns of water movement caused by the cilia.

6. Examine more closely at high power. If the ciliate changes direction (turning right or left, or especially when it reverses direction), how does the flow of water change near the surface of the cell?

7. Repeat your observations in Steps 4–5 using other ciliates, especially *Stentor*. Use a large drop of water for *Stentor* or the coverslip may crush it. *Stentor* have many cilia at their anterior ends. Observe the streaming action of the water in the vicinity of these anterior cilia. Are there differences in the pattern of streaming for these ciliates compared to *Blepharisma* or *Spirostomum*?

8. Repeat your observations in Steps 4–5 using *Vorticella*. Notice that *Vorticella* have no body cilia, but they do have cilia attached to the anterior end of their stalk. Observe the streaming action of the water in the vicinity of these anterior cilia. Are there differences in the pattern of streaming for these ciliates compared to *Blepharisma* or *Spirostomum*?

✔ Materials

- ☐ Compound microscope
- ☐ Slides, coverslips
- ☐ Eyedroppers with rubber bulbs
- ☐ Microspatula
- ☐ Carmine dye, or bottled mineral water
- ☐ India ink
- ☐ Protozoan slowing solution
- ☐ Cultures:
  Blepharisma
  Spirostomum
  Stentor
  Vorticella

2.2
INVESTIGATION

Discussion and Inquiry

The beating action of cilia can be compared to the motion of the arms of a human swimmer. The swimmer's arms push water backward, and this propels them forward. To swim backward, the arms are used to propel water forward, thus reversing direction. A similar pattern of activity occurs with the numerous cilia on the body of a ciliate. Backward-thrusting motions of the cilia propel the ciliate forward, while a reversal of beating thrusts water forward to reverse the direction.

Explain how the ciliates you have been observing change their direction of swimming. Do they turn to the right, to the left, or both? Can they go backwards? Compare the action of cilia in ciliates to the action of cilia on the surface of flatworms, and to the action of cilia that line the human esophagus.

How Ciliates Move

One of the primary characteristics of life is motion. Most forms of life exhibit motion at some level. In some cases there is only movement of streaming cytoplasm within each cell. This occurs within some single-celled organisms, like algae and other non-swimming protozoa, and in some plant cells. Plants do move their organs—they bend toward light, for example—but usually at a rate that is very slow compared to that of animals. Ciliates include a broad class of many types of protozoa that move by the beating action of their many fine, hair-like cilia. The internal structure of cilia is similar to that of flagella, but they are shorter. Cilia usually occur in groups on the surface of the ciliate. Their rhythmic beating action can be fully appreciated when students realize that it is the result of numerous flickering surface cilia. Though *Blepharisma* and *Spirostomum* are relatively sedentary ciliates, adding a slowing agent may make it easier for students to track their movement.

Encourage students to discuss how the cilia cause the ciliate to move. Each individual cilium can be compared to an oar on a boat or arm of a swimmer. The beating action propels the ciliate through the water. The ciliary beating is remarkably coordinated and forms a rippling pattern on the surface of the cell. If the organism is attached to anything, like the way *Vorticella* uses its stalk to remain fixed in position, then the beating of the cilia causes streams of water to pass near its surface. This brings food particles and fresh supplies of water to the ciliate's vicinity. Encourage students to explore how the structure and activity of cilia at various locations on a ciliate's body support a particular function. For example, cilia distributed in bands along the surface of the body largely aid swimming. Cilia near the feeding groove, as in *Blepharisma*, wash food-laden currents of water into the ciliate's mouth.

This investigation is most productive if you obtain cultures of ciliates from a biological supply company so students can observe each species individually. If this is not possible, a mixed culture can be established by filling a 2 l jar with pond water. Add some dried hay to occupy about 1/4 of the volume of the jar. If the jar is started 1–2 weeks before the class session, a variety of ciliates should be available. Ciliates may be

Micro-Macro Link
Most living things move at some stage in their life, and even the smallest organisms have highly coordinated motile activities that enhance their survival.

Time Management
This investigation may be completed in one class period.

Figure 4
Blepharisma.

especially abundant near the decaying hay.

A culture of *Blepharisma* (Figure 4) is easily maintained. Place some pond water or bottled mineral water into a small container with a loose lid. Boil some kernels of dried wheat and add them to the container about 2–3 days before adding the *Blepharisma*. Pipet about 0.5 ml of the *Blepharisma* culture into the prepared culture dish. Place the dish in a dark and cool location. After about a week there should be a large population, and some will be decidedly larger than others with a pink pigmentation. These giant individuals are often gathered near the wheat grain, and they frequently contain large food vacuoles filled with prey. This stands out vividly when India ink is added as a contrasting background dye in a wet mount slide.

A suspension of carmine powder can be mixed by adding a small quantity of powder, using the tip of a dissecting needle, to a test tube half-filled with water. Shake the tube well to thoroughly disperse the powder. Prepare this suspension immediately before class so the particles are not completely dissolved. Check your supply of India ink to be certain it is in a water base and is not toxic to the ciliates. Otherwise, some very fine charcoal powder or carbon black can be suspended in water in place of India ink.

Adaptations and Variations

If you do not have a viscous slowing agent, the ciliate can be slowed down by placing a very thin wisp of cotton fibers on the slide before adding the drop of ciliate culture. Cotton is also useful in slowing down larger ciliates because they become trapped in the small spaces among the cotton fibers.

◆

If you have some vital stain solutions, such as methylene blue or neutral red (0.01 g per 100 ml water), students can stain the ciliates and observe internal structures such as the nucleus and some of the small vesicles and other organelles.

◆

In addition to ciliary motion, students should observe other forms of motion, such as twisting of the body, contraction, and bending that occurs in some species. *Spirostomum* and *Stentor* have contractile bodies. The stalk of *Vorticella* is also contractile.

◆

Provide diluted acid, such as lemon juice, and have students introduce a very small drop to one side of the coverslip. They will notice that the ciliates swim away from this noxious stimulus. This response is an excellent example of how movement supports survival by allowing the ciliate to swim toward favorable environments and escape life-threatening situations.

◆

This investigation may be successfully linked to Investigation 2.3, on the movement of flagella in protozoan flagellates.

Assessment and Evaluation

Students should be able to identify how the ciliary action promotes the ciliates' survival. This includes the act of simply moving through water, which increases the probability of finding food, of avoiding noxious stimuli, and of locomoting to regions where oxygen is more available. Cilia also wash food particles into the feeding canal of the protozoan.

A functional understanding of ciliary action should include the ability to explain how beating action causes swimming motions, both forward and backward. Students should be able to label a diagram of a ciliate with arrows to show which direction of beating causes a forward movement, and which direction causes a backward movement. A backward-directed stroke propels the ciliate forward, and a forward stroke propels the ciliate backward. All living organisms demonstrate some coordination of physiological activity to achieve a rapid and efficient response to the environment. How is there evidence of coordination in the motion of cilia? The body cilia move in a rhythmic way to create a uniform flow of water. They also work together in gathering food particles and in washing them into the mouth region of the ciliate.

Scientific explanations are generated by dialogue among scientists. Accepted principles and observations are derived by community consensus based on accepted evidence. Allow students to offer explanations for why both the cilia and the ciliates behave as they do. List student explanations on the chalkboard or overhead projector. Evaluate how well students are able to respectfully entertain the ideas of other students, even (or perhaps especially) ideas that diverge from or contradict their own. To what extent do students critically evaluate evidence in support of one explanation or another? Do they attempt to find common themes in apparently diverse explanations? Do they provide defensible explanations based on a group consensus of what the evidence actually shows? Can they accept the idea that a scientific explanation is the best we are able to construct based on the evidence available at a particular time?

Encourage students to discuss their observations, either as the class proceeds or near the end when sufficient observations of motion have been made. These types of group discussions offer an excellent opportunity to develop a more coherent student appreciation of how scientific explanations are created, and to help students develop skills in identifying and applying relevant sources of evidence in defending explanations.

About the Author

O. Roger Anderson is Professor of Natural Sciences at Columbia University Teachers College and Senior Research Scientist at Columbia University. This investigation provides a way to encourage students to realize that even the smallest forms of life have highly coordinated motile activities to enhance their survival and explore their environment.

Resources

For distributors of protozoan slowing solutions and other biological supplies, see Appendix VI (pages 219–221).

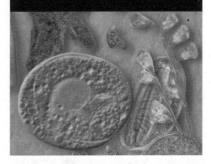

How Flagellates Move

Scientists studying protozoa have classified them according to how they move, or how they propel themselves through their environment. Protozoa with flagella are classified as *Mastigophora* and are refered to as flagellates. Flagella, as you will discover in this investigation, are long, whip-like appendages most often attached to or near the leading end of a protozoa's body (Figure 1). As you conduct this investigation, try to think of other types of organisms that use similar means of locomotion.

So What?

All living things move, even plants. The undulatory waves of the flagellates you observe in this investigation enable them to move somewhat as a snake does. Can you think of other organisms that move themselves the same way?

Figure 1
Flagella are long, whip-like appendages most often attached to or near the leading end of a protozoa's body. The flagellate depicted here is *Peranema trichophorum*.

2.3 Objective

To understand how a variety of different flagellates move.

✔ Materials

- ❏ Compound microscope, oil immersion objective preferable
- ❏ Slides, coverslips
- ❏ Two 2 l glass jars
- ❏ Eyedroppers with rubber bulbs
- ❏ Pond or stagnant water
- ❏ Sun-dried organic matter (hay or tall grass)
- ❏ Some dark, rich topsoil from garden or park
- ❏ 10 percent aqueous Nigrosin dye solution
- ❏ Carbon-black India ink
- ❏ Protozoan slowing solution
- ❏ Cultures:
  Euglena spirogyra
  Peranema
  Phacus
  Distigma
  Chlamydomonas
  Carteria

Procedure

1. Fill each of the 2 l glass jars about 3/4 full with pond or stagnant water. Add some sun-dried organic matter (e.g., dried leaves or grass) to one jar and about a 1/4 cup of rich soil to the other, as shown in Figure 2. Place the jars in a cool area with indirect sunlight for about one week.

Figure 2
Fill each of the 2 l glass jars about 3/4 full with pond or stagnant water. Add some sun-dried organic matter to one jar and about a 1/4 cup of rich soil to the other.

2. Take samples of the surface of the water using the eyedroppers, and make a wet mount slide. If you have some cultures from a biological supply house, also make some slides of each of these just before you are ready to examine them. If you choose, you can combine drops (one from each of several cultures) on a slide so you can compare different forms directly. If the protozoa move too rapidly, add some protozoan slowing solution and mix gently with a toothpick before adding the coverslip.

3. Using low magnification, look for spindle-shaped or nearly spherical protozoa moving slowly in the water. Some may be whirling and others spiralling as they swim. Place the microscope's condenser on low and close the diaphragm to get the best possible illumination.

4. Notice the protozoa that have fine, whip-like flagella extending from the surface. There may be one to several depending on the species. If necessary, add a small amount of India ink or Nigrosin stain to make the flagella stand out more clearly. They will appear

as long, undulating, bright, whip-like appendages moving against a dark background.

5. Examine your catch with a higher magnification, such as 40x objective, and observe the way the flagellates move. Look carefully at the color of the flagellates. What are the differences in the color? Are some colorless? If the flagellate is green, try to identify the plastids (small bodies containing the green pigment chlorophyll). How do these flagellates get energy? How do the colorless flagellates get energy? If you have an oil immersion lens, add a drop of immersion oil on the coverslip and rotate the lens into position to more clearly see the flagella.

6. Make another preparation using the Nigrosin stain, and allow it to dry. Mount under a coverslip for a more vivid view of the fixed and vivdly stained flagellum.

7. To find variations in the flagellate populations, choose several levels of the culture jars from which you will draw samples. Label the location—such as Near Top, Middle, and Bottom—on the outside of the jar. Then use the eyedroppers to draw the samples. Examine the flagellates under the microscope, then draw your observations. Below each drawing, record the magnification and the location it came from. Do flagellates from various locations move differently?

8. Compare the flagellates you find in the jar containing organic matter with the ones you find in the jar with soil. What do the flagellates look like that are in the very surface of the soil at the bottom of the jar?

9. Repeat Steps 2–8 each day for ten days. Continue to observe the changes in the population. Graph the changes on one axis and the time on the other.

10. Create a table of the data you collected during this 10-day period. For example, list Dates as row labels in your table. Make labels at the top of each column, such as Depth sampled, Color of flagellates, Number of swimming flagellates, and Number of non-swimming flagellates. If you are examining the protozoa on only one day, you can label the rows as Depth in the jar—Near Top, Middle, Bottom. Then use the entries in the columns to describe what you observe at each depth, color of flagellate, swimming or not, and so forth.

2.3
INVESTIGATION

Discussion and Inquiry

Draw the structures you observed in the flagellates, such as plastids, vacuoles (bubble-like bodies), and food reserve oil droplets or starch grains. As you draw, address the following questions:

- What is the function of each structure?

- What types of behaviors do the flagellates exhibit?

- Would other types of protozoa, such as those with cilia or pseudopods, exhibit the same or similar behavior?

- How do flagella affect the organisms' behavior?

- Based on your observations, do you think certain environments may be more conducive to flagellate populations?

Using the data table of flagellate movement you created in Step 10, can you find any patterns in your data? For example, are there more moving flagellates at one depth compared to another? Does the number of moving flagellatess vary from one day to another? What about the color of the flagellates? Do the flagellates near the top of the jar have a different color than those deeper down? How good are your data for answering these questions? Do you have enough data to answer all of them? Which questions do you think you can answer most confidently based on your current data?

How Flagellates Move

The locomotor organelles of protozoa are used to separate them into easily recognized groups, especially for ecological study. Protozoa with flagella are called flagellates, and those with cilia are called ciliates. Some protozoa move by extending pseudopodia as with the amoebae. Interestingly, some flagellates also have pseudopodia, and these are called amoebo-flagellates. They are common in soil water cultures. We now recognize that these broad groups (flagellates, ciliates, and amoebae) include organisms with very different evolutionary histories or phylogenies. Therefore, the grouping is not a phylogenetically natural one. Taken together the flagellates and ciliates have been included by some scientists into the larger group *Undulipodia*. Amoebae and related protozoa, that move by a creeping or crawling motion using pseudopodia, have been labeled sarcodines by some scientists, or *Pseudopodia* by others.

The taxonomy of protozoa is constantly changing as we learn more about them, and we need to remain flexible in our thinking about their higher level classification (above genera) until more complete data becomes available. In this investigation students focus on flagellate locomotory organelles that occur not only in protozoa but also in the specialized motility cells of plants and animals, including reproductive cells such as sperm.

Flagella are usually relatively long, and can be up to one or more times the length of a protozoan's entire body. They are most often attached to or located quite near the leading end of the body. Figure 3 shows examples of some common flagellates. As might be expected of locomotor organelles within the group *Udulipodia*, they cause motion through undulation in a variety of symmetrical and asymmetrical patterns. Encourage students to suggest similar ways that other organisms propel themselves in nature.

Adaptations and Variations

If you wish to involve students in the advance preparation for this investigation, have them assist in obtaining pond or stagnant water.

Micro-Macro Link

All organisms exhibit motility, whether bending toward a light source, finding a place to grow, or chasing prey. The movement of flagella, the motility organelles of protozoan flagellates, demonstrate some of the basic physiological ways in which organisms move.

Time Management

If cultures are grown about one week in advance, this investigation may be completed in about 40 minutes. For best results, this investigation should be done over several weeks, requiring one class period to begin and approximately 20 minutes each day for 10 days to complete.

2.3
TEACHER SECTION

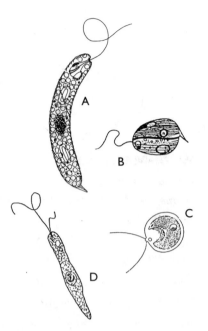

Figure 3
Examples of some common flagellates. (A) *Euglena spirogyra,*
(B) *Phacus,* **(C)** *Chlamydomonas,*
(D)*Distigma proteus.*

Water with a greenish-reddish color on its surface is the best source of flagellates. The water should be relatively uncontaminated, free of insecticides or detergents. The nutrient source, such as sun-dried straw, must be prepared one to two weeks prior to conducting the investigation.

◆

Students may wish to compare the results of jars supplied with dry straw or soil to those without it. They will need to prepare four jars, two with straw and two with soil, and if possible others without either hay or soil. Place half the jars with soil and with hay in darkness and the other half in diffuse light. This will allow comparison of the effects of light on the kinds of protozoa that grow up in soil or hay-enriched water. Consider breaking half the class into groups "with straw," "with soil" and "without added matter." Have students take samples of each type of jar at the same time over the ten days.

◆

This investigation may be success fully linked to Investigation 2.2, on the movement of cilia in protozoan ciliates.

◆

This investigation may also be successfully linked to Investigation 4.7, on the ecological effects of contaminants. If you have students use contaminants, such as insecticides and detergents, ensure that the substances used are handled properly under direct supervision. Contaminants can be added directly to the wet mount slide using a pipet, but they must be considerably diluted or they will kill the organisms before their effects may be observed.

Assessment and Evaluation

While this investigation follows a more or less standard observe-and-discuss format, it also provides an opportunity to generalize about locomotion in the context of evolutionary adaptation and the natural selection of species, among other unifying scientific principles. Have students demonstrate their understanding of such broader contexts as they answer Discussion and Inquiry questions as one means of assessment and evaluation.

This investigation allows students to develop skills in reflecting on the accuracy of data. How sufficient are the data to support a particular conclusion, and what additional data may be needed? In evaluating the success of their efforts, assess how critically students have made observations and how well they justify their conclusions. This is a good opportunity to encourage students to develop their own criteria for self-critical reflection. What ideals do they establish for becoming more critical and reflective scientists?

About the Author

O. Roger Anderson is Professor of Natural Sciences at Teachers College Columbia University. This investigation is a way to encourage students to think critically about the strengths and weaknesses of data. The protozoa are very useful since they are highly diverse and offer rich opportunities to make many different observations.

Resources

For distributors of biological supplies, see Appendix VI (pages 219–221).

How Amoebae Move

So What?

Some organisms adapt to environmental changes by changing their body structure.

When it rains, you wear a raincoat or use an umbrella. When it is sunny, you may wear shorts. Protozoa have also developed ways to adapt to unpredictable environments. The common amoeboid slime mold, *Physarum polycephalum*, has a particularly interesting adaptation method. Rather than adding garments, slime molds transform their entire physiological structure.

Slime molds live in cool, moist, shady places. They form a netlike structure on rotting leaves or decaying tree stumps and logs. Many are beautifully colored, ranging from brilliant yellows and oranges to deep blue, violet, or jet black. They are animal-like during most of their lives, engulfing food like an amoeba and then digesting it in food vacuoles. This is the plasmodium stage, during which the slime mold is a mass of cytoplasm. It requires relatively high humidity and a wet medium. If the environment begins to change for the worse, or if the slime mold is at a certain stage of development, it makes sporangia and spores. This is its reproductive stage. Figure 1 shows the life cycle of *Physarum polycephalum*.

If the environment dries slowly, however, the slime mold dries into what is called a sclerotium. The plasmodium begins to contract, and the cytoplasm divides into very small cysts. Each cyst forms a thin wall around itself, and the whole mass is enveloped by a crusty deposit holding the cysts together. When environmental conditions improve and sufficient moisture becomes available, the resting sclerotium becomes metabolically active, eventually protrudes outward at the periphery, and develops into a plasmodium again. During this investigation, you will work with both the plasmodial (motile) and sclerotium (encysted) stages of the slime mold.

**Figure 1
The life cycle of *Physarum polycephalum*.**

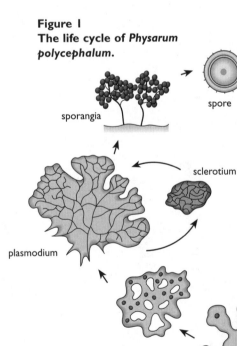

sporangia

spore

sclerotium

swarmers

plasmodium

Procedure

1. Cut some dried sclerotia into small sections using fine scissors, then moisten them with a few droplets of water. Using a blank sheet of paper, draw how the sclerotia appeared before and after they imbibed water. Take a small sample of the moistened sclerotium by dislodging it with a needle. Place it on a slide and make a wet mount. Gently disperse the sclerotium by pressing on the coverslip with a pencil eraser (see Steps 4–5). Alternatively, add some iodine as a stain instead of water before adding the coverslip.

2. Re-examine these cysts about 30 minutes later by making a wet mount (Steps 4–5).

3. To study motility, you will need to use a plasmodium on 9 cm diameter paper, set inside a sterile petri dish. Choose someone in your group to watch the time, and someone else to mark the plasmodium's position. Using a fine pencil, place a mark just at the side of the leading edge of one or more fans. Note the time. Place a small piece of rolled oat about 5 mm from the fan's edge. Every ten minutes, mark the new position of the fan's edge with a pencil, along with the time. Allow the plasmodium to move about for the duration of class.

4. To observe the non-motile stage, place a drop of pond or aged tap water on a glass slide. Use a dissecting needle to place some remaining pieces of the dried sclerotium in the water. Gently disperse the sclerotium by placing a coverslip over the preparation and pressing down lightly with the rubber end of a pencil. The sclerotium should be thinly smeared, so that light will pass through the sample. Note the many small spherical cysts released from the sclerotial mass. Each cyst is enclosed by a cell wall, which can be seen with a 40x objective. Record your observations.

5. Place a drop of methylene blue dye or other stain on one side of the coverslip. Use bibulous paper on the other side to draw it under the coverslip preparation. This will help you see the walls and internal contents of the cysts.

6. To observe the motile stage, obtain a sample of an active, feeding stage slime mold on a 9 cm diameter disc of filter paper. On your data sheet, draw its internal structural organization, as well as the yellowish fan-like leading edges that it may have developed. Label as many of the structures as you can.

7. Place a 4 cm diameter disc of filter paper on the bottom of a petri dish. Place a plasmodium on the filter paper, and a small piece of moistened oat just near the edge of the filter paper. The

2.4 Objective

To understand how the amoeba Physarum polycephalum *moves.*

✔ Materials

- ❑ Compound light microscope
- ❑ Slides, coverslips
- ❑ Fine scissors
- ❑ Petri dishes with covers, 9 cm
- ❑ Filter paper discs, 4 and 9 cm
- ❑ Pond or aged tap water
- ❑ Rolled dried oats
- ❑ Bibulous paper
- ❑ Blank paper, pencil
- ❑ Dried sclerotia of *Physarum polycephalum*

plasmodium will gradually move outward onto the clear surface of the petri dish over the next 24 hours. Observe the cytoplasmic streaming with a microscope under low power. Do not use a coverslip; it will destroy the specimen. Record your observations.

8. Before leaving class, calculate and record how rapidly your slime mold has moved. Do not remove the plasmodium from its petri dish. Use the data you collected every ten minutes, and add up the total distance traveled. Divide the total distance traveled in millimeters by the time in minutes:

_____ / _____ = _____
Total Distance   Total time   Rate of Travel

9. Gather stimuli you think the amoeba will be attracted to, and some you think it will avoid. (For example, a positive stimulus might be a potential food source. An aversive stimuli might be a piece of filter paper moistened with strong saline solution, or with an acid such as the acetic acid in vinegar.) Before you leave class, place the stimuli at different locations around the periphery of the culture dish.

10. Record the position of the plasmodium 24 hours after you placed stimuli close to it. Also, since the plasmodium leaves a thin translucent slime track behind when it advances, you should be able to see the different locations where the plasmodium has moved. If you are able to see the trail, record its pattern. Do not get the test stimuli directly onto the plasmodium. The underlying filter paper should be kept moist but not soggy.

Discussion and Inquiry

Address the following questions:

• Why does the sclerotium consist of numerous small cysts cemented together rather than as one large cyst?

• What advantage is there in having a cyst wall around each cyst instead of being simply embedded in a common cement?

• Why do you suppose the plasmodium forms a fan-like leading edge?

• The cytoplasm inside the small veins of the plasmodium flows in a reversible pulsating pattern, streaming forward and backward repeatedly. How does this streaming mechanism allow the plasmodium to move forward toward attractants and move backward away from harmful stimuli?

• What is the possible mechanism for the cytoplasmic streaming in the veins of the plasmodium?

How Amoebae Move

The excystment of sclerotia will occur more rapidly if the sclerotia are freshly prepared. To maintain a viable stock of sclerotia, it is advisable to reactivate them at regular intervals of about one month. If *P. polycephalum* is well nourished, during its feeding stage it will form viable sclerotia when allowed to dry slowly. Care must be taken to provide adequate food and not to allow it to dry out rapidly, or repeatedly dry and moisten it over short time intervals, or expose it to long periods of illumination or heat.

Additional sclerotia can be produced by simply allowing a well-nourished plasmodium to slowly desiccate. Place the petri dish in a darkened location and partially remove the lid to promote evaporation. Within one to two days, the plasmodium will typically contract into a dry sclerotial mass. Keep the sclerotia in a vial closed by a cotton plug. Avoid storing the sclerotia in warm places; keep the sample dark.

Healthy plasmodia can move toward food with a rate of about 3-5 mm in 45 minutes. Students are often surprised by how quickly the plasmodia move. Encourage them before the experiment to hypothesize how quickly their amoebae will move, and then compare their hypothesis to their actual findings.

To have fully motile slime molds during class, prepare several dishes the night before the class, or have students prepare them 24 hours before the investigation. Prepare two dishes per lab group—one for observing cytoplasm, the other for testing motility and reaction to stimuli, as shown in Figure 2.

Place two 9-cm filter paper discs in the bottom of a petri dish and deposit a small piece of sclerotium (4 mm^2) in the middle. Add sufficient pond or aged tap water to fully moisten the sclerotium and the filter paper. Do not leave excess water standing in the dish. Add two or three oat flakes near the piece of sclerotium. Put a lid on the petri dish, wrap it in aluminum foil or plastic, and place it in a dark location (about 20°C) until it is time to begin the investigation. The samples for observing cytoplasmic streaming should be prepared as above, but using only a small disc of filter paper about 4 cm diameter.

Micro-Macro Link

Many species of organisms, from the microscopic to the macroscopic, exhibit adaptive strategies in response to unpredictable or changing environments.

Time Management

This investigation may be completed in one class period, if preparation is performed the day before class. A 30-minute follow-up is required the day after the investigation.

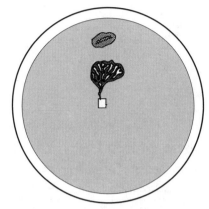

Figure 2
The arrangement of a petri dish containing moistened filter paper discs and a growing plasmodium emergent from a sclerotial mass in the center. The fan-shaped leading edge of the plasmodium migrates preferentially toward sources of food.

Distribute several small pieces of the dried sclerotium to each student at the beginning of the class. Also at the start of class, distribute the active stages that were started the previous night. Each sample will typically have one or more yellowish fan-like leading edge. If the preparation has developed more than one fan-like growing edge, each edge can be isolated by cutting out the piece of filter paper and placing it into a new petri dish lined with moist filter paper.

Adaptations and Variations

Students are often surprised at how quickly a large amoeba moves when food is present. Have them suggest further experiments, such as measuring the rate of movement of a fan edge without a piece of food nearby for comparison. Students may also want to measure the amoeba's rate of movement away from an aversive stimulus. Have them compare and contrast the rates for different stimuli.

◆

If time permits, have students experiment with the different life stages of the plasmodium. They can induce sporangia by very rapidly drying out the plasmodium's environment; by repeatedly drying and moistening it over short time intervals, or exposing it to long periods of illumination or mild heat.

◆

Students may also wish to observe the moistened sclerotia, using a microscope and smear preparation as described in Steps 4–5, one to two hours after they have been moistened. By this time the sclerotia will begin to form plasmodia. Students may see that some sclerotia are interlinked by thin cytoplasmic strands—this stage precedes full excystment and development of an amoeboid plasmodium, which will develop in two and a half to three hours.

Assessment and Evaluation

This investigation is designed to help students understand how adaptive strategies enable organisms to respond to unpredictable environments. The common amoeboid slime mold provides a microscopic example of an effective adaptive strategy. Students should be encouraged to extrapolate this particular example among macroscopic levels. Many species of organisms exhibit adaptive strategies in response to unpredictable or changing environments. Students' ability to understand such strategies within a broad ecological context should provide one instrument for assessment and evaluation.

Similarly, this investigation establishes links among several scientific disciplines, especially protozoology, biology, and ecology. Students should learn to view scientific activity as being characterized by both a wide range of conceptual and experimental systems and a fluid and dynamic spirit of inquiry. Their ability to apply these attributes of scientific activity to conducting the investigation and communicating its results provides another assessment and evaluation mechanism.

Possible student answers to some of the Discussion and Inquiry questions are outlined below. They are best used for organizational purposes, or as points of departure for more generalized debate.

- Why does the sclerotium consist of numerous small cysts cemented together rather than as one large cyst? Such a mass of numerous small cysts is less vulnerable to damage, since fragmentation does not destroy the viability of the encysted mass. Moreover, fragments of the sclerotial mass can be distributed to distant locations and still be viable.

- What advantage is there in having a cyst wall around each cyst instead of being simply embedded in a common cement? Individual cyst walls provide greater protection against predation, and also help each cyst to retain enough moisture to stay viable until there is enough environmental moisture for them to grow into new plasmodia.

- Why do you suppose the plasmodium forms a fan-like leading edge? The broad surface of the advancing plasmodium allows it to more effectively encounter potential food sources. Once it finds food, it can concentrate all of its movement toward those food particles. Also, if there are many small particles of food, the expanded edge of the plasmodium is able to engulf larger quantities of food. The cytoplasm inside the small veins of the plasmodium flows in a reversible pulsating pattern, streaming forward and backward repeatedly.

- How does this streaming mechanism allow the plasmodium to move forward toward attractants and move backward away from harmful stimuli? The duration of the direction of flowing determines the overall direction of the plasmodium's movement. If the forward-directed stream of cytoplasmic flow lasts longer than the reversal during each cycle, the plasmodium moves forward. If the reverse flow lasts longer, the plasmodium tends to move backward. Thus, it is a hydrodynamic balance between the forward force of the cytoplasmic forward versus the backward force that determines the plasmodium's direction of movement.

- What is the possible mechanism for the cytoplasmic streaming in the veins of the plasmodium? The walls of the veins are encircled by fine contractile filaments (actin that is chemically similar to that in the muscles of animals and humans). Contraction of the walls near the posterior parts of the plasmodium push cytoplasm forward. Contraction of the walls near the anterior of the plasmodium, push cytoplasm backward. These contractions occur alternatively, thus accounting for the reversible streaming of the cytoplasm.

- If the plasmodium is attracted to a stimulus, the posterior veins contract more forcefully than the anterior, causing a net forward flow of cytoplasm on each cycle of streaming. If an aversive stimulus is encountered, the veins contract more forcefully in the region nearest the negative stimulus, causing a net flow of cytoplasm away from the surface near the aversive stimulus. The plasmodium then gradually retracts in the opposite direction.

About the Author

O. Roger Anderson, who teaches protozoology at Columbia University, developed this investigation to invite students to explore the remarkable diversity of organismic responses to the changing demands of their environments. A major characteristic of all living things is their capacity to adapt, and thus to invade and inhabit diverse environments. This includes the simplest to the most complex of life forms.

Resources

For distributors of rolled dried oats, sclerotia, bibulous paper, and other biological supplies, see Appendix VI (pages 219–221). Oats may also be obtained from grocery stores.

Avoiding Predation

In order to survive, all species have developed ways to avoid predators. In the animal kingdom, many species avoid predators simply by moving quickly out of the way (Figure 1). You are probably familiar with the specialized ways that some animals avoid predators. Deer use their legs to run fast, birds use their wings to fly away, and monkeys use their tails to help them swing in trees. These are examples of physiological adaptations that certain species have developed to help them stay alive.

Some species of protozoa also avoid predators by moving quickly out of the way. But what physiological adaptations might a microscopic organism use to move quickly? How does a single-celled protozoan "jump"? What part of its body enables it to do so? How do they sense an enemy? In this investigation you will examine some of the physiological adaptations that microorganisms have developed to avoid predation. You will also contrast such adaptations with examples among more complex organisms.

So What?

Many organisms have to move just to stay alive, especially to avoid predators. Microorganisms, even though they don't have legs or fins or wings like larger organisms, have developed ways to move.

SCI**LINKS**®
THE WORLD'S A CLICK AWAY

Topic: predators
Go to: www.scilinks.org
Code: PROT04

Figure 1
In order to survive, all species have developed ways to avoid predators. In the animal kingdom, many species avoid predators simply by moving quickly out of the way.

2.5 Objective

To understand how protozoa move to avoid predators.

✔ Materials

- ❏ Compound microscope, oil immersion objective
- ❏ Slides, coverslips
- ❏ Filtration apparatus
- ❏ Separation funnel
- ❏ Glass fiber filters
- ❏ Several 1–5 l plastic bottles
- ❏ Pond, lake, or sea water samples
- ❏ EDTA-solution, MS-222, or other Calcium-binding quieting agents
- ❏ Inverted phase contrast microscope with camera equipment, counting chambers, and video system (optional)

Figure 2
A. Separator funnel in a darkened room, with flashlight lighting the tip. B. Bottle covered with aluminum foil, light shining into neck.

Procedure

1. Concentrate microscopic organisms in your sample. To do this, contain them first in a separation funnel or a bottle (Figure 2). Darken the room, and shine a concentrated light directly at the top of the container. After a few minutes, protozoa accumulate in the lighted, tip region and can be gently drawn off by opening the stopcock. Micropipet the top of the sample into a small vial or flask, and keep this enriched sample as cool as possible (room temperature) during repeated subsampling.

   Alternatively, a bottle can be covered with aluminum foil and filled with the plankton sample. Illuminate the botle at the top and use the same method to micropipet the protozoa into a small flask.

2. Take a subsample, make a wet mount slide (or preferably a small chamber), and look at it through the microscope. Check to see if further concentration is required; there should be tens of actively swimming organisms per milliliter.

3. Observe the movement of the microbes on your wet mount slide, and try to calculate their rate of speed. One way to do this is for one student to track the distance moved within the field of vision while another student records the time elapsed from beginning to end of movement, as signaled by the student observing the specimen.

4. Add one, two, or more droplets of the quieting agent to the subsample. The quieting agent absorbs calcium from the solution surrounding the protozoa. Some of the protozoans will disintegrate, but others will be immobilized within a few minutes. What can you conclude about the importance of calcium for protozoan motion, based on these results? Could these protozoa survive in water without calcium?

5. Make a new wet mount slide. As you now observe the immobilized organisms, you will notice that they are not dead but merely "quietened." Try to locate and identify individuals of the same species in both end and side view. Usually some *Halteria*, *Strombidium*, or *Mesodinium* species will be found in subsamples of lake or sea water. Few organisms in any subsample will survive more than 30 minutes, so take a new subsample.

Halteria (Figure 3), *Strombidium*, and *Mesodinium* are rounded cells with a fringe of ciliary structures at the forward end. However, the size and arrangement of these cilia, and others on the body, may vary within these three genera of ciliates. You may be able to recognize them by these general features and by their rapid movement. If they are not present, try the effects of the quieting agent on other ciliates you find. However, as a careful scientist, make a good drawing of each so you have a complete record. This will allow you to think clearly about your results when you review your notes, and to clearly communicate your findings to others.

Figure 3
***Halteria* sp.**

6. If a suitable species, such as *Mesodinium*, is present, create a table of pertinent data. Include such aspects as cell size, number of cirri, and ciliary rows or membranelles.

7. Based on your table, addressed the following questions:

   • What are the major features that characterize each of the species you observed?

   • Does one species seem to be more sensitive to the quieting agent than others?

   • Can you make an estimate if protozoa of different sizes respond differently to the quieting agent? That is, do ciliates of smaller size respond differently from those of larger size?

   • How confident can you be that you are correct? How many observations do you think you need to draw a conclusion about size and response to the quieting agent? Can you think of other kinds of protozoa you would like to examine for effects of the quieting agent?

Discussion and Inquiry

• Compare the size of the organisms and their swimming speeds.

• How fast are the main predators of the protozoa you observed?

• Is the number of cirri related to the cell diameter or is it constant in a population?

• Describe the physiological adaptations you observed that help microscopic organisms avoid predation.

• Contrast such adaptations with more complex organisms, such as worms, crickets, turtles, fish, cats, and humans.

Avoiding Predation

Micro-Macro Link

Organisms of all sizes have developed physiological means for movement, even protozoa.

Time Management

This investigation may be completed in one class period. Some practice may be required to perfect the lab skills, such as those outlined in Appendix I (pages 205–209), necessary for students to make their own subsample concentrations.

The ability to avoid predators is important for the survival of all species on Earth. Many organisms avoid predation simply by moving quickly out of the way when they feel threatened. While students are probably already familiar with a variety of specialized physiological organs macroscopic species use for such purposes—wings, legs, and tails, for example—they may have difficulty identifying comparable organs among microscopic species.

Most planktonic ciliates and a great number of flagellates play an ecologically important role in marine food webs. They are important grazers or primary producers in ponds, lakes, and seas. Many protozoans can to some extent avoid predators by fast swimming or jumping. Yet, because they are fast and fragile, they are hard to observe alive. *Mesodinium* is seldom present in net samples. When captured they often appear broken, contracted, or deformed by fixatives.

While live studies of these microbes require great patience and skill, many microscopic organisms may be easily narcotized. The quieting agents in this investigation work on a great number of protist species, especially ciliates and flagellates, but considerable patience is needed. EDTA and other quieting agents work well on cryptomonads, dino-flagellates, and euglenoids.

Adaptations and Variations

Concentration can also be accomplished by gravity filtration. Add approximately 200 ml of the water sample to a filter containing a piece of filter paper. Allow the water sample to drain through the filter until about 10-20 ml remains in the funnel. Use an eyedropper or pipet to gently swirl the suspension, and then withdraw it from the filter funnel. Store the enriched sample in a small vial or flask at a suitable temperature for repeated subsampling.

◆

The best results will be achieved if students are able to compare live organisms with preserved samples of the same species. This may be achieved using one or more of several techniques. If you have camera equipment available, photograph several fields of view at low magnification using a 1/4 second exposure. Also photograph an object micrometer at all magnifications to facilitate cell measurement and the identification of motility organelles. Size, number of cirri, and behavior of ciliary rows and membranelles can also be checked from slides—remember to have a slide of the scale. Measurements may also be taken with a microfilm monitor. The scale can then be drawn on tape at the edge of the screen or on a ruler. Students may want to make a poster using any good photographs they have taken of protozoan species.

◆

If film is used, the tracks on the film will indicate the approximate swimming speed. Speed and behavior can also be noted on a video screen. If a photographic record is not possible, encourage students to suggest alternative ways to work together to estimate speed and distance in their microscopic environments. For example, how much time is required to move through one half of the distance of the diameter of the microscopic field?

Assessment and Evaluation

Before initiating this investigation, ask students how they think a single-celled organism "jumps." Have them keep a record of their responses to contrast with their findings upon completing the investigation.

This investigation provides a good opportunity to evaluate how well students work with data they have compiled and how they arrive at conclusions based on their data. A student's ability to compile, organize, and interpret data provides a mechanism for assessment.

About the Author

Tore Lindholm is Senior Lecturer at the Åbo Akademi University in Åbo, Finland. He has worked with protists and phytoplankton from the Baltic Sea and the coastal lakes of Finland, especially the marine protist, *Mesodinium rubrum*. He developed this investigation to teach students the skills required to physically handle fragile but fast protozoans.

Resources

Lindholm, T. 1982. "EDTA and oxalic acid—two useful agents for narcotizing fragile and rapid microzooplankton." *Hydrobiologia*, 86: 297–298.

Patterson, D.J. 1992. *Free-living Freshwater Protozoa: A Colour Guide.* Sydney, Australia: Wolfe Publishing, Ltd.

For distributors of EDTA-solutions and concentrations, MS-222, and other Calcium-binding or quieting agents, as well as other biological supplies, see Appendix VI (pages 219–221).

How Protozoa Eat

So What?

All living organisms need energy to live. From the smallest to the largest, they all consume and digest energy, and excrete wastes.

Seeing the organelles or cell structures protozoa use to eat and digest food can be difficult even with a high-power microscope. In this investigation, you will use a method that reveals the way certain ciliated and flagellated protozoa eat or use photosynthesis (Figure 1) to make food, particularly *Euglena*, *Blepharisma*, *Paramecium*, *Euplotes*, and *Vorticella* (all ciliates). You should be able to clearly see the flagella and cilia such protozoa use to engulf food, the details of their mouth structures, and their internal digestion and excretion organelles.

The word "morphology" refers to the biological form and structure of living organisms. As you observe the feeding morphology—the biological structures used to eat—of the ciliated protozoa in this investigation, think about how other kinds of organisms perform the same function. Can you identify differences or similarities between the feeding morphology of ciliated protozoa and that of other organisms?

Figure 1
When we think of photosynthesis, our first thought is of green plants, which absorb sunlight and convert it into usable energy. *Euglena* are also photosynthetic. As you conduct this investigation, think of ways in which *Euglena* are similar to green plants, as well as ways in which they are different.

National Science Teachers Association

Procedure

1. To stain the yeast, place a small piece of the yeast cake into the previously-prepared Congo red stain. Bring to about 95°C for 10–15 seconds to drive the stain into the yeast. Let cool to room temperature before using.

2. To slow the protozoa down enough to see them feeding, you must immobilize them with a protozoan slowing solution.

3. Use a dissection microscope (or a good hand lens) and micropipet to capture several *Paramecium* and transfer them to the center of a ring of protozoan slowing solution on a glass slide. Add a drop of Congo red-stained yeast and a small amount of Nigrosin. Gently mix by using the edge of a coverslip. Carefully cover this preparation with a glass coverslip. Observe the beating action of the cilia and the currents of water carrying the red-stained yeast. Watch carefully where the yeast are gathered into the *Paramecium*'s cell body.

What happens to the Congo red-stained yeast, if available, within the food vacuoles? Is there a color change? What does this indicate? Compare the feeding behavior of a *Paramecium* to that of a *Euglena* (Figure 2). Does *Euglena* eat yeast? Like plants, *Euglena* are green: do they necessarily need to eat solid food particles? Repeat the procedure using some other ciliates.

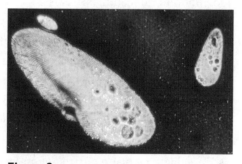

Figure 2
Paramecium and *Euglena*. **Compare their feeding behavior, as well as their respective sizes and anatomies.**

4. Using 400x magnification, observe how the ciliates plow through the yeast, ingesting it, and concentrating it in their vacuoles as they go. You will be able to focus on fewer ciliates and see even better details with 1000x magnification. Record and label your observations on a data sheet. Be sure to label as many morphological details as you can.

5. Prepare a slide with a drop of *Euglena* culture or one of the ciliate cultures. Add a drop of Nigrosin. Apply the coverslip and observe the flagellar action of *Euglena*, or the beating cilia on the ciliates. Remove the coverslip, and allow the slide to dry. This will result in a permanent preparation, which is a better way to clearly see

✔ Materials

- ❑ Stereo binocular dissection microscope
- ❑ Compound light microscope, oil immersion objectives
- ❑ Glass slides, coverslips
- ❑ Immersion oil
- ❑ Micropipet
- ❑ Pasteur pipets
- ❑ Bunsen burner
- ❑ Rubber bulbs
- ❑ Forceps
- ❑ 2 finger bowls
- ❑ Wheat germ kernels
- ❑ Charcoal-filtered pond water (CHPW) or bottled spring water
- ❑ Caked baker's yeast
- ❑ Congo red stain
- ❑ 10 percent (weight/volume) aqueous Nigrosin (black) stain
- ❑ Protozoan slowing solution
- ❑ Permanent mounting medium
- ❑ Cultures:
  Euglena
  Blepharisma
  Paramecium
  Colpidium
  Euplotes
  Vorticella

specific morphological details, such as the cavity where food enters the cell of ciliates. Record and label your observations on a data sheet.

6. Repeat this procedure with *Paramecium*, *Colpidium*, *Euplotes*, and *Vorticella*.

Discussion and Inquiry

All forms of life assimilate matter to meet their energy requirements, although it may be only very small molecules dissolved in the surrounding medium. How do organisms in this investigation, such as *Euglena*, obtain energy? Does *Euglena* require particulate (solid) food if it can make its own food by trapping light energy? How did you decide this? What materials may be dissolved in the growth medium that the *Euglena* can absorb through its outer membrane? Can they absorb nitrogenous molecules, phosphates, and small organic acids?

Living organisms vary in their metabolic activity and in their rate of locomotion and feeding. This is also true among higher organisms; some relatively large animals move rapidly to pursue prey, such as leopards, wolves, certain lizards, and others. Other animals are more slow moving, such as snakes and turtles.

Protozoa also vary in motility rate and feeding activity, and it is worthwhile to note differences in the swimming rates and food particle-gathering abilities among the ciliates you observe in this investigation. *Blepharisma*, for example, is rather slow moving and sometimes halting, as is the large elongate ciliate *Spirostomum*. Some smaller ciliates move more continuously and, apparently, more rapidly as they gather food. Which of these ciliates is likely to metabolize most rapidly and which less rapidly? Which is likely to be able to survive when food is more limited?

How Protozoa Eat

One of biology's organizing principles is that all living organisms require energy to live. Some produce food through photosynthesis. Others ingest solid food, digest it, and excrete waste materials. Despite often dramatic differences in feeding morphology and actual physical structures, all living organisms nevertheless perform these same biological functions. Protozoa exhibit both of these energy-getting strategies, and this investigation provides an opportunity for students to observe them in action.

Have students look for details of flagella or cilia. Students should also identify patterns on flagellates and ciliates, respectively, as well as patterns on the cell surfaces when stained with Nigrosin. These will appear white against a blue-black background; chloroplasts will be green. Cells and membranes will fill with the Nigrosin dye and stand out clearly. Ciliary structures will beat continuously. *Paramecium*'s horn-shaped and *Colpidium*'s triangular mouth become increasingly apparent as the dye concentrates at their mouth regions (Figures 3 and 4). The ingestion of the stained yeast will be followed by lysosomal activity, and the contents of food vacuoles will change from red to blue as digestion proceeds and

Micro-Macro Link
Ciliated and flagellated protozoa are single-celled, but they obtain and digest solid food using a process remarkably similar to that used by multi-celled organisms.

Time Management
This investigation may be completed in one class period. If you wish to involve students in preparation (outlined in Adaptations and Variations), protozoa must be cultured about one week in advance.

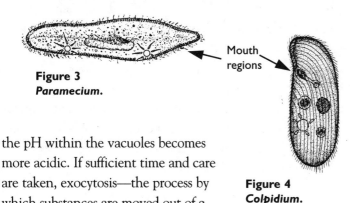

Figure 3
Paramecium.

Mouth
regions

Figure 4
Colpidium.

the pH within the vacuoles becomes more acidic. If sufficient time and care are taken, exocytosis—the process by which substances are moved out of a cell—may also be seen.

As the investigation proceeds, encourage students to compare and contrast the feeding morphologies of organisms from different feeding levels. Encourage them to observe the parallels between the ciliates' oral groove and the human mouth, between the buccal cavity and the esophagus of humans, and between the digestive vacuole of ciliates and the stomach of humans. Both the oral groove and the human mouth become acidic during digestion. Later on in the digestive process, vacuoles become alkaline just as food does in the human small intestine. Finally, waste material is excreted from the ciliate at a specialized, posterior region (anal pore) analogous to the anus of higher organisms.

Adaptations and Variations

To prepare glass micropipets, have students follow the instructions in Appendix IV (pages 215–216).

◆

To prepare the Congo red stain, add 0.1 g to 100 ml of water. Warm gently to disperse. Nigrosin stain is prepared by dissolving 10 g in 100 ml of distilled water. Mix thoroughly and place in a stoppered bottle to prevent evaporation. Prepared stain solutions can also be purchased from biological supply companies.

◆

To prepare charcoal-filtered pond water, add 2 g of activated charcoal to 1 l pond water in a large flask or jar. Mix for 20 minutes, and filter out the charcoal through large circular filter paper. Repeat if necessary until no charcoal remains.

◆

Purchase protozoa cultures from a biological supply company, or culture them in the classroom. Place 200 ml of charcoal-filtered pond or bottled spring water in a shallow culture bowl and cover it with a piece of glass. Alternatively, use a glass jar with sufficient volume to provide a large enough surface area for the culture medium. Wash four dried wheat germ grains or kernels with distilled water, and add them to the culture bowl. Then add several drops of concentrated protozoa. Let the culture stand for about one week in an area with indirect illumination and no drafts.

◆

If a video camera is available, students can watch all this activity from a TV monitor and make observations during specific feeding stages. This method will also help you point out specific organelles, such as food vacuoles, that are important during this process.

◆

Have students make a chart of the mouth region and digestive vacuoles in a ciliate. Place it beside a similar chart of a human digestive system, and have students make comparisons between the two.

Assessment and Evaluation

Scientific investigations require creative thought based on clear and accurate observations. Assess how carefully students are able to describe the events that occur when the ciliates eat yeast. Do students understand that this is a series of functionally interrelated events?

Yeast particles are gathered by the cilia in a compact mass at the base of the feeding canal. This permits efficient digestion of the particles of food. The food becomes isolated from the cytoplasm in a vacuole "like a stomach" where the digestion can occur without harming the rest of the cell. The movement of the vacuoles ensures that digested products are distributed throughout the cytoplasm and permits an orderly sequence of continuous feeding, allowing room for new food vacuoles to form at the mouth region. Eventually the digested waste is expelled, preventing the cell from filling with useless matter.

An organizing biological principle is that structure and function are complementary, that they are mutually supportive. Students should note how the shape of the cell, the arrangement of the beating cilia, and the form of the buccal cavity promote food gathering. Following the discussion of photosynthetic forms of protozoa versus the heterotrophic ciliates, students should be able to state why *Euglena* does not need to eat particulate food, and why the ciliates must do so to survive. *Euglena*, like some other larger, less active protozoa, conserve energy and store food, and they can therefore survive better during periods of short food supply. Small, fast-moving protozoa metabolize more rapidly, and therefore may deplete their food reserves when food is scarce, thus dying out faster. These are quite successful during "feasts," but die out quickly during "famines."

About the Author

Arthur Repak teaches protozoology, environmental microbiology, and freshman biology at Quinnipiac College in Hamden, Connecticut. Microbial feeding strategies involve eating and growing quickly. The method of using a negative stain to reveal ciliate feeding and locomotor organelles along with pH indicators allows students to see that single-celled organisms also have mechanisms for ingestion and digestion of food materials.

Resources

For distributors of permanent mounting media, protozoan slowing solutions, and other biological supplies, see Appendix VI (pages 219–221).

How Paramecia Eat

So What?

All organisms have to eat, and even the tiniest single-celled organisms have developed specialized ways to ingest and digest food.

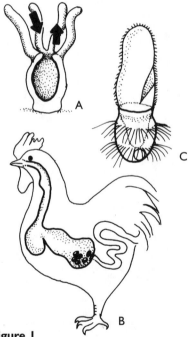

Figure 1
Digestive diversity: (A) the incomplete digestive tract of a sea anemone—food enters and residues exit through the same opening; (B) the complete digestive tract of a bird—food is pushed to the back of the pharynx and swallowed into the esophagus, from where it passes into the crop where it is stored; (C) a *Didinium* engulfs a larger *Paramecium*—this digestive behavior is what you will observe in this investigation.

Different organisms have different feeding strategies, depending on their morphology and nutrient requirements (Figure 1).

Single-celled organisms like paramecia gather food into small compartments in the cytoplasm called vacuoles. This feeding strategy is called endocytosis. The two modes of endocytosis are phagocytosis and pinocytosis. Phagocytosis involves ingestion of large particles, such as other cells or cell debris, into large vacuoles called phagosomes. In pinocytosis, very small particles and fluid are ingested via vesicles that are smaller than most phagosomes. These vesicles form either at the cell surface or at the base of tapered channels that penetrate deeply into the cell. One way to think of the difference is that phagocytosis is cell eating, while pinocytosis is cell drinking.

In this investigation, you will explore how paramecia undergo phagocytosis. The beating of their external cilia allows them to gather food particles, which are then enclosed in a food vacuole at the cytostome, and the vacuole is acidified as digestion begins.

On the face of it, endocytosis sounds pretty different from the way multi-celled organisms derive nourishment. Yet, despite some rather obvious morphological differences—complex organisms lack food vacuoles and external cilia, for instance—can you think of any similarities in the feeding strategies of single- and multi-celled organisms? The primary similarity is the basic process itself. Both types of organisms bring food inside their bodies, begin digestion through acidification, and excrete waste after digestion.

As you perform this investigation, try to make this type of simple connection between the feeding strategies of microscopic and macroscopic organisms. Try relating phagocytosis to the way you yourself get nourishment.

Procedure

1. Place a drop of *P. caudatum* on the microscope slide, and add a drop of the suspension of Sephadex containing yeast stained with Congo red. Congo red is a pH indicator which changes from red, at pH 5 or above, to blue at pH 3. (Sephadex is very small plastic beads that help slow down the swimming motion of the paramecia.) Gently apply a coverslip.

2. Search the preparation at low magnification to find cells that are either immobile or moving very slowly. Once you've identified such cells, observe them at the highest magnification. You can increase the contrast by adjusting the height of the condenser, the light intensity, and the condenser diaphragm opening. This will help you distinguish between the stained yeast and the cytoplasm.

3. Examine the cell's morphology (its shape or body structure), and identify the pre-oral groove. The pre-oral groove is a depression in the anterior, ventral surface, which leads to the oral (buccal) opening, approximately in the middle of the cell. Cilia in the groove are difficult to distinguish, but you should be able to recognize the red-stained yeast as the beating cilia propell it quickly across this region. The cilia of the buccal cavity are easier to distinguish, since they are arranged in clusters, or membranelles.

4. Use a piece of blank paper as a data sheet, and divide it into four sections. In the first section record your observations for Step 3. Use colored pencils to depict the yeast within the pre-oral groove and the buccal cavity. Be sure to label the yeast, the pre-oral groove, the buccal cavity, membranelles, the cytoplasm, and any organelles you observe. Use the second section of your data sheet to draw a close-up picture of the pre-oral groove and the buccal opening with membranelles.

5. Many yeast cells are first propelled into the buccal cavity and then rejected in a continuous stream. However, a few yeast cells will enter the cavity and be transported to its bottom by the beating of the membranellar cilia. Notice the yeast particles accumulating in a sac-like depression of the cytostome, located at the cavity bottom. The cytostomal depression is the forming food vacuole, which will grow larger as yeast cells enter it. This new food vacuole then pinches off and moves posteriorly into the cytoplasm.

6. Use the third section of your data sheet to record the food vacuole while it forms, and how it looks as it breaks away.

7. After you observe the formation of several food vacuoles, follow one of them as it moves through the cytoplasm.

2.7 Objective

To understand phagocytosis, the feeding strategy by which paramecia gather and derive nourishment from food particles.

✔ Materials

- ❑ Compound microscope
- ❑ Slides, coverslips
- ❑ Eyedroppers with rubber bulbs
- ❑ Scale accurate to 0.1 g
- ❑ Congo red stain
- ❑ Baker's yeast
- ❑ Sephadex G-150
- ❑ Blank paper, colored pencils
- ❑ Culture: *Paramecium caudatum,* concentrated

Topic: endocytosis
Go to: www.scilinks.org
Code: PROT05

8. Use the final section of your data sheet to track the progress of the vacuole through the paramecium's cytoplasm.

Discussion and Inquiry

- In addition to food vacuoles, did you see any other objects, such as granules or other cell organelles within the paramecium moving in the cytoplasmic streaming ("cyclosis")?

- Do all cells form the same numbers and sizes of food vacuoles?

- Does yeast become blue in all vacuoles?

- The blue color demonstrates that the vacuole has become acid. How rapidly does acidification occur? Is it a question of seconds, minutes, or hours?

How Paramecia Eat

In this investigation, students will observe two fundamental biological phenomena. First, students will see the formation of food vacuoles and the changes within them during digestion. Second, students will see the process of filter feeding whereby some ciliated organisms are able to remove, concentrate, and derive nourishment from particles suspended in their aqueous environment.

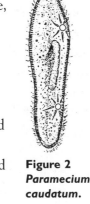

Figure 2
Paramecium caudatum.

P. caudatum (Figure 2), with its specialized oral ciliation, cytostome, and complex intracellular digestive process, is remarkably well adapted to this feeding strategy. Some *P. caudatum* cells will be more immobilized than others, depending upon how many cilia adhere to the surrounding Sephadex beads. Even cells well attached to beads will rotate some during observation, so students will have to frequently adjust the microscope's fine focus knob. The immobilized cells also provide an ideal opportunity to study the functioning of the contractile vacuole/radial canal complex.

Phagocytosis is a feeding strategy of many protozoa and some animal cells (white blood cells, for example), in which food particles pass from the extracellular medium into the cell's cytoplasm. In paramecia, the food vacuole (phagosome) is formed when a food particle enters the buccal cavity and is enveloped by a membrane. Another method of phagocytosis is exhibited by amoebae. Amoebae first surround the food particle with pseudopods, then use their plasma membrane—the outermost membrane surrounding the cell—to form a food vacuole membrane.

This investigation, however, concentrates on the mode used by paramecia and many other ciliated protozoa. Here, the food vacuole forms in a specific region of the cell, the cytostome, and the membrane for the food vacuole is derived from vesicles present in the cytoplasm immediately below the cytostome. In paramecia, such vesicles are flattened and disc-shaped, and they do not appear to contain digestive enzymes. In certain other ciliates, such as *Pseudomicrothorax*, these vesicles are lysosomes, rich in digestive enzymes.

Micro-Macro Link

All living organisms have developed specialized ways for obtaining and processing nutrients. Compare the human stomach's acidification process with how some protozoans break down food to illustrate this organizing biological principle.

Time Management

This investigation may be completed in one class period. If you wish to involve students in preparation and set up, follow the procedure outlined in Adaptations and Variations.

Once formed, food vacuoles undergo a series of modifications during the digestion process. In both paramecia and amoebae, the first clearly demonstrated change is a sharp drop in vacuolar pH. Acidification may serve several purposes. It may kill or render less offensive the ingested prey organisms, it may facilitate their digestion, and it may reduce the pH of the vacuole to one which favors the activity of digestive enzymes.

The acidification results from the fusion of the food vacuole and the acid-containing vesicles called acidosomes (acidosomes have been identified by electron microscopy, but they are too small to be observed by light microscopy). Subsequently, lysosomes transporting the digestive enzymes fuse with the acidified vacuole.

Adaptations and Variations

To prepare the Congo red stained yeast, add 10 ml of distilled or deionized water to 0.1 g of Congo red and heat gently over a low flame with stirring to dissolve the dye well. Add 2 g of fresh baker's yeast, mix until the yeast cake is dispersed, and continue gentle heating with stirring for about 5 minutes. Do not boil. Fresh yeast is preferable to lyophilized yeast, but if only the latter is available, use 0.1 g in place of the 2 g of fresh yeast. Add 90 ml of distilled or deionized water. This suspension may be stored in the refrigerator for at least 1 week.

◆

To prepare Sephadex G-150, add 1 g of Sephadex to 50 ml of distilled or deionized water. Let swell with intermittent agitation for 20 minutes. Let the Sephadex settle out of suspension and gently pour off the water above the Sephadex layer. Again add 50 ml of water, mix 5 minutes, let settle out and pour off the water. The washed Sephadex may be stored in the refrigerator for several weeks, or frozen.

◆

To prepare the Congo red stained yeast and Sephadex, add 25 ml of the stained yeast suspension to the above washed Sephadex; the final settled volume of Sephadex is about 25 ml. Mix briefly. This suspension may be further diluted with water if desired. It may be stored at least one week in the refrigerator, or frozen, until use.

◆

These preparations last 30–40 minutes before drying up, or before the cells are killed from the heat of the microscope lamp. Encourage students to observe several cells, rather than spending too much time on one cell that may ingest few or no yeast cells. The time it takes for acidification will vary, both from cell to cell and among vacuoles within the same cell.

◆

The Congo red stained yeast may be used alone if the Sephadex is not available; however, the latter considerably aids observation by slowing down these rapid little beasts. Alternatively, a small wisp of cotton placed on the slide prior to depositing the paramecia and yeast will entrap some paramecia in small spaces under the cover slip and immobilize them sufficiently for observation.

◆

Students can estimate the rate of filter feeding in these ciliates. Since each newly formed food vacuole is clearly visible by the red mass of yeast in it, have them determine how many food vacuoles are formed per unit time. This can be done by noting the time when one vacuole has filled with yeast, and then noting the time when a number of other vacuoles have filled. Dividing the number of vacuoles by the time interval will give the number of vacuoles formed per minute. Also, by using very high power, it is possible to count the number of yeasts per vacuole, and thus estimate the number of yeasts consumed per minute.

Assessment and Evaluation

Students should be able to compare the feeding strategies of the paramecium to larger forms of life including vertebrate animals and humans. For each step in the paramecium's feeding sequence, students should be able to cite the corresponding or similar step in the feeding of more advanced organisms. For example, the pre-oral groove and buccal cavity are analogous to prehensile elements, such as tentacles, arms, and teeth. The cytostome is analogous to the mouth and esophagous. The digestive vacuole is at first acid like the stomach; later it is alkaline like the small intestine. The waste is excreted through an anal opening as in higher organisms.

Students should also be able to recognize the differences. Higher animals have a continuous digestive tract, while paramecia have vacuoles. The digested food must move out of the vacuoles into the cytoplasm without the aid of advanced structures, while in animals the digestive tract has highly complex absorbing surfaces.

Students should also be able to evaluate to what extent the feeding strategy of paramecia is active (pursuing prey) versus passive (lie and wait). Both strategies are apparent among these ciliates. Forward swimming movement allows more food particles to be gathered but, even when the paramecium is not swimming, food is gathered by the beating action of the cilia. Any food particle that happens to be present in the stream of water propelled by the cilia can be engulfed if it is not too big.

If paramecia have the capacity to accept or reject food particles, where in the sequence of feeding events would this most likely occur? It should be clear that after the particle is swept into the food vacuole, it is probably too late to reject it. However, at the earliest stages where particles enter the region of the pre-oral groove, or the buccal cavity, there is a possibility of propelling unwanted food away.

Paramecia belong to a large group of organisms known as filter-feeders. Students should be able to describe why the paramecium is considered a filter feeder. Since the food is swept into the pre-oral groove in a stream of water and "filtered out" from it by enclosure in the food vacuole, the category is appropriate. Other filter feeders include clams, mussels, some floating (planktonic) invertebrates, and other lower organisms that gather suspended food particles out of the water column. Students should be able to appreciate the similarities and differences among these various micro- and macroscopic organisms.

About the Authors

Robert Peck, Jose Fahrni, and Francoise Duborgel teach at the University of Geneva in Switzerland. They employ protozoan cells as research organisms and, in their teaching, use them to illustrate basic biological processes, such as phagocytosis.

Resources

For distributors of biological supplies, such as Sephadex G-150, see Appendix VI (pages 219–221).

How Ionic Stimuli Cause Cellular Movement

All living things, including microbes, are made of protoplasm. Therefore, it isn't surprising that the behavior of single-celled microorganisms is determined by the same biological principles that govern multi-celled organisms. In your study of biology you might have learned how, in nerve cells, depolarization and a change in the cell membrane's ion permeability mark the passage of a nerve impulse. The same signals also precede function in other cells.

Although most are single-celled, microorganisms employ this same biological principle to propel themselves through their environments. In this investigation you will examine the biological effect of ionic stimuli on protozoan locomotion. You will expose *Paramecia* (Figure 1) and *Halteria* (Figure 2) to different kinds and concentrations of ions. In this investigation, you will use potassium chloride (KCl) and calcium chloride ($CaCl_2$), which are plentiful in the natural environment and play a role in biological responses.

So What?

Often without even thinking about it, you move your arms to pick up something or your legs to walk down the hall. But how does your brain tell your legs to move? What biological process translates your brain's command into your legs' action? Protozoa use the same biological process, called ionic stimulation, that you use. Here you will examine ionic stimulation in protozoa to understand how your own body moves.

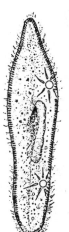

Figure 1
Paramecium caudatum.

Figure 2
Halteria sp.

2.8 Objective

To understand how ionic stimuli cause movement.

✔ Materials

- ❏ Stereoscopic microscope
- ❏ Slides, coverslips
- ❏ Several 1 l glass jars
- ❏ Glass eyedroppers with rubber bulbs
- ❏ Graduated cylinders
- ❏ Flasks
- ❏ Rack of 12 test tubes
- ❏ Balance
- ❏ Potassium chloride (KCl), calcium chloride (CaCl$_2$), barium chloride (BaCl$_2$), and acetic acid
- ❏ Olive oil, or oleic acid
- ❏ Pond or aged tap water
- ❏ Powdered skim milk
- ❏ Cotton, graduated pipets (optional)
- ❏ Water plants with *Halteria* sp.
- ❏ Culture: *Paramecium caudatum*

Procedure

1. Prepare the following solutions. *Be sure to follow the instructions of your teacher carefully!*

   - 1.0 molar (M) solution of KCl in water
   - 80 millimolar (mM) solution of KCl in water
   - 80 millimolar (mM) solution of CaCl$_2$ in water
   - 1.0 percent acetic acid in water
   - (optional) 40 mM BaCl$_2$ plus 0.5 mM CaCl$_2$ in water.

2. Place three drops of culture medium containing numerous paramecia on a glass slide. Use a stereomicroscope to observe the normal movements of the paramecia. Record your observations.

3. Now place three drops of 80 mM KCl solution next to the pool of culture medium on the slide. Mix the two fluid volumes rapidly with a dropper, pipet, or other clean object. The result is a 40 mM KCl-culture medium solution. Observe the movements of the paramecia, and record any new movements and their duration.

4. Repeat the above procedure, using one drop of 80 mM KCl solution to three volumes of culture fluid, to get a 20 mM KCl-culture medium solution after mixing.

5. Repeat Steps 3–4 with a culture of numerous *Halteria*.

6. Place a glass slide on the stage of the stereomicroscope, and then use a pipet to place a few drops of olive oil or oleic acid on the slide. Now carefully release a single drop of *Halteria* culture into this pool of olive oil or oleic acid. Observe and record the results.

7. Following the procedure in Step 4, mix one volume of the 80 mM CaCl$_2$ solution with three volumes of *Paramecium* culture. The result is a 20 mM CaCl$_2$-culture medium solution. Observe and record the results.

8. Repeat the above procedure, but this time use about one volume of the 80 mM CaCl$_2$ solution to nine volumes of paramecia culture. The result is a concentration of 8–10 mM CaCl$_2$. Observe and record the results.

9. Repeat Steps 7–8 using the *Halteria* culture. Or mix equal proportions, of 40 mM BaCl$_2$ plus 0.5 mM CaCl$_2$ solution with culture medium pools containing, respectively, paramecia or *Halteria*. Observe and record the results.

10. Place a few drops of *Halteria* culture on a slide placed on the stereomicroscope's stage. Make sure the pool of culture isn't too

deep. With a micropipet, carefully release a single drop of 1.0 M KCl at a single locus in this fairly shallow pool. Shake the slide gently to cause *Halteria* to swim to the drop of 1.0 M KCl. Observe and record the results.

11. Now release a single drop of 1.0 percent acetic acid elsewhere into the same culture pool. Shake the slide gently to cause *Halteria* to swim to the acetic acid drop. Observe and record the results.

12. Place a pool of several drops of either moving paramecia or moving *Halteria* on a separate glass slide. Allow it to sit out in the air. As the culture begins to dry, place a single drop of distilled or aged tap water into the culture. Observe and record the results.

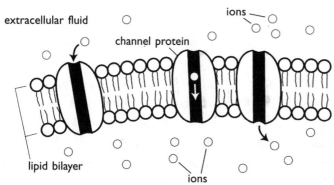

Figure 3
An enlarged segment of the living membrane enclosing the ciliate cortex and cilia. The cell cortex and each cilium are covered by a living membrane.

Discussion and Inquiry

How are the ciliates able to detect differences in the kind and concentration of ions? Look at the diagram of an enlarged segment of the ciliate cortex with cilia (Figure 3). The cell cortex, and each cilium, are covered by a living membrane. Compare this to a diagram of a neuron enclosed by a living membrane and surrounded by a multilayered insulating sheath known as the myelin sheath (Figure 4). Discuss how ion channels in the membrane permit changes in the ionic composition, resulting in changes in the electrical potential across the membrane.

Compare and contrast the changes that occur when a neuron is depolarized by Na ions crossing the membrane, and those that occur when Ca ions enter the cell across the ciliate plasma membrane. Both involve the entrance of positive-charged ions across the membrane, reversing the negative charge internally contributed by anions and negatively-charged large macromolecules within the cytoplasm. Discuss the general principle that signaling by membrane depolarization is a widely occurring mechanism at the cellular level across a wide range of organisms from protozoa to larger animals.

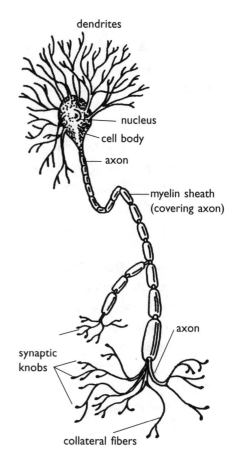

Figure 4
A neuron enclosed by a living membrane.

How Ionic Stimuli Cause Cellular Movement

Micro-Macro Link

The basic biological principle—a negative potential passes over a cell, changes its membrane's ion permeability, enabling muscular function—holds true for single-celled and multicellular organisms. Locomotion in ciliates is governed by this principle.

Time Management

This investigation may be completed in one class period. If you wish to involve students in advance preparation, follow the procedures outlined in Adaptations and Variations. Prepare solutions before class to speed the investigation.

In nerve fibers, depolarization and a change in the cell membrane's ion permeability mark the passage of a nerve impulse. Depolarization occurs when the electrical potential across the membrane (positive outside and negative inside) is abolished. This occurs mainly because the positive ions move into the cell across the membrane. This movement is possible because ion channels open to allow the positive ions to diffuse into the cell. The passage of a negative potential over the cell and a change in the cell membrane's ion permeability precede function in the muscle and other cells of multicellular organisms.

This is a basic biological concept. Locomotion in ciliates is governed by the same electrophysiological principles. Furthermore, ionic stimuli affect specialized parts of a ciliate's cell plasma membrane endowed with transducer properties, resulting in an initial change in the membrane's permeability to ions and depolarization. A similar process occurs in receptor cells (such as taste cells).

Both *Paramecium* and *Halteria* will show continuous ciliary reversal (CCR) in the final 40 mM KCl and 20 mM KCl dilutions. However, the ciliary reversals of the two species will differ greatly in speed and duration. If a drop of medium containing *Halteria* is placed in a volume of olive oil or oleic acid, within 30 seconds the *Halteria* will start to perform continuous ciliary reversal at great speed and maintain it until close to death after 4–13 minutes. In the $CaCl_2$ mixtures, as well as in the 40 mM $BaCl_2$ plus 0.5 mM $CaCl_2$ dilutions, one can expect to see periodic ciliary reversal (PCR). In PCR, the organisms alternate between reversal and forward spiraling. This will be more clear-cut in *Halteria*.

Halteria will do continuous ciliary reversal through a discrete drop of 1.0 M KCl carefully deposited into the pool of culture fluid on a microscope slide, and resume forward swimming on the other side. It will not, however, enter a drop of 1.0 percent acetic acid. Both *Paramecium* and *Halteria*, when subjected to drying culture fluid on a microscope slide, will concentrate in a drop of distilled water or aged tap water that is carefully placed in the middle or at the edge.

Prepare solutions as follows:

- 1.0 M KCl. Weigh 7.5 g and bring to 100 ml with water in a volumetric flask or accurate graduated cylinder, mix thoroughly.

- 80 mM Kcl. Take 8 ml of 1.0 M KCl and bring to 100 ml with water.

- 80 mM $CaCl_2$. Begin with calcium chloride (hexahydrate) crystals ($CaCl_2 \cdot 6 H_2O$). Weigh 1.75 g and bring to 100 ml with water. If you have the dihydrate form ($CaCl_2 \cdot 2 H_2O$), then use 1.2 g and bring to 100 ml with water.

- 0.5 mM $CaCl_2$. Take 0.63 ml of the 80 mM $CaCl_2$ using a 1 ml pipet, and bring to 100 ml with water.

- 40 mM $BaCl_2$. Begin with $BaCl_2 \cdot 2 H_2O$. Weigh 9.77 g and bring to 1000 ml with water. If you do not have a container that is graduated to 1000 ml, first bring the 9.77g to 100 ml with water, then take 10 ml of this solution and bring it to 100 ml with water.

- 1.0 percent acetic acid. Take 1 ml of acetic acid and bring to 100 ml with water. A good quality of table vinegar is close to 1.0 percent acetic acid.

Adaptations and Variations

Have students prepare several hay infusions and innoculate them with paramecia 10–14 days before the investigation. To culture *Halteria*, use quart-sized or larger jars to hold several samples of pond water and water plants. The samples should be drawn from different locations. For best results, try to use dense protist cultures.

Add a small quantity of skimmed milk powder to some of the jars. To insure obtaining good numbers of *Halteria*, prepare a series of test tubes containing 20 ml of pond water from the unused samples of pond water. Place some wheat grains in a few of the test tubes. If possible, place a dead house fly or a third of a dead cricket in each of the test tubes. Then seal all the tubes with a tuft of cotton. This can be done 3–4 days prior to the investigation.

◆

Alternatively, a good *Halteria* culture in which the number of specimens has been allowed to drop to a low level can be brought back up to high numbers by adding a source of nutrition 3–4 days prior to the investigation. This will work a second or third time.

Assessment and Evaluation

Upon completion of this investigation, students should be able to make some generalizations about their findings. If given a list of each of the chemical compounds (and their concentrations) they have used, the students should be able to write a brief statement of the effect on the ciliate. They should be able to discuss why ions are important in the responsiveness of living things to their environment. For example, they should recognize that the irritability of living cells, particularly the neuron, depends on the imbalance in concentration of ions across the cell's surface membrane (the outside is more positive than the inside).

Certain ions are more likely to affect the responsiveness of the cell than others, depending on their size and charge. Calcium has two positive charges per ion, while potassium has one. These differences in charge, plus the difference in size and chemical activity owing to differences in the number and arrangement of electrons surrounding the nucleus, may produce differences in physiological response to the ions.

Students should especially note the significant effect of calcium ions. Calcium ions are important regulatory ions in maintaining a healthy state of the cell. Changes in internal concentration of calcium at the proper concentrations can cause changes in behavior such as the reversal of ciliary beating in ciliates. Calcium ions must be present in the proper concentration and in balance with other chemical compounds in the cell for normal healthy functioning. Students should be able to discuss what evidence supports this conclusion based on their investigation. They should also be able to explain the response of the ciliates to noxious stimuli such as the dilute acetic acid, which they avoid by swimming away from it.

About the Author

Henry Tamar researches protozoa at Indiana State University. His interest is in the movements and responses of ciliated protozoans, and he determined that the jumps performed by many ciliate species are avoidance movements. This led to studies of how well such jumps enable certain ciliates to escape predators. Such reactions among protozoans provide a unique opportunity to study the effects of stimuli on a relatively simpler system—a single (although complex) cell. In higher, multicellular organisms what happens in a receptor cell, such as a taste cell, is just the first step in a series of events involving many cells. By using ciliate clones having single mutations affecting the stimulus-response system, it is also possible to investigate individual steps in this system.

Resources

For distributors of biological supplies, see Appendix VI (pages 219–221).

3 Interacting with Other Organisms

Life on Earth forms a complex web. Each organism depends on others for its health and well being. These relationships assume many forms. Some relationships are symbiotic, some are parasitic, some involve direct competition for nutrients and space, and some involve more subtle forms of evolutionary adaptation.

This section explores how such relationships are essential for maintaining balanced ecosystems. Students conduct investigations into mutualistic and parasitic ecological relationships, competition, and predation. As they do so, students will come to learn that all creatures, regardless of their size or complexity, play important roles in maintaining Nature's equilibrium.

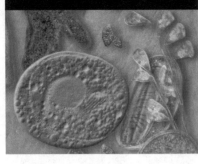

Symbiosis: The Termite as an Ecological Community

So What?

Some species of organisms have adapted to environmental changes by developing biological relationships with organisms from entirely different species.

SCI LINKS
THE WORLD'S A CLICK AWAY

Topic: symbiosis
Go to: www.scilinks.org
Code: PROT06

Microbial organisms like protozoa have adapted over time to a surprising variety of ecological niches. Some microbial organisms have adapted by developing what ecologists call a symbiotic association with a host organism of an entirely different species.

There are three types of symbiotic relationships. Parasitism is when one organism benefits at the other's expense. Commensalism is a symbiotic relationship in which one species benefits and the other species is neither helped nor harmed. When both organisms benefit, it is called mutualism.

A good example of mutualism is the relationship between certain termite species and several species of protozoa and bacteria. Termites can find and chew wood, but they can't digest cellulose, wood's main ingredient. The microbes within the termite's enlarged intestine, however, can digest cellulose and chemically change it into nutrients for the termite. Together, the host termite and the symbiotic micro-organisms can consume wood, digest it, and turn its cellulose into nourishment so that both can survive. In addition, the microbes have a sheltered environment.

You probably think a termite's intestine is a pretty strange place to live. How did this relationship develop between termites and microbes? Remember that organisms evolve over very long periods of time, perhaps thousands of years. A very general definition of evolutionary adaptation is that, over time, organisms develop better and better ways to get food and to avoid being gotten as food. According to Darwin's principle of natural selection, organisms that develop better ways of doing both these things tend to survive and reproduce, while organisms that don't change tend to be selectively weeded out.

But adaptation doesn't occur only because of adversarial relationships, such as predator-prey competition. There are other forms of interaction between species besides competition. Some such forms result in mutually beneficial adaptations, like the relationship between termites and microbes. These, more subtle forms of interaction between species are called co-evolutionary adaptations, and this investigation provides an opportunity for you to explore a particularly interesting one.

Procedure

Maintaining termites

1. Termite cultures purchased from supply companies come in small plastic jars with a few pieces of wood. Add a little water every few days just to moisten the wood. Too much water will cause mold growth and even termite drownings. *Do not shake or tap the jars. Do not leave them on sunny windowsills.* The cultures may last 2–3 weeks.

2. Termites collected from the wild may be left in the wood they were nesting in and enclosed in plastic trash bags or in plastic trash buckets. Add a moist sponge and close the container tightly. The termites will not need much oxygen. Break off pieces of wood and termites as needed. The cultures could last for months.

3. Termites may be maintained for several days on moistened filter paper in a petri dish. This is a convenient culture method for some experiments.

Removing the symbiotic microorganisms for study

1. Have on hand 0.6 percent NaCl, slides, coverslips, dissecting needles, and fine forceps.

2. Place a drop of saline on a slide.

3. Remove a termite from the culture by picking it up with forceps by the neck.

4. Keep holding the termite with forceps and place it against the glass slide. Cut off its head with a dissecting needle. Figure 1 shows where to make your incision on the termite.

5. Hold the headless neck with forceps and use the needle to press down on the tip of the posterior end. Slowly draw the two instruments apart, thus pulling out the intestine.

6. Discard the body and mince up the digestive system in the saline. Add coverslip and observe first on low power and then at 400x–1000x.

7. If you cannot get the digestive system out neatly, simply mince up the whole termite to make a messy but usable preparation.

8. Look carefully over an entire slide of microorganisms. Note the corkscrew-like movements of the long, helical spirochete bacteria and the gliding movements of the long, rod-like bacteria. Many of the small rod-like, coccoid (spherical), and spiral-shaped bacteria move with bacterial flagella, not visible in this preparation. Note that many of the protists move with long, undulating whip-like organelles. Some have internal mechanisms for motility, such as undulating membranes and motile bundles of microtubules called

3.1 Objective

To investigate the ecological niches of symbiotic protozoa, and develop an understanding of co-evolutionary adaptation.

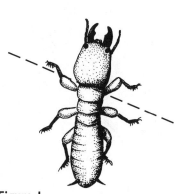

Figure 1
Make the incision to remove the termite's head and intestine as indicated.

✔ Materials

- ❏ Compound and dissecting microscopes
- ❏ Slides, coverslips
- ❏ Saline solution (0.6 g NaCl in 100 ml water)
- ❏ Fine forceps, dissecting needles
- ❏ Filter paper, hole puncher
- ❏ Antibiotic discs
- ❏ Petri dishes
- ❏ Dyes prepared as 1.0 percent aqueous solutions:
    Methylene blue
    Phenosafranin
    Nile blue
    Methyl orange
    Bromocresol blue
    Phenol red
- ❏ Blank paper, pencil
- ❏ Termites *Zootermopsis* or *Reticulitermes*

axostyles. Some of these protists have been described as looking like "a snake in a bag." Figure 2 depicts some typical protozoa found in termite intestines.

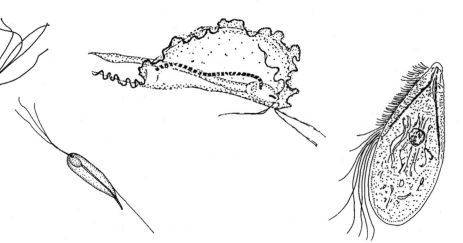

Figure 2
Some typical flagellates found in termites' intestines.

Disrupting the community

1. On filter paper in petri dishes, feed ten or more termites for two days. The number of termites depends on how large an investigation you plan to conduct.

2. Remove termites to two or more petri dishes, set up as follows:
    Control: 5 termites, with 3–4 filter paper discs punched out from filter paper. Moisten the discs.

    Experiment: 5 termites, with 3–4 moistened antibiotic discs. Set up as many experimental plates as you like.

3. Check the community (by sacrificing a termite) on day 1, 2, 3, etc. Check the termites' general health daily.

Testing the digestive system's eH (redox potential) and pH conditions

The eH of a solution is an expression of its oxidizing or reducing capacity—its potential to serve as an oxidizing medium (removing electrons from compounds) or a reducing source (adding electrons to compounds). This redox potential is expressed in terms of millivolts (mV), comparable to voltage that can drive an electrical current. The more negative the eH, the greater the reducing potential, while the more positive the eH, the greater the oxidizing potential.

1. Prepare 1.0 percent solutions of methylene blue, phenosafranin, and Nile blue.

2. Prepare nine termites by feeding them on filter paper discs for two days to clean the wood particles from their systems.

3. Feed termites for an additional two days on filter paper discs moistened with one of the three dyes. Use three termites per dye treatment.

4. Carefully remove the termite's digestive system, and then *quickly* observe colors in the different sections with a hand lens or dissecting scope. Record the eH using the following guide:

   Nile blue becomes white at eH = –186 to –63 mV
   Phenosafranin becomes pink at eH = –312 to –192 mV
   Methylene blue becomes white at eH = 50 to 70 mV

5. Observe over a period of time how the colors change as oxygen enters different sections of the digestive system. Try piercing the large intestine to let in oxygen, thus changing the color of the dye.

6. Look at the microorganisms to see if there were any effects from the dyes.

7. Test the pH (acidity and alkalinity) of the termite's digestive system by setting up the entire investigation again. This time, use 1.0 percent solutions of the following pH indicating dyes:

   Methyl orange changes from red to yellow at pH = 3.1 to 4.4
   Bromocresol blue changes from yellow to purple at pH = 5.2 to 6.8
   Phenol red changes from yellow to red at pH = 6.8 to 8.4.

Discussion and Inquiry

The termite's intestine provides several ecological niches, habitats where a diversity of other organisms survive and thrive. How many species of microbial organisms, including bacteria, live in the termite's intestine? Use a key, such as the one provided in Figure 2, to identify the different protozoa you removed from the termite's intestine. If you have collected termites from your own geographic region and if you know the species, try to get information from the library as to what protozoa species to expect.

How does the biological diversity of this particular ecological community compare with that of larger communities more familiar to you, such as a forest, grassland, or tidal pool? What does the diversity of the microscopic community suggest to you about the uniformity of the intestinal environment?

When you disrupted the community, which types of bacteria or protozoa seem to have been missing or were changed due to antibiotic treatment? How did missing members of the community seem to affect

Note

The termite's intestine will probably have a very negative eH—there is very little oxygen present. Most of the microorganisms that live there are anaerobes with fermentative metabolisms.

other microorganisms and the termite itself? Did it appear that any particular species were essential for the well-being of the symbiotic relationship? What would be an equivalent investigation among macroscopic ecosystems? What characteristics does this unique ecological system share with larger ecosystems, and what makes it different?

What are all these different microorganisms doing? How important are they to each other and to the termite? What happens when we remove certain members of the community? What are some of the physical parameters of the intestine?

Do humans have symbiotic relationships with other species? Are such relationships parasitic, commensal, or mutualistic?

Symbiosis: The Termite as an Ecological Community

Students are probably already aware that evolutionary adaptation occurs through direct competition between predator and prey species. Lions have developed sharper teeth and claws for catching and chewing, and deer have developed longer legs for running away. This is an example of evolutionary adaptation by "tooth and claw," so to speak, and students may be able to suggest other examples from their own experience or from things they've read or seen on television. But this investigation provides an opportunity to expand their knowledge of natural selection processes by helping students understand that evolutionary adaptations can also be subtle, and not all of them are characterized by direct competition through the aggression or elimination of competitors.

The most important symbiosis for the termite involves those microorganisms digesting cellulose to a form usable by the termite. However, other symbioses may be found as well. These include motility symbioses, as well as numerous other microbial interactions of unknown function. The microorganisms display a diverse array of motilities including the corkscrew motions of spirochetes, the gliding of bacterial rods, the churning and mixing motions of some of the larger protozoa, and the movements of other protozoa using highly visible motility organelles. Some motility occurs via motile bacterial symbionts arranged on the surface of a larger cell.

Many of the protozoa may have bacteria in and on them. Some of these are casual associations, but others appear to be symbioses. The physical connections between associates can be quite elaborate (although not visible in this preparation). Many of the functions of the symbioses are not yet known, but some have been shown to involve motility. That is, motile bacteria arranged on the surface of a protist propel themselves and the protist through the medium. Another possibility is that some of the internalized bacteria may even be helping the protozoa digest wood particles.

Termites and their intestinal communities are highly accessible and inexpensive research subjects for the classroom. Depending on the

Micro-Macro Link
Evolutionary adaptations can involve the development of mutually beneficial relationships between species, and aren't all characterized by direct competition through aggression.

Time Management
The basics of this investigation may be completed in one class period. Depending on how many adaptations and variations you wish to incorporate, allow up to two weeks.

3.1
TEACHER SECTION

focus of the class or their personal interest, students can study various themes, including the adaptations and variations outlined below. If students object to dissecting termites, you may prepare the gut isolations in advance, or divide the class into groups to perform different aspects of the investigation.

Termites may be purchased from biological supply companies or collected from the wild. If you purchase your termites, they may be maintained for several weeks in the original cultures with wood. Alternatively, an exterminator may be able to help you locate a colony. Termites collected from the wild may be left in the wood they were nesting in and enclosed in plastic trash bags or in plastic trash buckets. Add a moist sponge and close the container tightly. The termites will not need much oxygen. Break off pieces of wood and termites as needed. The cultures could last for months.

Before the investigation, prepare the dyes (methylene blue, phenosafranin, Nile blue, methyl orange, bromocresol blue, phenol red) as 1.0 percent solutions. Use one gram of dye in 100 ml of water. The solutions can be stored tightly capped for several years. In addition, dozens of different antibiotic discs are available, and may be purchased from biological supply companies.

Adaptations and Variations

Additional experiments might include looking at parameters that might change the diversity of the micro-community. These could include: starvation (provide only drops of water); different types of wood including some with preservatives designed to deter termites (provide tiny shavings or chips and keep them moist); comparisons of different castes and instars, if available. Reproductives, soldiers, and young instars often eat pre-digested wood provided by workers. Is the diversity of the community different when the food is pre-digested? An example of each caste and instar may be collected and preserved in 75–80 percent alcohol.

◆

Try to have students identify as many protozoa and bacteria species as they can. You may want to have students create nicknames for the species they identify so they can easily discuss them.

◆

Have students tabulate data on the increase or decrease of the protozoa population after the termites have been reared during eight weeks in the laboratory. Draw a population curve graph showing the number of protozoa recovered in each isolate from the intestine at intervals of several days during the eight weeks of growth of the termites in the laboratory.

◆

Have students study the degree of activity of the protozoa and their rapidity of movement when the termites have been fed a diet of different kinds of wood. Collect wood from different trees in your locale. Try feeding the termites wood from trees that have resinous secretions such as spruce, larch, or pine. Or try wood from oak, gingko (Chinese fan tree), sweet gum, or sassafras trees to determine their effects on termite flagellates. Which kinds of wood produce the greatest increase in flagellate numbers in the termite gut and which wood seems least supportive of flagellate growth?

Assessment and Evaluation

If students have fully grasped the significance of symbiotic relationships, they should be able to state why a symbiotic association tends to stabilize co-existing populations of organisms. Both the host and the enclosed symbionts benefit from survival-promoting advantages.

Students should also be able to discuss how diverse the populations are in the termite gut. For example, how many different kinds of flagellates were observed, and how numerous were they relative to one another? The larger the number of different kinds and the more close in number they are to one another, the higher the diversity.

The ecological role of other inhabitants of the gut, including bacteria, should be noted as part of the complex community in the termite. For example, some of the flagellates and bacteria are essential since they convert the wood into digestible smaller molecules. Other flagellates and bacteria utilize some of these molecules for their nutrition.

Your students isolated the protozoa from the termite gut in salt water (NaCl). Do they understand the importance of having a mild salt solution? Ask them what they think composes the fluid in the termite gut. Is it pure water, or does it have some dissolved salts in it? Do they understand what happens to cells that are adapted to living in a mildly saline environment if they are suddenly immersed in pure water?

More advanced students should be able to discuss why we conclude that this symbiotic association has developed on an evolutionary time scale rather than being a fortuitous association of the host and symbionts. The strict dependence of the termite on the symbionts and the complex set of physiological and ecological linking factors between host and symbiont suggest a long evolutionary co-adaptation for this association.

Teaching Note

Termite symbionts are sensitive to air and light. To ensure that the coverslip is airtight, spread a thin film of petroleum jelly on the palm of your hand and scrape all four edges of the coverslip along it. This sealing process will also prevent premature drying of the specimens.

About the Author

Betsey Dyer teaches cell biology, genetics, and parasitology at Wheaton College in Massachusetts. Termite microbes are among her favorite organisms because they are fascinating to watch, convenient to study, and wonderful models for all sorts of symbiotic interactions.

Resources

For distributors of termites and other biological supplies, see Appendix VI (pages 219–221). Not all termites native to North America and Europe contain protistan symbionts, and some species contain only bacterial fauna. If you collect termite species in the wild, check to ensure that they contain protists.

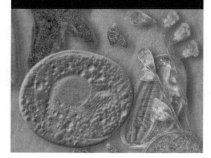

Parasites

Parasitism is an ecological relationship in which two organisms live together, but one derives its nourishment at the expense of the other. Typically, parasites don't kill their hosts the way predators kill their prey, although a host organism may die from secondary infection, or suffer from stunted growth, emaciation, or sterility. Parasites display an astonishing variety of ways and adaptations for exploiting host organisms. The parasites with which you are probably most familiar—such as a tapeworm or a tick—are those that simply attach themselves directly to a host organism and acquire nourishment directly from its cells.

But other forms of parasitism include insects that inject their eggs into a host organism and, by the time the larvae have metamorphosed into their adult form, the host's soft tissues have been completely consumed. Viral infections are another form of parasitism. The presence of a heavy load of such infections is referred to as a disease. Parasites can be plants or animals, and they may in turn parasitize plants or animals or both.

The usual approach to classifying parasites has been taxonomic, meaning they are classified according to species. But parasites may also be distinguished on the basis of their size, as microparasites or macroparasites. Microparasites include viruses, bacteria, and protozoa, while macroparasites include worms, fleas, lice and mistletoe. In this investigation you will examine a protozoan from the phylum Apicomplexa, the *Gregarinidae*. Gregarines are protozoan endoparasites, who live inside a host organism. You will examine the gamont, or sexually reproductive, stage of the gregarines.

So What?

Parasites develop an ecological relationship with host organisms, deriving their nourishment at the expense of the host.

SCI LINKS.
THE WORLD'S A CLICK AWAY

Topic: parasites
Go to: www.scilinks.org
Code: PROT07

3.2 Objective

To understand the parasitic relationship of certain insect species and the protozoa that live in their intestines.

✔ Materials

- ❏ Compound microscope
- ❏ Glass slides, coverslips
- ❏ Eyedroppers
- ❏ Graduated cylinder and jar or flask
- ❏ Forceps and dissecting needle
- ❏ NaCl
- ❏ Distilled or aged tap water
- ❏ Grasshoppers, crickets, cockroaches, and/or meal worms

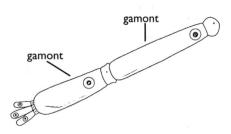

Figure 1
Two *Gregarina socialis* gamonts linked to form a syzygy.

Procedure

1. Prepare a solution of about 0.9 percent NaCl. The preparation does not have to be exact.

2. Put a few drops of this salt solution on a slide.

3. Obtain the intestines of a grasshopper, cricket, cockroach, or meal worm by removing the insect's head with forceps. The gut frequently pulls out along with the head but, if not, squeeze or dissect the insect to get to the intestines.

4. Place the insect's intestine into the salt solution on the slide.

5. Macerate the intestine using the forceps and dissecting needle, so that the intestinal contents are well mixed with the salt solution.

6. Cover some of this macerated material with a coverslip. With the microscope, look for large oval bodies about 100 µm to 500 µm in length. These are the gamonts (sexually reproductive stages) of the gregarines. You may also find two or more such bodies joined one behind the other. This linkage is called syzygy (Figure 1).

7. Look for gliding movements and also for immotile, large cysts; typically spherical bodies 100 µm or larger. The cysts are dormant stages that permit the gregarine to survive during adverse conditions. Observe the body parts of the gamonts. Record your observations. Identify the species using these observations and the attached figures, or a resource book your teacher will provide.

8. If you did not find gregarines, repeat this procedure on a different type of insect. Each type of insect will most likely have different types of mutualistic protozoa.

Discussion and Inquiry

- Why might an organism evolve into a parasite? How does parasitism benefit an invading organism?

- Make a list with two columns, and label one column Advantages and the other Disadvantages. Under Advantages, write down all the benefits that a parasite might derive by invading a host and living there. Under Disadvantages, write down all the benefits a parasite loses by not being free-living in the natural environment.

- Identify examples of parasitic macroscopic organisms with which you are familiar that behave the same way or similarly to the protozoan parasites you observed in this investigation.

Parasites

Parasites live upon or invade the bodies of hosts where they obtain nourishment at the expense of the host's health. Parasitism is very widespread in both the animal and plant kingdoms. Among the protozoa an entire phylum, the Apicomplexa, obtains nutrition by parasitism. This phylum includes endoparasites such as the human malaria parasite, *Plasmodium*. All these pose significant threats to human health.

The parasitic mode of existence is readily demonstrated to students with species of insect parasites in a family of the Apicomplexa, the *Gregarinidae*. Large life stages of these species are easily found in common insects, providing a laboratory experience that is practical for virtually all classrooms. Encourage students to compare this intestinal parasite to parasites of other organs. Students may conduct research to learn how some parasites occupy the muscles, others the glands, and some may be found largely in the nervous or circulatory system. The human malarial parasite is a blood-dwelling parasite in humans, but dwells in the gut of the mosquito before migrating to the mosquito's salivary gland. This is how it is introduced into another human, through the salivary fluid of the mosquito when it bites.

Encourage students to compare the location and parasitic role of the microparasitic gregarine in insects with parasites of humans. For example, the micro-parasitic amoeba *Entamoeaba histolytica* invades the intestine of humans and causes ulceration of the large intestine and diarrhea. Likewise, the flagellate *Giardia* causes an unpleasant but usually not fatal diarrhea. There are certain macroparasites in the human digestive system including tape worms. Discussion can include the similarities and differences between these forms of parasitism and that of the gregarines in insects. Students should be encouraged to describe the major differences in morphology of the species of gregarines, as shown for example in Figure 2.

Micro-Macro Link
Parasitism is widespread among plants and animals, from the micro- to the macroscopic.

Time Management
This investigation may be completed in about one hour.

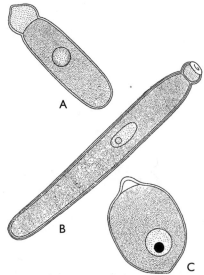

Figure 2
(A) *Leidyana erratica* gamont
(B) *Cnemidospora lutea* gamont
(C) *Sphaerocystis simplex* gamont

Adaptations and Variations

If slides of other protozoan parasites are available from biological supply houses (e.g., prepared slides of trypanosomes, *Entamoeba histolytica*, or the large flagellate *Opalina* living in amphibian guts, etc.), more advanced students can compare the morphological features of these parasites to those of gregarines. The students should evaluate how the life cycle and morphology of the parasite relates to its infective site in the host. For example, trypanosomes have a very prominent undulating membrane attached to the flagellum to help it swim in the serum of the blood. *Entamoeba histolytica* moves by pseudopodial motion. Thus it can creep into crevices in the intestine where it is protected and can invade the underlying tissue causing lesions. The gregarines are able to attach to the gut of their host and glide into places that may be more protected.

◆

If time is available, students may prepare bar graphs showing the number of gregarines observed in the gut of each insect species. The name of the insect or its description forms the x-axis along the bottom of the graph, and the number of gregarines counted in the gut (y-axis) is the height of the bar. This will provide some estimate of the intensity of infection and also which insect species is likely to harbor the most parasites.

Assessment and Evaluation

Parasitism is an important concept in biology. Students should be able to discuss the advantages and disadvantages of parasitism, as opposed to being free-living in natural environments. The lists they construct for Discussion and Inquiry should discuss the advantages of a parasitic form of existence in relation to its limitations. Below are some examples of potential student observations about the advantages and disadvantages of parasitism.

Parasites have the advantage of ready sources of nourishment in a host, they can be protected if properly concealed within a safe site, and they may avoid predators by growing and reproducing within a portion of the host where there are no predators. They have the disadvantage of sometimes becoming dependent on the host for their nutrition. This means that if they are fatal to the host, they must have some way of being transmitted to another host. In some cases this can be as a resting stage such as a cyst that is resistant to drying and can be passed out of the host body and ingested by another host. Other parasites use an intermediate host to carry them from one primary host to another.

For example the human malarial parasite is carried by a mosquito from one human to another. Free-living organisms must search for their food, may be more vulnerable to predators, and sometimes must face harsh environmental conditions. However, free-living organisms are less dependent on one environment for their survival. They are free to move about and find more favorable environments, and they may be less specialized to inhabit a particular niche. In the long run, they may have greater genetic variability and thus greater potential for evolutionary adaptation.

Students should understand the differences in size and morphology between microparasites and macroparasites. If given a list of parasites, students should be able to categorize them into micro- or macroparasites. Also, students should be able to explain how the parasite invades a new host, especially if the parasite is fatal to the host.

More generally, students should know that the gregarines are classified within a larger taxonomic group of protozoa, the Apicomplexa, that also includes the blood parasite of human malaria, *Plasmodium*. The gut of an insect is a very specialized environment, meaning its salinity, oxygen, and pH are probably different from natural aquatic environments. Students should discuss what features of the parasite allow it to survive in these specialized conditions. For example, it may not use oxygen in respiration and have a form of anaerobic respiration, as in some yeasts or bacteria that dwell in oxygen-depleted environments. Students should also understand the role of the cyst as a way of avoiding unfavorable environments, and as a stage in the parasite's life cycle that allows ingestion by a new host.

Advanced students may devise experiments to determine the host range of a parasite. For example, if parasite-free individuals of a potential host species can be obtained, the parasite can be introduced to the host, and the number of each species infected tabulated as a way of estimating susceptibility to infection.

About the Author

Henry Tamar has taught protozoology at Indiana State University. He believes the personal experience of discovering parasites in a host organism might well be an initial stimulus that leads to a research career in an area of parasitology.

Resources

For distributors of biological supplies, see Appendix VI (pages 219–221).

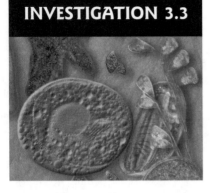

Competitive Exclusion and Environmental Adaptation

So What?

Species that adapt to environmental changes easily and quickly tend to outcompete species that don't.

In the 1930s, ecologist G.F. Gause was interested in the way species compete with one another. To study the interactions between competing species from the same genus, he reared together under constant conditions a population of *Paramecium caudatum* (Figure 1) and its competitor, *Paramecium aurelia*, in a test tube. Gause found that *P. aurelia* out-competed *P. caudatum*. Indeed, *P. aurelia* drove *P. caudatum* to extinction in Gause's controlled environment.

Then, Gause changed the conditions in the test tube by adding sediment to the bottom of the tube. Under these new conditions, *P. caudatum* took refuge in the sediment and continued to multiply, coexisting with *P. aurelia*. By hiding in the sediment *P. caudatum* adapted to the changed environmental conditions.

Gause's investigation was at the microscopic level, but the ecological principle he demonstrated has since proven true for organisms at macroscopic levels too. This principle of competitive exclusion, which states that a more adaptive species tends to displace a less adaptive one, must be demonstrated using mathematics. In this investigation, you will conduct an experiment similar to Gause's, and you will use math skills to analyze your results.

Figure 1
Paramecium caudatum.

Procedure

1. Prepare glass micropipets by following your teacher's instructions.

2. Maintain stocks of two separate and distinct genera of micro-organisms using charcoal-filtered pond water (CHPW) or bottled spring water and wheat germ kernel in clean glass bowls. *Blepharisma* (Figure 2) and *Euplotes* (Figure 3) will work particularly well for this investigation.

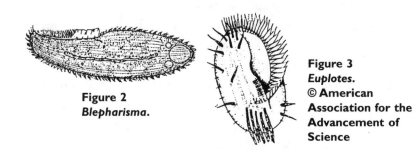

Figure 2
Blepharisma.

Figure 3
Euplotes.
© American Association for the Advancement of Science

3. Before undertaking the investigation, fill each of a Falcon™ dish's six wells with 5 ml of CHPW. Place one *Blepharisma* in each depression along with 0.5 ml of a distilled water-washed wheat germ kernel or grain. Do the same for the other genus, *Euplotes*.

4. Count the number of single-celled protozoa present each day for about a week. This may be done using a micropipet and a stereoscopic dissecting microscope. If necessary remove the organisms one by one to a separate container. When finished, return them to the well from which they originally came.

5. Make a growth curve by plotting the data on a daily basis. Use Figure 4 as a model. Plot the number of single-celled organisms you observe each day on the Y axis and the number of days on the X axis.

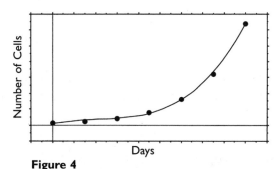

Figure 4
A growth curve showing the increase in cell count over time. The cell number doubles every 1.5 days.

✔ Materials

- ❑ Compound light microscope, oil immersion objectives
- ❑ Stereoscopic dissecting microscope
- ❑ Glass slides, coverslips
- ❑ Immersion oil
- ❑ Falcon™ 6-well plastic culture dishes, covers
- ❑ Wheat germ
- ❑ Pasteur pipets
- ❑ Bunsen burner
- ❑ Rubber bulbs
- ❑ Grooved forceps
- ❑ Charcoal-filtered pond water (CHPW), or bottled spring water
- ❑ Magnetic stirrers
- ❑ 1 l Erlenmeyer flask
- ❑ Finger bowls, 200 ml
- ❑ Blank paper, pencil
- ❑ Two distinct genera of microorganisms

3.3
INVESTIGATION

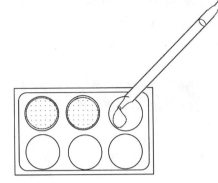

Figure 5
Preparation of a 6-well Falcon™ plastic culture dish containing 5 ml of charcoal-filtered pond water (CHPW) per well.

6. To set up the competition experiments, place one individual of each of the two genera into each of four wells in a six-well dish (Figure 5). Each well will now contain two cells, one of each genus. Also prepare two control wells in the six-well dish, one for each genus. Each control well will have two identical cells of the same genus. For example, there should be two cells of *Blepharisma* in one control well and two cells of *Euplotes* in the other control well.

7. Count the number of cells per well daily for one week using a stereoscopic dissecting microscope. With some practice, you should be able to estimate the number of cells of each genus by scanning the contents of each well. Slow-moving ciliates such as *Blepharisma* are easy to count by eye. Counts can be made manually using fine-tipped Pasteur pipets fitted with rubber bulbs. Remove each organism as it is counted to a separate container while viewing through a stereo dissecting microscope. Some practice is necessary to develop skill at this procedure. All of the organisms must be replaced in their respective wells to continue the experiment, so be certain to keep accurate records as you conduct this investigation.

8. Plot a growth curve for each genus on the graph you developed in Step 5, along with the controls, for comparison.

9. Through the creation of growth curves for each species, both separately and together, determine which genus will outcompete the other. What do the generation rates suggest about this competition?

Discussion and Inquiry

An interesting measure of growth is the generation number, which is the number of times the single-celled organisms have divided during a growth interval—how many generations of daughter cells have been produced. For example, suppose you begin with two cells. When these two cells divide, they produce four cells. This is the first generation of daughter cells. These four cells will divide to produce eight cells, the second generation, and so on.

How many generations have occurred by the time there are 64 cells? We can determine this using the formula for the generation number as follows:

$$\text{Generation number } (g) = (\log B - \log A)/\log 2$$

A is a count of the cells at a point when the growth has entered the logarithmic phase, and B is the count of cells at a later point in time. Using our example above, B = 64 (the final cell count) and A = 2 (the beginning cell count). The log of 64 = 1.806, and the log of 2 = 0.301; g = (1.806–0.301)/0.301 = 5. By the time there are 64 cells in the culture, five generations of daughter cells have been produced. The rate of generation or rate of cell division is D = g/t where t is the time in days between taking counts A and B. The generation rate will be expressed in this case as cell divisions per day.

Using our above example of an increase from 2 to 64 cells, assume that this took 10 days (i.e., t = 10, D = 5/10 or 0.5). At this rate of reproduction the number of cell divisions was 0.5 per day. Or, stating it in other terms, it requires two days on the average between cell divisions or each doubling of the protozoan population.

By determining the generation number and rate, you can see that the species that is able to outgrow its competitor has the ecological advantage within a particular environment.

Competitive Exclusion and Environmental Adaptation

Micro-Macro Link

Competitive exclusion—a more adaptive species tends to displace a less adaptive one—is one of ecology's organizing principles, and occurs from micro- to macroscopic levels.

Time Management

This investigation requires approximately one class period for initial setup, and 30 minutes each day for one week to tabulate student findings.

This investigation provides an easy way to demonstrate a basic ecological principle—competitive exclusion—using competing ciliates. But competitive exclusion is not limited to microbes. For example, Gause's contemporary, A.G. Tansley, demonstrated the effect of this principle on the distribution of two species of bedstraw plants. One species grows in acidic and the other in alkaline soil. When the two were grown together in the same soil (either acid or basic), the survivor was the one normally found there.

In yet another competition experiment, this one during the 1970s, N.G. Hairston studied competitive exclusion between salamander species in the Great Smokey Mountains. At lower elevations, *Plethodon glutinosus* (Figure 6) dominates, while at higher elevations, *P. jordanii* (Figure 7) is prevalent. Because some overlap does occur, Hairston removed species from different test plots in overlapping ranges; some plots he left untouched as controls. For five years, nothing happened in the control plots: the two species coexisted. In those plots where one species was allowed to exist while the other was removed, that species proliferated.

Students may want to research Gause's competitive exclusion studies. If they do so, it can then be informative to have them consider what they learned through their research as they conduct this investigation. Students can conduct this investigation critically, and retrace Gause's steps to make sure he did everything scientifically. How, for example, might this investigation be varied or altered to address interesting factors Gause may have missed? Students should be encouraged to understand that they are themselves contributing to the relatively young science of ecology.

Figure 6
Plethodon glutinosus.

Figure 7
Plethodon jordanii.

This investigation provides an opportunity for students to see firsthand the practical application of mathematical principles in both learning and doing science. As they conduct this investigation, encourage students to understand that they are engaged in a real-world scientific experiment just like the one Gause undertook more than half a century ago. They are doing an actual scientific study using real scientific tools and skills, particularly mathematics, not performing a truncated version for the purpose of teaching basics only. Gause's competition studies have provided one of ecology's most important organizing principles, one that has served as a model for continued scientific investigation of predator-prey relationships for decades.

Adaptations and Variations

If you are interested only in demonstrating growth curves, *Blepharisma* is particularly useful. Have the students add about two individuals by carefully pipetting them into a culture dish containing a wheat kernel. It is preferable to boil the wheat kernel about three minutes to soften it before cooling and use. The small culture dish should be covered to prevent evaporation. The number of *Blepharisma* can be counted at one- or two-day intervals by examining them with a dissecting microscope. Keep the culture dishes in the dark, and the *Blepharisma* will become decidedly pink due to the blepharismin pigment. They are easily seen against a black background when illuminated from above. If the cultures are not disturbed much when moving them to the microscope, most of the *Blepharisma* will be on the bottom and can be counted very easily by eye. Figure 4 shows a sample growth curve for protozoa.

◆

A quantitative variation of this experiment could involve determining the volume of the cells used—*Blepharisma* has a 3-dimensional shape resembling an oval with the following formula: $V = 4/3\Pi r^2 h$, where V = volume, r = radius, and h = length of the *Blepharisma*. *Euplotes* has the general shape of a hemisphere, and the formula for volume is $V = 2/3\Pi r^3$. By determining the approximate volume of each you can determine the approximate number of cells needed of each organism to be equal in mass. For example, it might be that the volume of four *Euplotes* would be equal to the volume of one *Blepharisma*. This might provide a better starting population for comparison, if cell volume is a key factor in the competitive exclusion process.

Assessment and Evaluation

Have students discuss other examples of competitive exclusion, such as different species of duckweed in a pond or different species of birds at different levels on a tree. Do humans compete among themselves like

Teaching Note

If you would like to involve students in preparation, and if time allows, they can help prepare filtered water as a substitute for sodium-free, bottled mineral water. Prepare charcoal-filtered pond water by adding 2 g of activated charcoal to one liter of pond water. Mix for 20 minutes, then filter out the charcoal through a large piece of circular filter paper. Repeat if necessary until no charcoal remains. The result is charcoal-filtered pond water (CHPW).

other animals, plants, or protozoa?

How do various environmental factors affect this kind of competition? From other examples of competitive exclusion, students can learn that each species has certain requirements for existence. This investigation provides a good way to introduce students to scientific library research, and to highlight the importance of researching the work of other scientists in conducting any scientific investigation. Suggestions for getting students started on library research are provided in Resources.

Students should be able to discuss the advantage of using mathematics and graphs to support and prove a point. Students should demonstrate an understanding of what is meant by "a scientific argument." Some lawyers argue for a living, but that doesn't mean they're always angry. Scientists also argue, and students should understand the value of supporting a scientific argument with proper data presentation.

About the Author

Arthur J. Repak teaches protozoology, environmental microbiology, and freshman biology at Quinnipiac College in Hamden, Connecticut. Since protists do not exist independent of their environment or other microorganisms, studies of competitive exclusion and growth curves demonstrate that contests for survival are ongoing, realistic events in nature.

Resources

Begon, M., Harper, J., and Townsend, C. 1990. *Ecology: Individuals, Populations, and Communities*. 2nd edition. Sunderland, MA: Sinauer.

Gause, G.F. 1934. *The Struggle for Existence*. Baltimore: Williams and Wilkins.

Hairston, N.G. 1980. "The experimental test of an analysis of field distributions: competition in terrestrial salamanders." *Ecology*, 6(1): 817–826.

Jacobs, V. and Repak, A.J. 1989. "Competitive exclusion between the marine heterotrich ciliate *Fabrea salina* and the marine hypotrich *Euplotes vannus*." Unpublished paper presented to the Society of Protozoologists at Hofstra University.

Tansley, A.G. 1917. "On competition between *Galium saxatile* l. and *Galium sylvestre* poll. on different types of soil." *Journal of Ecology*, 5: 173–179.

For distributors of biological supplies, such as CHPW and Falcon™ dishes, see Appendix VI (pages 219–221). Wheat germ is also available from health food stores.

Predators of Protozoa

The relationship between a predator and its prey is often quite complex. One interesting aspect of such relationships involves natural mechanisms for maintaining population densities, so that both predator and prey populations can coexist. Without such natural mechanisms, one population or the other might grow too large, causing the other to suffer and decline. If a predator population significantly outgrows that of its prey, for example, the latter might even become extinct. If that were to occur, the predator population would also be placed at risk because it would have no food.

Evolution, however, has developed natural mechanisms to keep the populations of both groups substantially balanced over time. One such mechanism is heterogeneity, which means that a prey population remains dispersed according to no fixed pattern. Such a 0scattered arrangement decreases the chances that an entire population of organisms will be wiped out by predators. Another mechanism is a predator's ability to switch foods when its usual prey becomes scarce. Through such adaptive mechanisms, nature has developed a sustainable community, in which neither prey nor predator is ever significantly outnumbered.

In this investigation, you will examine a third adaptation known as predator-induced defense. Predator-induced defense means that prey respond to their predators by changing their behavior or their form. This investigation uses *Euplotes* (Figure 1), a protozoan species that changes its physiological structure when predators are nearby.

So What?

Some organisms can change their shape when threatened by a predator.

Figure 1
Euplotes.
© 1985 American Association for the Advancement of Science

3.4 Objective

To understand how protozoa adapt in response to predation.

✔ Materials

- ❑ Compound light microscope
- ❑ Slides, coverslips
- ❑ Pasteur pipets
- ❑ Several 10–100 ml glass jars
- ❑ Cotton
- ❑ Pond water
- ❑ India ink, or picric acid
- ❑ Wheat stalk, or rice grains

Procedure

To conduct this investigation, you must first isolate and grow *Euplotes* cells as prey organisms, as well as at least one protozoan or metazoan predator organism that will feed on them. You also will need smaller ciliates or flagellates to feed both *Euplotes* and their predators. If you already have some suitable feed organisms—such as *Colpidium campylum, Tetrahymena thermophila, Chilomonas paramecium,* or *Chlorogonium elongatum*—proceed to Step 4. Otherwise follow these procedures.

1. Fill each of several jars 2/3 full with filtered pond water, and place them on a window sill where they will be kept cool and receive indirect sunlight. The jars should contain small, single-celled organisms, but they should lack large predatory protozoans and metazoans. To some of the jars, add some pieces of wheat stalk or two to three grains of rice as a nutrient source.

2. After several days, use a Pasteur pipet to draw up from some of the jars fluid containing small food organisms at a relatively high density. Transfer these food organisms to new jars containing heat-sterilized pond water, and either no or the same nutrients as before. You should find photosynthetic flagellates in the jars with no added nutrients, and non-photosynthetic flagellates (as well as some small ciliates) in the jars with added nutrients.

3. Wait several more days to allow the food organisms to regain their high densities.

4. From natural pond water, isolate *Euplotes* cells, as well as large predatory ciliates and metazoans, especially tiny worms such as turbellarians and oligochaetes. Place several individual organisms of the same species into small glass jars. Try to feed *Euplotes* and the other organisms you have isolated from the natural pond water with the small food organisms you grew previously. Every other day, feed *Euplotes*, predatory ciliates, or metazoans only as much food as they will eat within a few hours. Keep the jars in a cool, dark location, and do not add any nutrients other than the small food organisms.

5. After several weeks you should have at least one culture of *Euplotes* and some other cultures of predatory protozoans or metazoans. At that time, mix a few starved predators with *Euplotes* and observe whether or not the predators feed on them. If they do, conduct the following investigations.

6. In a 10 ml glass jar, mix a few well fed predators, about 10–20 turbellarians or about 50 ciliates, with at least 100 well fed *Euplotes*.

Leave some *Euplotes* in the original culture; do not mix them with the predator organisms. If you have larger numbers of single-celled and other organisms, use the same ratio as above but mix as many individuals as possible in as little medium as possible.

7. Make a wet mount slide and study the form of the *Euplotes* you took from the original culture. To observe a living sample, add India ink to the *Euplotes*; to view a fixed sample add picric acid. Twenty four hours after mixing *Euplotes* with their predators, find out whether or not there are still any *Euplotes* left in the mixture with their predators. With a narrow-tipped pipet, isolate some of the remaining *Euplotes* and study their cellular form. *Euplotes* taken from the mixture will probably have a different, greatly enlarged, circular form, such as that shown in Figure 2. Can you explain this result?

8. Fill two jars with 2 ml medium, and add a fixed number of predator cells. Add the same number of transformed *Euplotes* cells to one jar, and the same number of non-transformed *Euplotes* cells to the other jar. *Be sure to use the exact same number of both* Euplotes *and predator cells in each jar.* Shake the jars gently every five minutes for one hour, then count the remaining *Euplotes* cells in each jar.

9. Transfer a few transformed *Euplotes* cells into a jar filled with filtered pond medium. What happens to *Euplotes* after the cells are separated from their predators? Re-examine the shape of these cells a few days later.

10. Continue feeding the *Euplotes*/predator mixtures with the flagellates and/or ciliates culture. How long will *Euplotes* survive when co-cultivated with its predator?

Discussion and Inquiry

Living cells change their shape, or other characteristics, to better survive during predation or other environmental pressures. This investigation illustrates subtle forms of communication among populations of organisms within an ecological community. Consider what kind of signal induces the *Euplotes* to change its shape. Is the shape change due to contact with the predator, chemical compounds produced by the predator, or that only smaller forms of the *Euplotes* are eaten and thus the larger forms are selectively favored? The latter is not likely, since the shape change is so remarkable that it cannot be explained simply by larger ones being favored by not being eaten. It is more likely that some chemical substance released by the predator induces changes in the shape of the prey. Devise an investigation to test the idea that a predator-released chemical substance is present in the medium.

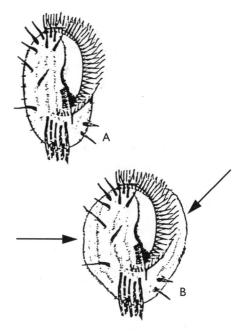

Figure 2
(A) *Euplotes* **with a normal shape is transformed into (B) an expanded shape when cultured with a predator. The flared enlargements, marked by arrows, are called "wings," and they make it more difficult to be ingested by the predator. The oral aperture is lined by a complex set of beating cilia; the longer projections at the posterior end are bundles of cilia, called "cirri." © American Association for the Advancement of Science.**

Predators of Protozoa

Micro-Macro Link

Predators and prey don't always compete directly, by "tooth and claw." Their competition can involve more subtle physiological and behavioral adaptations, such as a chameleon's ability to camouflage itself or a skunk's noxious release.

Time Management

If advance preparation is performed by the teacher, this investigation may be completed in one class period. If you wish to involve students in preparation, perform Steps 1–6 up to four weeks in advance.

Student findings may be generalized to macroscopic ecosystems. At least 30 multicellular animals—including rotifer species, cladocerans, bryozoans, and barnacles—and more than 100 species of terrestrial plants are capable of inducible defenses in response to signals emitted by predators.

This investigation provides an opportunity to discuss the evolutionary significance of physiological and behavioral adaptive mechanisms. Encourage students to describe the subtle ways living organisms can compete and survive by rather "simple" adjustments in shape and size. Not all predator-prey relationships involve direct competition, and students should be encouraged to appreciate the evolutionary basis for physiological and behavioral adaptation strategies.

This investigation provides a good illustration of the biological roots of adaptive behavior, whether physiological or behavioral. *Euplotes*, for example, transforms into an expanded shape when cultured along with a predator (Figure 3). Subtle physiological capabilities that typically do not appear under low predatory pressure can become readily apparent as adaptive features when predatory pressures increase.

Hormones in higher organisms are compounds released by one tissue that affect the activity of other body tissues. These signaling molecules induce physiological or structural changes in the target tissues. In a very

Figure 3
Optical transverse sections through *Euplotes* before (A) and after (B) exposure to a predator. The long ventral projections are some of the cirri, which *Euplotes* uses to "walk" on a substrate. © American Association for the Advancement of Science.

primitive way, the induction of changes in cell shape of *Euplotes* by substances released by the predator is an example of this kind of signaling among different populations of organisms.

The primary point of this investigation—living cells change their shape, or other characteristics, to better survive during predation or other environmental pressures—can be related more broadly to other examples. Changes in human cell shapes can help prevent attack by parasitic organisms. Sickle cell anemia, for example, is a disease that affects human red blood cells. It occurs with high frequency in people of African descent or those from the Mediterranean area near Africa. Sickle cell anemia may appear to be maladaptive, but in regions of high malaria it actually helps protect red blood cells against malarial parasites. Such a survival "trade-off" favors continuation of the genetic trait, even though it causes stress and some physiological disability. The red blood cells become sickle-shaped when they pass through tissue where oxygen is low. The shape prevents easy passage of the red blood cell through narrow vascular tissue and causes pain and discomfort. However, the sickle-shaped cells are more resistant to the malaria parasite that is common in tropical climates in Africa and surrounding regions. It is unfortunate that the sickle cells cause so much human suffering, but we can understand why the shape change has been positively selected in the populations where it occurs. Though the disease is debilitating, it provides a survival trade-off by helping to protect the individual against predation by the malarial parasite, a usually fatal disease in early life.

Adaptations and Variations

As a source of predators and prey organisms such as *Euplotes*, collect samples of pond water from several different freshwater ponds. Alternatively, if you have not been successful isolating *Euplotes* from a natural pond, ask the American Type Culture Collection (ATCC) for a test tube of *Euplotes aediculatus*, strain No. 30859.

◆

A suitable substitute for the predatory ciliates and turbellarians in this investigation is the rhizopod, *Amoeba proteus*, which can be used as a predator of *Euplotes*. In this case, an induced avoidance response of the prey (instead of or, in some *Euplotes* species, in addition to the physiological transformation) can be observed after about 24 hours.

Assessment and Evaluation

Life exhibits many remarkable forms of adaptation to support species survival and reproduction. In some cases, the survival of a species may involve getting sources of energy and nutrition with greater efficiency than other species. In this investigation, changes in shape that occur in response to the presence of a predator can give a species survival advantage by making it less available to its predators. Students should realize that these changes are induced by a predator's presence, through chemical signal molecules, and not by the protozoan "intentionally" altering its shape. Here is a good opportunity to determine if students can explain these observations in scientific, mechanistic terms rather than by anthropomorphic reasoning.

For example, students should note that protozoa do not have a nervous system as in higher forms of life, and they also lack the sophisticated brain structures of humans. It is therefore unlikely that any behavioral responses among protozoans are intentional. Ask students to evaluate how likely it is that the mere presence of the predator is enough to cause the shape change. What possible signal could be presented by the mere presence of the predator? If students recognize that a chemical signal is likely, encourage them to devise an experiment to test the idea. Elicit a statement of hypothesis, such as "Predator-induced shape change is due to a chemical substance released by the predator that triggers changes in the shape of the cell." Evaluate how well students construct their hypotheses. Do they clearly cite the variables and indicate how the variables are related to one another? Are the variables stated in a way that they can be implemented in an experiment?

Assess how well students devise a plan to test their hypotheses. This can be done by group discussion. Elicit suggestions such as: (1) "Grow a large quantity of the predators in a small container," or (2) "Take samples of the culture fluid each day, ensuring no predators were included in the sample. Add it to the *Euplotes* culture and observe whether shape change occurs."

Determine if students understand the need for a control in an experimental investigation. For example, a control culture of *Euplotes* should have something added in the same manner as the predator culture fluid, but lacking the predator signal. Every aspect of the control should be the same as the experimental treatment, except no predator extract should be introduced. One control might be to set up a culture dish with the same culture medium as was used for the predator, but no predator would be added. This culture fluid could be used as the control treatment. It could be added to the control *Euplotes* culture in the same amount and at the same time as the addition of the predator culture medium to the experimental treatment. If the experimental *Euplotes* change shape but the control does not, this helps support the hypothesis.

About the Author

Hans-Werner Kuhlmann teaches protozoology at Münster University in Germany, and is affiliated with the Institut für Allgemeine Zoologie and Genetik.

Resources

Kuhlmann, H.-W. and Heckmann, K. 1985. "Interspecific morphogens regulating predator-prey relationships in protozoa." *Science*, 227: 1347–1349.

Kuhlmann, H.-W. and Heckmann, K. 1994. "Predation risk of typical ovoid and 'winged' morphs of *Euplotes* (Protozoa, Ciliaphora)." *Hydrobiologia*, 284: 219–227.

Kusch, J. 1993. "Behavioral and morphological changes in ciliates induced by the predator *Amoeba proteus*." *Oecologia*, 96: 354–359.

For distributors of biological supplies, see Appendix VI (pages 219–221).

4
Comparative Ecology

All species of organisms live in communities and occupy ecological niches. Humans are purely terrestrial. Protozoa, by contrast, live in a wide variety of habitats, including soils, water, and inside other organisms. And, despite their microscopic size, protozoa live in well-organized communities and exhibit identifiable responses to environmental changes just like humans do.

This section explores the varied habitats of protozoa, especially how they form communities and how they are distributed within those communities. As they conduct these investigations, students will learn how the ecology of microscopic communities compares and contrasts with the ecology of macroscopic communities. Students will explore colonization and succession, the relationships between nutrient quality, gradients, and distribution, net respiration and carbon cycling, predator-prey interactions, and the ecological effects of contamination and pollution. As they examine how protozoa interact with their particular environments, students will develop a better understanding of how humans interact with their own environments.

Species Colonization

So What?

Every time a new habitat is created, whether it's a mountain raised by a volcano or a drop of water left after a rainfall, it becomes colonized by many species of organisms.

New habitats are created in many ways. In some cases catastrophic disturbances eliminate all the living things in a certain area. In other instances, naturally or artificially created habitats alter the balance of life that already exists. New habitats may be created at a variety of different scales. A new large-scale habitat may be created after a volcanic eruption, for example, while a new small-scale habitat may be created by a pool of standing water left after a rainfall. New habitats are like barren ecological islands, and the process by which communities of different species develop on such islands is called colonization.

The creation of any new habitat invites a host of species that are especially suited to being good colonists. The first organisms to colonize a newly created or a substantially altered habitat are called opportunistic or pioneer species. These first colonists are succeeded by those slower to take advantage of the new habitat, and by those that are dependent on changes that the first colonists make to that environment. In this way, the composition of the community changes over time. Figure 1 shows how plant organisms have colonized a newly created or disturbed habitat.

The most important factor affecting which species colonizes a new habitat is nutrient availability. Is there enough of the right kind of food to make colonization productive and worthwhile? Other important factors are the new habitat's ecological conditions, such as temperature, water and oxygen, and stability. In this investigation, you will create new "island" habitats out of polyurethane foam (PF) blocks, monitor the microscopic species that colonize them—especially protozoa—and form hypotheses about why you think those particular species were the first to take advantage of the new habitats.

Figure 1
The first organisms to colonize a newly created or disturbed habitat are hardy pioneer species. In this diagram, the first colonizers were the lichens at right, followed by larger plants such as mosses, ferns, and shrubs. These are eventually replaced by pioneer tree species, such as those shown progressing toward the left.

112

Procedure

1. To make artificial substrates from polyurethane foam (PF), cut the foam into blocks about 4×5×6 cm using the serrated knife. *Be extremely careful when using the knife, and do so only under the supervision of your teacher.* Blocks of smaller or larger size can also be used. Wet or wash the blocks in distilled water before using them—this step is essential for the organisms' growth.

2. Decide on an organizing question. You can pose many questions about the way new habitats are colonized, but a few examples might include: Which PF islands accumulate species most quickly and in the greatest diversity? What kinds of organisms are likely to be pioneers? How did you alter the environment to either help or hinder colonization? What kinds of organisms are likely to arrive last and why?

3. Once you have decided on your organizing question, you will need to think about how you want to arrange the PF blocks in the aquarium. The arrangement and number of blocks you use will be determined by your organizing question. For example, if you want to investigate how a habitat's size affects its colonization, you might place PF blocks of differing sizes equal distances from a starting point, a central or epicenter block. In general, the colonized PF blocks serve as the source of species, the epicenters from which species colonize the barren PF blocks. The epicenters are analogous to a "mainland," while the barren PF blocks represent newly created "island" habitats.

4. Measure the distance between the epicenters and barren PF blocks in some regular way, such as between centers or between nearest edges. A good distance is 10–15 cm. The barren blocks should range from very small—perhaps 1 cm³—to about twice the size of the epicenters.

5. After deciding how to arrange the blocks in order to address your organizing question, place enough water in an aquarium or tray to cover the blocks. You may want to find a way to anchor the blocks, such as hooks glued to the bottom with non-toxic silicon caulk.

6. Cover the tray or tank with plastic film to keep the blocks from drying out. Use a form of uniform illumination to further assure the protists survival. Let the set up sit undisturbed for two to three weeks to allow ample time for species colonization to occur.

7. To sample a PF block, lift it from the colonization aquarium or tray and immediately squeeze the contents into a collection receptacle,

4.1 Objective

To understand how species colonize newly created habitats.

✔ Materials

- ❑ Compound or video microscope
- ❑ Slides, coverslips
- ❑ Eyedroppers
- ❑ 5–10 l aquaria or trays
- ❑ Pasteurized pond or aged tap water
- ❑ Polyurethane foam (PF) blocks
- ❑ Serrated knife
- ❑ Collection receptacles
- ❑ Blank paper, pencil

such as a beaker or jar. Let the sample settle for a few minutes; the organisms will sink to the bottom and concentrate there.

8. Make a wet mount slide using a sample taken from the bottom of the collection receptacle. Examine the sample on a microscope by systematically scanning from left to right. The best views will be at higher magnifications (200–400x), but a good estimate of species abundance and diversity can be made at 100x. Sketch the organisms you observe and identify them using a field guide or textbook. Be sure to look at the algae as well as the protozoa. The protozoa usually will be moving, but they will settle down after a few minutes on the slide.

9. Record which species were present on which PF blocks at what intervals, and estimate their numbers. Build a life list—a list of the species you observe and identify—for each of the different islands.

Discussion and Inquiry

• If you repeated this investigation using the exact same conditions, would the results be exactly the same? Why do you think there might be variations between your replicate investigations?

• How would you expect species to change over time once they colonize a barren PF block? Would there be fewer or more species? Would there be fewer or more individuals within a particular species? How might the species interact? Would you expect small islands to hold fewer or more species of organisms? Would you expect islands nearer an epicenter to hold fewer or more species than islands farther away? As you answer these questions, try to use the language of ecology, framing your answers in terms of species abundance, diversity, and competition.

• In science there is a strong connection between an investigator's organizing question and how an investigation is designed. In Step 2 you were asked to decide on your organizing question, and in Step 3 you were asked to arrange the PF blocks in a way that might provide answers to your question. Now that you have completed the procedural portion of this investigation, reexamine your organizing question and your investigation's design (i.e., the arrangement of the PF blocks). Do you feel that there is a strong enough connection between your question and your design to support your conclusions? If not, how would you reframe your question and/or redesign the investigation to support a stronger connection?

• During this investigation, you have examined species colonization of newly-created habitats at the microscopic level. Can you think of examples at macroscopic levels of the same or similar ecological processes? Describe any differences and similarities between microscopic and macroscopic species colonization.

Species Colonization

Micro-Macro Link

Colonization of new habitats, whether microscopic or macroscopic, always involves some agent of disturbance.

Time Management

If preparations are made in advance, this investigation may be completed in one class period. Allow between two and three weeks for organisms to colonize PF blocks, whether collected from the wild or prepared in an aquarium.

Students should understand that a "new habitat" at the microscopic level may consist of no more than a fresh dung heap, a fallen acorn, or a pool of standing water. Regardless of the scale of a new habitat's creation, the ecological principle by which all species colonize any newly created habitat is the same. This investigation provides a way to demonstrate that principle at the microscopic level, and establish links among habitats at macroscopic levels.

Colonization, and the succession of species that follows, is a complicated and much debated process. Ecologists generally agree, however, that it is a dynamic process that always involves some agent of disturbance. Encourage students to think about different ecosystems and the different kinds of disturbances that are likely to occur there. For example, in a forest ecosystem, fire and human action are two agents of disturbance that occur regularly. An intertidal ecosystem regularly experiences disturbances caused by waves, rising and falling tides, and wind.

In all ecosystems, animal activity regularly creates new habitats ripe for colonization by a host of different species, from microscopic to macroscopic levels. Examples of such activity include carcasses left after predation and natural death, excrement, and migration. In each case, a new habitat is created that may be colonized by different species.

Protists may be collected from the wild using the procedure outlined in Appendix III (pages 212–214), or you can establish a varied culture of protists in an aquarium by following the classroom protist cultivation procedure outlined in Appendix II (pages 210–211).

PF foam is sold as cushion or pillow material at fabric stores, or as sheets of foam in variety and department stores. The easiest material to work with is five cm thick, medium density foam—it is also the most common kind sold in stores. Pond or stream water may be used in the aquariums in which students will monitor species colonization, but this water will need to be "pasteurized." A simple method is to heat the water to about 50°–70°C and then cool it by aeration. The water used should be more or less free of organisms, and definitely should NOT be distilled or deionized—organisms need the trace elements and nutrients to survive.

A protozoa field guide, such as those cited in the Appendix VI (pages 219–221), will help students examine the details of the morphology and structure of microorganisms. An estimate of species diversity can be achieved by having students sketch the organisms they observe and record how many different species are present in the samples. Alternatively, students may class the organisms they observe according to broader groups, such as photosynthetic or heterotrophic and ciliate, flagellate, or amoeba. A good starting point is to have students practice sketching before starting the investigation. Using this technique, students can develop a starting life list for the source ecosystem.

Teaching Note
Use tap water aged 24–48 hours to eliminate chlorine.

Adaptations and Variations

This investigation provides an opportunity for students to create and discuss growth curves, using the records they have developed of species abundance, diversity, and rates of colonization. They may already have some idea of growth curves based on their observations of the numbers of individuals they observed in the PF blocks over the course of this investigation. Have students make a graph, such as the one shown in Figure 2, of the number of protozoa found in the PF block as a function of time. This will give a graphic portrayal of how the numbers increase with time, a growth curve. Students may then compare growth curves obtained from different PF blocks, and especially those in different environmental conditions. Based on the trace of the graph, students should deduce which PF blocks showed the most rapid increase in number of protozoa with time, and which the least. Are there differences in the shape of the trace of the graph? Do some graphs show a slow increase with time, while others seem to increase very rapidly or abruptly over time?

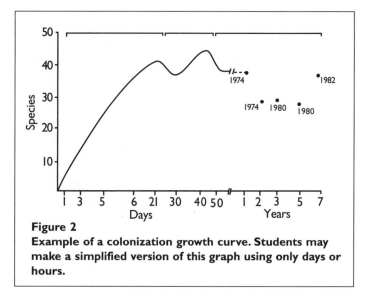

Figure 2
Example of a colonization growth curve. Students may make a simplified version of this graph using only days or hours.

Why are these differences likely to occur? The protozoa and other organisms within the PF block gradually condition the environment so growth often increases more rapidly at later stages of sampling.

◆

As time allows, you may want to introduce some mild contaminants—such as ink, soap, or chalk—to the aquarium in which colonization is taking place. Using the procedure outlined above as a control, encourage students to hypothesize about the effects of certain contaminants on the colonization process in subsequent procedures. This will not only help students extrapolate their investigations to larger ecosystems, but will highlight an appropriate scientific methodology involving hypothesis and experimentation.

◆

This investigation may be successfully linked to Investigation 4.2 (pages 120–126) on species succession, as the preparation requirements are identical for both.

Assessment and Evaluation

Why is it that a new PF block that has not been invaded previously by protozoa is so favorable as a new habitat? In any habitat, there are supportive and competitive interactions among organisms. What are some of the supportive interactions that may facilitate colonization by a wide range of protozoa in the PF block? What are some of the competitive interactions that may suppress some species in the PF block over time? Students should realize that invasion by photo-synthetic algae and protozoa can provide food sources for heterotrophic species. Waste products from some of the early colonizers provide nourishment for bacteria that can bloom and provide additional food for bacteria-eating protozoa. Competitive effects may include crowding that limits the growth of less vigorous species, or some species may be able to get food more effectively than others and thus exclude them by reducing the food available. Eventually, waste products may accumulate and limit growth.

Encourage students to reflect on the logic of this set of experiments. Why is a longitudinal study (over time) of this kind an effective way of getting scientific information? Why do we use different environments (pond, stream, aquarium) in making comparisons among the colonization experiments? What are the controlled conditions in this experiment? Students should recognize that longitudinal studies provide information on the dynamics of communities of organisms with time. This infor-mation allows us to make better models to predict how both the biotic and abiotic components of an environment are likely to change with time, and so forth. Different environments are used to better document how colonization varies across different habitats and with different initial communities of organisms. Students should recognize that we use the same colonization material—PF blocks—in each portion of this investigation, and thus the substrate itself serves as a control.

Scientific investigations often involve group effort with several scientists cooperating to bring their particular expertise to bear on the issue. Encourage students to engage in a discussion of what each one has learned from this set of experiments. Collate their contributions either by writing them on the chalk board or on an overhead display. Focus discussion on contributions that seem to be complementary or supportive, and encourage students to discuss how this knowledge could be used to devise new investigations or draw new conclusions. Likewise, highlight divergent or different information offered by other students, and discuss how this might lead to innovative or different approaches to this investigation's research problem.

An important aspect of this investigation is establishing a strong connection between the organizing question and the investigation design. In every realm of scientific activity, each informs the other, and each can and should be reevaluated continually in light of emerging data. Students should be encouraged to practice reframing questions and redesigning investigations as data emerges. Their ability to grasp this connection conceptually may be linked to their adeptness at redesigning experiments, and constitutes one mechanism for performance assessment.

As the investigation progresses, encourage students to discuss how their data relate to other, larger ecosystems that have undergone disturbance, and to the species that inhabit them. It might be desirable to perform this microscopic investigation in conjunction with an imaginary or real macroscopic ecosystem so students will develop an appreciation of temporal and spatial scale. Some guidelines for relating micro-systems to macro-systems are provided in the Discussion and Inquiry portion of the student section. Student appreciation and comprehension of the link between micro- and macro-ecosystems provides another assessment mechanism.

About the Author

James R. Pratt is Director of Environmental Sciences and Resources at Portland State University in Oregon. He specializes in protozoology, and his work has ranged from basic studies of the ecology, distribution, and biogeography of protozoa to their use as indicators of contaminant effects in freshwater and estuarine ecosystems. Dr. Pratt's work has taken an experimental approach to biogeographic questions by studying the dynamics of island colonization using protozoa as model systems.

Resources

Pratt, J. and Cairns Jr., J. 1985. "Long-term Patterns of Protozoan Colonization in Douglas Lake, Michigan." *Journal of Protozoology,*" 32 (1): 95–99.

For distributors of biological supplies, see Appendix VI (pages 219–221).

Ecological Succession

Succession is a fundamental idea in ecology. Put simply, ecological succession means that one species is gradually replaced by another species in an ecosystem. There are many variables that determine which species replaces another species, when the process begins, and how long it takes. But the most basic variable is nutrient availability—what kind of nutrients are available and how much of them there are.

Like communities of larger organisms, microbial communities grow large and then small according to how much nutrients are available to them. At certain times, one species of organism may dominate an environment while at other times another species may dominate. This change in species dominance within a particular environment is called ecological succession.

Think about the way different plant species appear in a field after all the trees have been removed. The first species to appear are the pioneers or colonizers. After that, a succession of different species appears depending on what nutrients remain available. This same process occurs at the microscopic level.

Ecological succession happens differently among terrestrial and aquatic ecosystems because of differences in how their respective food webs make nutrients available. A food web in an open ocean is different from a food web in an open field, for example, and it's this basic difference that has the greatest effect on which species succeeds which other species.

In this investigation, you will take samples from different depths in a culture vessel that represents an aquatic ecosystem. You will monitor and record the successive appearance of different protozoa species, and you will relate your observations of protozoan species succession to species succession among larger aquatic organisms.

Procedure

1. Fill each of the 4 l jars about 3/4 full with pond or aged tap water.

2. If the pond water does not already contain sediment, add about a tablespoon of good quality soil to each jar.

3. In one of the jars, add some organic matter—hay, dried wheat, or other dry matter—as a nutrient source.

4. Place each jar under fluorescent illumination or on a window sill where it will remain cool and receive indirect sunlight—a north window works well.

5. At regular intervals over a period of two weeks, use the 200 mm Pasteur pipets to sample the water at different levels in the jar—near the surface, at mid-depth, and near the sediment at the bottom. Using a pipet or eye dropper, make a wet mount slide. Record the different protozoa species you observe from each level in the jar.

6. Tabulate the data to show how the kinds of organisms change over time. The abundances of different kinds of protists can be shown as a bar graph, using drawings beneath each bar to denote the kind of protist observed, as in Figure 1.

4.2 Objective

To understand ecological succession in an aquatic habitat.

✔ Materials

- ❑ Compound microscope
- ❑ Slides, coverslips
- ❑ Eyedroppers with rubber bulbs
- ❑ 200 mm Pasteur pipets
- ❑ Two or more 4 l glass jars
- ❑ Pond or aged tap water
- ❑ Soil, or pond water with sediment
- ❑ Hay, dried wheat leaves, or other dry organic matter

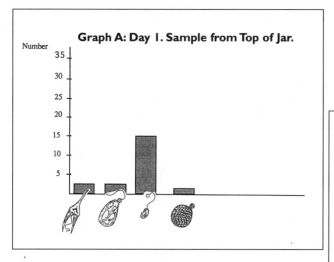

Figure 1
Examples of protist succession in laboratory cultures plotted as bar graphs.

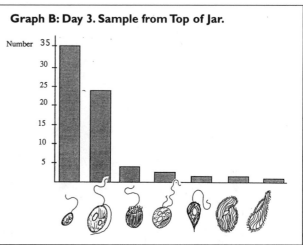

7. Examine your data from the two jars, and determine if there are differences in the kinds of organisms observed and their changing abundances over time.

Discussion and Inquiry

- Based on the observations you collected, what general trends can you identify in the succession of species in this invesitigation? Do green pigmented cells usually appear first. If so, what tends to follow them in the sequence?

- How does the diversity of species change over time? How do the numbers of different kinds of forms observed change with time? What is the variation in total numbers of organisms over time?

- To what extent can your data on variations in numbers be generalized to other environments?

- What are some of the limitations of using a jar compared to using a much larger body of water, such as a stream or pond? What differences are likely to be introduced? How well does the jar serve as a "model system" to represent the natural environment? What are some advantages of this model system to help us understand the world? What are some limitations?

- During this investigation, you will have noticed other, non-protozoan organisms under your microscope. Are those organisms involved in ecological succession, or is it just the protozoa that are succeeding one another? Judging by the shape and size of those other organisms, are they from a higher or lower order than the protozoa? On what evidence have you based your conclusions?

Ecological Succession

Succession is an important—and complicated—ecological concept. There are many variables involved in determining which species will colonize a newly created habitat, the order of appearance of succeeding species, and why those species appeared in that particular order. These variables include, but are not limited to, nutrient availability, predators, reproductive strategies, length of life cycles, environmental disruptions and interactions, and so forth. This investigation, however, is designed to help students visualize over a relatively short period of time only the fundamental concept of ecological succession: that one species replaces another species according to nutrient requirements.

Protozoa provide a convenient classroom tool to enhance student understanding of the concept of ecological succession by illustrating in a relatively short period of time the dynamics of population changes. Students can identify the protists they locate either by drawing them and simply keeping a record of the abundances of each kind, or by using a standard key to identify them to species. They may classify them into broad groups such as flagellates, ciliates, and amoebae and then make further refinements. They can identify ciliates and amoebae by body shape, and flagellates by the number of flagella and body shape.

To compile their data, students can create a large wall poster as a graph to illustrate succession over time, or, as in Figure 1, to demonstrate differences in species composition and diversity in different habitats at different levels in the culture jar. One way to demonstrate these differences might be to arrange drawings of the protists in layers on the wall chart, showing all of those found near the top on the top line, those in the middle part of the water column on the middle line, and those from the bottom on the bottom line of the poster.

The bar graphs shown in Figure 1 provide an example of the changes in protozoa over a three-day period in a culture jar. Each species is shown

Micro-Macro Link

Many variables determine which species succeed which other species, but the most important is nutrient availability.

Time Management

This investigation requires about 30 minutes for initial set up, or you may set it up in advance. Completing this investigation requires about 20 minutes per class over the course of several weeks.

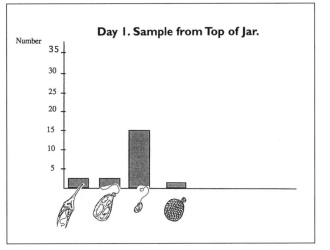

Day 1. Sample from Top of Jar.

below the X-axis as a simple drawing, similar to those made by a student. This provides an opportunity for students to learn to identify and visually represent the major morphological features to accompany the quantitative data represented by the height of the bar graph. Since observing and drawing may occupy a large amount of time, students can be assigned to different groups, with each group focusing on drawing the kinds of organisms observed at a particular level within the water column.

Student findings from this investigation may be generalized to other ecosystems, such as succession in marine environments. To help the students understand the broader implications of their analyses, encourage them to apply their knowledge to other ecosystems. For example ask students to cite some of the kinds of organisms they might expect to find in a marine coastal environment. Encourage them to think about all size ranges and kinds of organisms. This list should include invertebrates such as small algae, protozoa, bacteria, and worms. Small fishes and fish predators, such as the moray eel, as well as larger aquatic vertebrates, such as seals, are also examples. Ask students to predict which ones would most likely appear first in an ecological succession and which ones later. Students should recognize that the smaller photosynthetic species would likely appear first, followed by heterotrophic microorganisms, small fish, larger fish, and then fish predators.

Variations and Adaptations

You may want to use cultures of known organisms—such as all primary producers with no predators, all predators, or various mixtures of both—in this investigation. These cultures may be grown separately under varied conditions, such as different light or temperature. Using known organisms enables students to identify the "players" beforehand, and they may then spend more time observing and recording changes in community structure. Varied mixtures of six or more different protist taxa should work well.

◆

This investigation can be modified to include the effects of pollutants on the kinds of protista observed and their composition over time. Have students add different pollutants to different samples, and then record species succession among control (no pollutant) and variable (pollutant) samples. If time allows, students can compare the differences in succession of organisms in samples of water taken from different locations. They can also compare the differences in organisms grown in cultures of pond water inoculated with samples of soil from different locations.

◆

Students may also wish to devise their own adaptations to this investigation. It may also be linked to Investigation 4.1 (pages 112–119) on species colonization, as the preparation requirements are identical for both.

Assessment and Evaluation

Follow up on the suggestion that students should discuss the merits of their jar cultures as a model for the natural environment. Determine to what extent they understand the jar's limitations—students should be able to cite the small volume, as well as the likelihood that light would not penetrate throughout the depth of a deep pond to the same extent that it does in the transparent jar. However, oxygen may be more available in a shallow pond since the surface area will be greater compared to the volume. Also, there may be very different sediments in a natural body of water compared to those in their jars.

Students should understand that scale is very important in biology. The simple fact that the jar is small in volume can produce different combinations of physical, chemical, and biological effects not found in larger bodies of water. Likewise, the jar may heat up during the day if exposed to light, but larger bodies of water would be less likely to do so. However, the jar may be a very good model for shallow ponds because shallow ponds can warm up considerably during sunny days.

Evaluate how accurately students are able to generalize from the succession observed in their jar to that likely to occur in the natural environment. Do students cite reasonable species for the habitat to which they are extrapolating their information? Are they adequately aware of the range in size and kind of organisms that are likely to occur in the natural habitat? Do they suggest a reasonable sequence of succession of these organisms, with primary producers largely appearing first, especially small efficient ones, followed by larger organisms that are consumers and/or larger primary producers? Do they understand the concept of a food chain, and that producers appear first since they can use sunlight as a source of energy, and need only mineral nutrients? Do they understand that producers are followed by consumers, and then by larger, secondary consumers that prey on the primary consumers?

About the Author

Daniel Hanley teaches environmental science at the High School For Environmental Studies in New York City. While earning his Masters degree in science education, he developed this unit of study to expand students' understanding of habitat selection and succession of protozoa living in pond water. He found that students' experience with protozoa was a static representation based on prepared slides and purified cultures. In contrast, this investigation allows students to observe dynamic protozoan communities, possessing a variety of adaptations that enable them to exploit diverse habitats.

Resources

For distributors of biological supplies, see Appendix VI (pages 219–221).

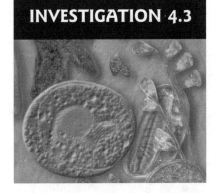

Nutrient Quality and Population Distribution

Have you ever seen a cow pasture? Most contain a variety of organisms, such as birds, grass, some wildflowers, maybe a few trees. Think for a moment about how those organisms are physically located in your cow pasture. Can you identify a pattern to their distribution? A pattern might be, for example, if all the brown cows were lined up facing east, all the white cows were lined up facing south, and all the birds were lined up facing west. You've probably never seen a cow pasture where the organisms were distributed so uniformly.

Uniform distribution patterns like this imaginary one are extremely rare in nature. In most environments, organisms are distributed heterogeneously, like the cows shown in Figure 1. This means that they are not distributed uniformly, according to a pattern, but are all mixed or clumped together. Ecologists call this clumpy distribution "patchiness," and organisms are distributed this way for several reasons.

A main reason for patchiness is nutrient distribution, where the food they eat is located. If you think about the cows in your pasture, you'll remember they usually move to the area with the most and best grass. Sometimes all the cows together will move as a group to a new section of pasture. At other times, individuals or small groups will move away in search of food.

Careful examination of protozoa species in their natural habitats reveals that many of them also exhibit patchy distribution patterns. In this investigation, you will examine some of the causes of patchy distribution among microscopic organisms, and you will consider your findings regarding microorganisms and what those findings might mean among macroscopic populations.

So What?
Organisms are distributed throughout an environment mostly according to where their food is located and how good it is.

Figure 1
Cows "randomly" distributed throughout a pasture, the result of nutrient availability and quality.

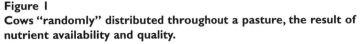

4.3 Objective

To understand how nutrient quality and location affect population distribution.

✔ Materials

- ❑ Dissecting microscope
- ❑ Slides, coverslips
- ❑ Petri dishes, 100 &150 mm
- ❑ Sea water
- ❑ Agar
- ❑ Autoclave or pressure cooker
- ❑ Large zipper-locked plastic bags
- ❑ Cork borer, 1–2 cm
- ❑ Ethyl alcohol (80 percent)
- ❑ Sterile eyedroppers
- ❑ Micropipets, or Pasteur pipets
- ❑ Microspatula
- ❑ "Hockey stick" spreader
- ❑ Hypotrich culture: *Euplotes vanus*
- ❑ Prey organism cultures: *Dunaliella salina* *Amphora* sp. *Nitzschia* sp. *Navicula* sp. *Fragilaria* sp.

Procedure

1. Pipet 0.5 ml of the test alga onto a seawater-agar solidified media in 100 mm sterile petri dishes. Use a different, labeled petri dish for each algal type.

2. Sterilize the "hockey stick" spreader by dipping it in alcohol and touching it briefly to the blue part of a bunsen burner flame. Repeat this step three times. Make sure the sterile spreader has cooled before using it during Step 3.

3. Spread the algae uniformly on the surface of the agar using the "hockey stick" spreader.

4. Place the petri dish in a zipper-locked bag and incubate it under a cool, white fluorescent light source with a timer (18 hours light and six hours dark), or simply use continuous illumination for 7–14 days. The cultures also may be grown with illumination from bright light on the window sill with northern exposure. Avoid direct sunlight.

5. After incubation, alcohol-sterilize a cork borer following the procedure in Step 2. Use the borer to cut discs of lawns of the various diatom species being tested.

6. Obtain a previously prepared 150 mm test petri dish containing only 3 mm of agar. After alcohol-sterilizing the cork borer again, use it to remove agar discs from predetermined sites. These discs will be replaced by those cut out of the lawns of diatoms above.

7. Alcohol-sterilize a microspatula and carefully slide it under one of the agar discs you just cut. Use the spatula to lift and discard it.

8. After discarding all six discs from the large petri dish, resterilize the microspatula. Use it to lift and transfer the algal discs to the empty disc spots you just made around the edge of the large petri dish. The dishes will contain six discs of potential food, in an otherwise barren agar substrate.

9. Gently pipet seawater over the petri dish, taking care not to agitate the lawns.

10. Carefully place the petri dish with its overlying water over a template on the stage of a dissecting microscope. Gently pipet the ciliates into the petri dish's central well by removing an agar disc.

11. Make counts of the ciliates at 1–2 hour intervals.

Discussion and Inquiry

- Think about the distribution of human populations across the United States, and use a map to identify the major population centers. Identify and list why Americans are distributed the way they are.

- Before the Industrial Revolution, Americans had to rely much more heavily on their ability to find and grow food than we do today. Use a historical atlas to observe how population centers were distributed across the United States before the Industrial Revolution. Identify differences and similarities in the way Americans were distributed then and the way they are distributed now. What reasons might be responsible for those differences and similarities?

- Now think about the microorganisms you observed in this investigation. Compare your findings about how Americans were distributed before the Industrial Revolution with your findings about how microorganisms were distributed in your investigation of protozoan patchiness. If protozoans were able to use technology to help them find and grow food, what do you think might happen?

Nutrient Quality and Population Distribution

Micro-Macro Link

All organisms within a species population, even the smallest microbes, exhibit one of the three ecological distribution patterns: patchy, random, or uniform.

Time Management

Preparing the agar-filled petri dishes will take about half an hour. Students will need 15–20 minutes to prepare this investigation, followed by one class period 1–2 weeks later. They will also need time to make observations after the initial class.

Ecologists have determined three types of population distribution patterns: patchy or clumped, random, and uniform (Figure 2). The most common is patchy, and this investigation provides an opportunity for students to link population distribution and density with nutrient availability and quality.

While many factors affect a species' overall distribution pattern— such as their own reproductive strategies and migratory habits, and those of predator populations—the need for most organisms to forage for nutrients is a primary determinant. From this basic need arise many contributing variables, including the abundance and quality of different nutrients; the different amounts of energy gained from them; the differences in energy expended in searching and processing different nutrient types; the degree of satiation at each encounter; and many other less well defined characteristics.

For protozoans, one of the primary determinants of patchy distribution is the patchy distribution of nutrients. This investigation

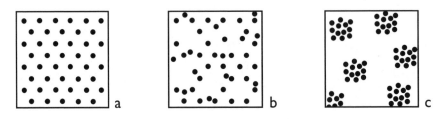

Figure 2
Patterns of distribution: (a) uniform, (b) random, (c) patchy.

provides an opportunity for students to observe, examine, and extrapolate the causes of microbial population distribution. For example, the marine ciliate *Euplotes vannus* grows much faster on diets of certain species of algae. The ciliate also grows and reproduces much faster on patches of high quality nutrients than it does on mixtures of nutrients with varying nutritional qualities.

This investigation is a good way to introduce students to population density. Ecologists use two measurements of density: crude and ecologial. Crude density refers to the number of individuals of a particular species per unit area. The *U.S. Census of Population* provides an example of crude density. Like the microorganisms in this investigation, human populations also are distributed in patches. Before the Industrial Revolution enabled humans to radically manipulate their environments, towns and cities tended to spring up where the environment was most agreeable to sustaining human life. Microorganisms also tend to be distributed in patterns that reflect the availability of resources and favorable support for reproduction and growth.

But populations don't occupy all the space within a unit of area. They congregate in areas that adequately meet their requirements. (For example, an area may include a field and the stream that runs through it; yet fish will exist only in the stream.) Ecological density, therefore, refers to the amount of area available as living space. Density is an important parameter of populations not only because it helps determine distribution patterns, but also because it affects energy flow, resource availability and utilization, physiological and environmental stress, and productivity.

Adaptations and Variations

This investigation is most informative if counts of the ciliates can be made at 1–2 hour intervals. If you have several classes meeting in one day, each class might observe the experimental and control preparations and pool their data to be shared by all classes. Alternatively, the preparations can be made one day and the number of ciliates on the experimental food patches and the control patches counted the following day. This does not show the rate of accumulation as clearly, but does show the overall trend for longer time periods.

◆

This investigation can be modified for freshwater ciliates by using only freshwater agar as a base, supplying freshwater diatoms or algae, such as *Chlorella*, as food in the food wells, and adding a suitable alga-eating ciliate (supplied by biological supply companies). Some appropriate genera include *Amphora* sp., *Navicula* sp., and *Nitzschia* sp.

◆

This investigation is ideal to discuss sampling and statistical tests of the validity of results. Depending your background and the availability of computers and programs, the statistics can be as simple as comparing means and standard deviations. The more computer-familiar teacher might use Clarisworks™, Cricket Graph II™, or Excel™ to perform analyses like Chi-square comparisons or t-tests.

Assessment and Evaluation

This investigation elucidates how nutrient availability influences the patchiness of protozoan populations. Students should not only be able

Teaching Note

When preparing seawater-agar solidified media in 100 mm sterile petri dishes, carefully control the depth of the medium. It should be exactly 3 mm deep.

Preparation Note

Procedures for preparing the "hockey stick" spreader appear in Appendix IV (pages 215–216).

to describe the results of their study—to cite which dishes had the most ciliates gathered around the food—but also to explain why. They should recognize that abundance and quality of nutrients provide necessary energy to sustain life, that under these conditions growth of the organisms is likely to be promoted and reproduction more successful. As a result, nutrient sources become colonized more readily and maintain a more stable population of higher density than environments with less available nutrient sources.

Students should be able to explain why the nutrient sources chosen for this investigation were algae—photosynthetic flagellates and diatoms. These are good primary producers and the ciliate is herbivorous. The students' understanding of the limitations of the investigation should be explored. For example, do they realize that it would be rare for a nutrient source in the natural environment to contain only one kind of alga? This investigation focuses on only one kind of predator. In a natural environment, most nutrient patches would be invaded by several different species of protozoa. This kind of variable introduces complications of community dynamics including competition, possible changes in numbers due to predation, and so forth.

If students fully understand this investigation, they should be able to propose modifications using different organisms. For example, how could they find out if these same principles applied to aquatic snails? Can they devise an experiment to see if these same principles of patchiness apply to insects or terrestrial snails? The plan would be the same, except an appropriate food source would be provided in place of the algae. The test organisms should be placed in an appropriate container with and without the nutrient source, and the distribution observed over time. The ability to apply scientific principles and experimental designs to new situations is an important cognitive skill that should be monitored as students mature in using inquiry investigations.

About the Author

John Lee is a Distinguished Professor of Biology at City College of CUNY, where he teaches microbiology and microbial ecology. His work with salt marsh microbial food webs, and his searches for protozoa and micrometazoa for the first feeding larvae of marine fish, led him to develop this investigation to stimulate students to appreciate the qualitative aspects of food webs involving small creatures. This investigation also stimulates thinking about the biological aspects of niche separation, marine blooms, and patchy distribution of micro-herbivores.

Resources

For distributors of biological supplies, see Appendix VI (pages 219–221).

Net Respiration and the Carbon Cycle

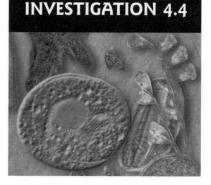

Humans and other animals consume oxygen (O_2) and release carbon dioxide (CO_2). This is called respiration or respiratory activity. Do microbial, single-celled organisms respire? If so, how rapidly do they produce CO_2 compared to other organisms? Are there differences among the various microbial organisms that produce carbon dioxide? What are those differences?

These are important questions, especially to ecologists and biologists. They are important not just because scientists want to understand how individual organisms maintain their life's functions, but because the respiratory activity of entire communities of organisms contributes to an ecosystem's net respiration, which in turn contributes to the global carbon cycle.

Think about net respiration this way. Sitting in your classroom, you are continually consuming oxygen and producing carbon dioxide. You do this at a certain rate, meaning you produce so much carbon dioxide over a certain length of time. But you are just one individual, and there are others in the classroom besides you. Together you make up a community of individuals, and you are all consuming oxygen and producing carbon dioxide. Just as there is a rate at which you yourself produce carbon dioxide, there is also a rate at which the entire community of your classmates produces carbon dioxide. The rate at which all the individuals in your class produce carbon dioxide is your community's net respiration.

If your class were an ecosystem it would contain mostly a community of human organisms. But real ecosystems contain a wide variety of communities of individual organisms, and each community has its own net respiration. What happens if you add together all the net respirations of all the communities of individual organisms in an ecosystem? What if you add together the net respirations of all Earth's ecosystems? What might this value tell you about Earth's ecological health? This investigation will help you find ways to answer such questions, and it will give you a new appreciation of the contribution microbial organisms make to a healthy Earth.

So What?

All breathing organisms contribute carbon dioxide to their ecosystems, and the rate at which they do so is that ecosystem's net respiration. The carbon dioxide is used by plants during photosynthesis, and the plants in turn add oxygen back into the atmosphere.

SC*L*INKS
THE WORLD'S A CLICK AWAY

Topic: carbon cycle
Go to: www.scilinks.org
Code: PROT09

4.4 Objective

To analyze respiration of protozoan communities, and to understand the role of net respiration in the global carbon cycle.

✔ Materials

- ❑ Compound microscope
- ❑ Slides, coverslips
- ❑ Large test tube, 20×150 mm
- ❑ Rubber stoppers
- ❑ Filter paper discs, 9 cm
- ❑ Absorbent cotton
- ❑ Petri dishes, 9 cm
- ❑ Bromothymol blue solution, 0.01 percent or less
- ❑ Sodium bicarbonate solution, 0.001 percent w/v
- ❑ Dried baker's yeast
- ❑ Pasteur pipets, 225 mm length, or dropping pipets with fine tips
- ❑ Mixed protozoan and microbial cultures
- ❑ Photosynthetic protozoa: *Euglena* sp.

Procedure

1. Place 1.0 ml of bromothymol blue (0.01 percent) in a test tube. Blow into the test tube vigorously enough to displace air. Agitate the dye by swirling it and continue to blow into the test tube with intermittent shaking. Note the gradual change in color against a white sheet of paper. How long does it take for the color to change to green and then to yellow?

2. Use test tubes filled with 1.0 ml of bromothymol blue (0.01 percent) to record how many drops of bicarbonate, equivalent to carbon dioxide, are required to produce each different color: intense blue, pale blue, blue-green, dull green, emerald-green, yellow-green, and yellow. Record your results. *If possible, use a pipet that can measure the drops to .01 ml; even if you use an unmarked pipet, consider the volume of each drop to be .01 ml.* Multiply each of total volume of bicarbonate times 0.0016 to find out how many micromoles of bicarbonate, equivalent to carbon dioxide, are needed to produce each color change. Show all your calculations, and record your final results.

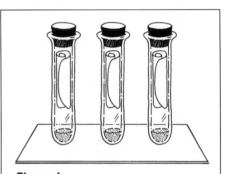

Figure 1
Arrangement of test tubes. When you add bromothymol blue in Step 3 be careful not to splash it up onto the test tube walls.

3. Set up three stoppered large test tubes, as shown in Figure 1. These will be used to observe the rate of respiration produced by microbial cultures suspended in cotton webbing and layered between two filter paper discs.

4. Add 0.5 ml of 0.01 percent bromothymol blue solution into the bottom of each test tube. The blue dye will be an indicator of respiratory activity as demonstrated by the effects of your breath on its color in step one.

5. Prepare three petri dishes, and label them Dish A, Dish B, and Dish C. In each dish place a 9 cm filter paper disc and add a thin layer of cotton that has been gently pulled out into a very thin layer. All dishes should contain a filter disc covered with a thin layer of cotton. Figure 2 provides an illustration of this set up.

6. Add only clean water to Dish A, thoroughly moistening the cotton and filter paper. This is a control, it has no living organisms.

134

7. Swirl the culture of microorganisms and add a sufficient amount to Dish B to saturate the cotton and filter disc.

8. Swirl a culture of yeast and add it to Dish C.

9. Place a filter paper disc on the top of the cotton in each dish, and be certain it is fully saturated with the cultures added to the dish.

10. To prepare a control test tube, gently roll the paper discs from Dish A into a spiral. The roll should be just large enough to fit easily into the test tubes (see Figure 1). Insert the paper roll into the first test tube and gently push it down until it will just clear the stopper when inserted. Label this Test Tube 1. It is a control preparation, and contains no living organisms.

11. Make a roll of the paper discs from Dish B and add it to a second test tube. Be certain the paper discs are drained before inserting into the test tube. Label this Test Tube 2.

Figure 2
Arrangement of petri dishes. Each contains a 9 cm filter paper disc and a thin cotton layer.

12. Remove the filter disc pad in Dish C and drain it fully. As before, be very certain no culture fluid is dripping from it. Roll it loosely and place it into the upper part of a third test tube. Label this Test Tube 3. Seal each test tube with a rubber stopper. Immediately record the time and the color of the dye in your Lab Record Sheet.

13. Gently swirl each of the test tubes at about two minute intervals, and record the color of the dye in Table 1 immediately after you finish swirling. If there is sufficient respiratory activity in the cultures, the dye color will gradually change from intense blue to pale blue, then to blue-green, and then sequentially to dull-green, emerald-green, yellow-green, and yellow. Typically, a blue-green or green color is sufficient evidence of respiratory activity, and the time required for Tubes 2 and 3 to each reach a green color should be recorded in your Table 1. The color of the dye in the Tube 1, the control test tube, should not change appreciably and can be used as a reference color in checking the progress of color change in the other two tubes.

14. Based on the final color observed in Tubes 2 and 3, calculate how many micromoles of carbon dioxide were absorbed. Divide this

4.4
INVESTIGATION

value by the amount of time in minutes required to produce the color change. You now have a rough estimate of the rate of respiration by the microbes in each tube expressed as micromoles of carbon dioxide per minute. Record your results in Table 1.

Discussion and Inquiry

- Bromothymol blue dye can be used as an indicator of respiratory activity. Bromothymol blue changes color from deep blue to pale blue, then to green and ultimately yellow as carbon dioxide is absorbed, thus indicating CO_2 presence. What causes the color change? What is being absorbed from your breath? Can you suggest what chemical reaction is occurring to cause the change in color?

- In Step 12, which of the test tubes changed color most quickly? Examine a sample of the yeast and of the protozoan culture with the high power of your microscope. Adjust the substage diaphragm to produce sufficient contrast to note presence of bacteria in addition to protozoa. Based on the size and number of microbes in the cultures, can you explain the differences in the rate of activity?

- Based on your observations of carbon dioxide production by these different microbial communities, can you make an estimate of how much carbon dioxide might be produced in a small pond? Estimate how much volume of culture you poured into your Dish B. Using this in relation to the estimated volume of a small pond, you can use proportions to calculate your estimate of respiratory activity in the pond. Likewise, how much respiratory activity might be produced in a lake, or in the ocean? Where does the carbon come from that the microbes use for respiration? That is, how do these small organisms obtain food with carbon compounds in them to produce respiratory carbon dioxide? Are there similar processes on land among terrestrial microorganisms? How much respiratory activity do you think is occurring on the planet Earth all totaled?

- Carefully and critically consider your estimates for respiratory activity. What are the likely sources of error in your estimates? Are your samples of microorganisms used to estimate respiratory activity typical of those found in lakes, ponds, and oceans? Is the concentration in your samples typical of these other aquatic environments? If not, what is the likely difference in concentration? Is it more or less than your cultures? Can you alter your estimate of global respiratory carbon dioxide production by correcting for the differences in concentration in these other environments?

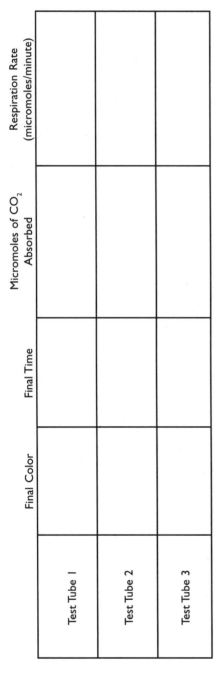

Table 1
Respiration rate of *Euglena* sp. (Use calculations from Step 2 to determine the amount of Co$_2$ absorbed.)

Net Respiration and the Carbon Cycle

Biology students understand that individual organisms respire, meaning they consume oxygen and produce carbon dioxide. They also may understand that individual organisms respire at a certain rate, that a value may be assigned to that rate, and that this value is called net respiration. But they may not yet be able to apply this concept to entire communities of organisms or to integrated communities, like an ecosystem. This investigation presents students with a simplified explanation of net respiration in order to establish a connection between individual respiration, community respiration, and the global carbon budget.

True net respiration equations include a variety of variables other than simply how fast and how much. For example, scientists trying to determine an ecosystem's net respiration will assign values to such variables as species emigration and immigration, biomass accumulation, birth and death rates, and many others. One of the most significant variables, is how much CO_2 is contained in humus, Earth's second largest carbon sink after the oceans. Microbial organisms like protozoa are intimately associated with biogeochemical cycling among detrital communities, like forest floors, bogs and swamps, and aquatic sediments. This investigation highlights the importance of microbial communities to Earth's natural cycles.

It is important for students to be aware of the breadth of the concept of net respiration, especially as it provides a good example of holistic scientific inquiry. Encourage students to expand their conception to encompass an integrated interpretation of individual, community, and global respiratory activity. Such an integration will help students appreciate, for example, that the CO_2 flux among land, sea, and atmosphere has been disturbed since the industrial revolution by a rapid injection of CO_2 into the atmosphere from the burning of fossil fuels and the clearing of forests. Clearing increases the input of CO_2 from burning and decomposing forest biomass, and it reduces the forest sink for storing CO_2 scrubbed from the atmosphere by photosynthesis and biomass accumulation.

Micro-Macro Link

Net respiration describes the connection between individual respiration, community respiration, and the global carbon budget.

Time Management

This investigation may be completed in one class period if preparation is performed in advance. Follow the preparation procedure outlined in Adaptations and Variations.

Adaptations and Variations

If you wish to set up this investigation in advance, prepare a mixed community of actively growing protozoa and bacteria. Either obtain a mixture of protozoa from a biological supply company and establish them in laboratory culture enriched with organic nutrients, or start a mixed culture as follows. Obtain pond water or put some garden soil into aged tap water in a gallon jar. Add some dried hay and/or nutrient source, such as yeast extract. Keep in a cool place for about one week or until a vigorous community of protozoa and other microbes develops. More vigorous growth can be expected if the culture is gently aerated using an aquarium pump. Add additional replacement water if there is evaporation. You may need to add small quantities of nutrient powder periodically over a two week period, but add it sparingly to avoid excessive eutrophication. It is essential, to have a relatively dense growth of microbes to achieve results within the time of one class period.

◆

If you choose to show the contribution of photosynthetic protozoa, begin a culture of *Euglena* or other photosynthetic protozoa. These may be purchased from a biological supply company. To start a photosynthetic protist culture on your own, place some pond water in a north window or in a location away from direct sunlight, or use continuous fluorescent illumination. Add mineral nutrients, such as algal nutrient solution or small quantities of a mineral fertilizer. In one to two weeks a supply of photosynthetic protozoa will usually appear.

◆

Within an hour before beginning the investigation, suspend a packet of baker's yeast (approximately 7–8 grams dry weight) into 500 ml of warm water (approximately 45° C). The water must be warm to activate the yeast. Add about two tablespoons of glucose powder. Glucose is needed to ensure vigorous respiration. Swirl the suspension until the yeast is fully dispersed. Keep the culture at room temperature. It will remain viable for several hours. If it has been prepared in advance of the class, add some more glucose immediately before the students use it.

◆

To calculate the equivalent amount of carbon dioxide required to produce the color change in the test tubes, the students need a glass pipet with a very fine tip. Have them follow the instructions outlined in Appendix IV (pages 215–216). The tip must be sufficiently fine to deliver a drop of approximately 0.01 ml volume. The pipet is fitted with a rubber bulb to control the release of drops of the 0.001 percent (weight/volume) bicarbonate solution. Bromothymol blue solution (0.04 percent) can be diluted before use to 0.01 percent concentration by adding one part of the solution to three parts water.

◆

If students are available to make observations 18–24 hours later, you can demonstrate the effect of adding organic carbon sources on respiration. Take about 30 ml of the thoroughly mixed microbial culture into each of two test tubes. Immediately before the experiment, add glucose powder (approximately 1/2 teaspoon) into one of the tubes. Then, use each preparation to saturate separate cotton pads as explained in the methods. Insert each one into a labeled test tube, and stopper securely. Usually within 18–24 hours, the bromothymol blue solution in the test tube with the glucose enriched culture will be a bright yellow while the other preparation will be only green. This shows the effect of available carbon as glucose on enhanced respiration. It is important to roll the cotton pads loosely to promote diffusion of the expired carbon dioxide into the test tube and into the bromothymol blue solution. This laboratory experience is particularly useful if you have classes that are scheduled in close succession. The test tubes need only to be emptied and rinsed by the students at the end of the class session, and they are ready for the next.

◆

When helping students address the Discussion and Inquiry portion of the student guide, encourage them to realize that the cultures are enriched in microbiota, and most aquatic environments will have fewer respiring organisms, perhaps by hundreds of times less. They must adjust their estimates by dividing by this correction factor.

◆

What happens if photosynthetic protozoa are added to the microbial community? You may choose to make a mixture of photosynthetic and non-photosynthetic microbial organisms by adding green photo-synthetic protozoa in with the microbial community used in Tube 2 and compare it to the rate you obtained above. You need to set up a new test tube following the procedures you used for Tube 2, but this time include the mixture of green and colorless protozoa when saturating the pad of cotton. How much carbon dioxide was produced in each test tube containing microbes?

◆

Students can determine how much CO_2 is needed to produce each of the color changes in the test tubes by using a solution containing a known amount of carbon dioxide molecules present as bicarbonate ions (HCO_3). Have students add small drops one by one and observing changes in the color.

◆

In a test tube, add 1.0 ml of 0.01 percent bromothymol blue dye. Also obtain a sample of a 0.001 percent bicarbonate solution. Using a fine pipet, carefully add drops of the solution and note how many drops are required to produce a blue-green color. Continue adding drops and determine how many are required to produce a green and ultimately a yellow color. If your pipet has a fine tip, each drop is about 0.01 ml. For a 0.001 percent solution each drop contains 0.0016 micromoles of bicarbonate ions. A micromole is one millionth of a mole.

Assessment and Evaluation

This investigation provides an opportunity for students to develop an appreciation of global carbon cycling and of the role of microbial communities in global carbon budgets. Potential student answers to some of the specific questions in the Discussion and Inquiry portion of the student section are outlined below, but students should be encouraged to address these questions within a larger context of biological and ecological systems. How students apply the results of their investigation into the respiration of *Euglena* sp. to their understanding of such systems should provide one mechanism for assessment and evaluation.

Students should be able to explain some of the sources of evidence used in this investigation. For example, the bromothymol indicator is blue in alkaline solution. When, however, carbon dioxide is absorbed in the solution carbonic acid is formed with the water. This mild acid causes a chemical change in the bromothymol blue molecule that shifts its color toward yellow. Yeast are rapidly metabolizing unicellular, fungal organisms that produce substantial amounts of carbon dioxide. This is why we add them to bread dough; the yeast release carbon dioxide gas causing the bread dough to swell or rise. The yeast are much more active than the less dense community of protozoa and bacteria, producing the most dramatic change in the color of the bromothymol dye solution.

In the Discussion and Inquiry portion of the student section, students were asked to examine the protozoan community suspension under the microscope and compare it to the yeast suspension. Students should be able to describe the difference in density of the organisms, and discuss differences in metabolism that may explain the differences in carbon dioxide production, and thus differences in bromothymol color reaction that they observed. Some students will have difficulty in using proportional analysis to solve the problem of estimating the total activity in a pond based on the activity in their test tube experiment. However, providing them with a simple clue may be helpful: If students are told that a pond is likely to contain 10,000 times the amount of water as their experimental sample, they should then be able to deduce that they need to multiply their results by 10,000 to extrapolate their findings to the natural environment. Students should be able to critically analyze this estimate by noting that the pond may not have a uniform concentration of microorganisms equivalent to that in the test tube. Their estimates may be on the high side, since some areas of the pond may contain fewer organisms.

About the Author

O. Roger Anderson, who teaches protozoology at Columbia University, developed this investigation to encourage students to expand their appreciation of respiratory activity beyond the individual organism. Students who think in terms of the net respiration of communities of organisms develop a broader understanding of important biological and ecological processes, such as global carbon budgets, biogeochemical cycling, and population dynamics.

Resources

For distributors of biological supplies, such as bromothymol blue solution, see Appendix VI (pages 219–221).

Predator-Prey Interactions

So What?

Predation pressures can act as a "brake" to limit the populations of fast-reproducing species and help to maintain an ecosystem's diversity. Without such a brake, one species could multiply so much it would completely dominate all other species.

The diversity of an ecosystem depends on two factors: the amount of nutrients available and the level of predation. In many habitats, a predator can act as a "keystone" for the community of species, limiting the competion from fast-growing species that might otherwise exclude other species and reduce diversity. The starfish, which preys on mussels in the ocean's rocky intertidal zone, is one example. Without the starfish, mussels would eliminate other organisms—such as chitons, barnacles, and limpets—by outcompeting them. Protozoans may act similarly to limit fast-growing bacteria and maintain diversity at the microbial level.

Bacteria, and the protozoa that prey on those bacteria, are important in decomposing dead organic material and releasing nutrients from it for plant and algal growth. Diversity of bacteria is important to the efficiency of this process: the greater the diversity of bacteria, the faster and more completely the organic material is decomposed and the nutrients recycled. The protozoan biomass formed from consuming bacteria also becomes part of an ecosystem's food web by serving as prey for other organisms.

Predators and prey exist in a balance between predator efficiency and prey defense. Some prey populations escape predation by growing fast, being distasteful, or having shapes that are difficult for predators to deal with. Many bacteria have chemicals that are toxic to protists, thus inhibiting predation. Many insects and some plants also have chemicals that inhibit predators from eating them. Frequently, these toxins are the pigments that we see in bacterial colonies grown on agar plates. Bacteria also may have slime layers on their surfaces, layers that make it dificult for protozoans to feed on them. Many bacteria grow in clumps or filaments, a strategy that makes it physically difficult for protozoans to ingest them.

In this investigation, you will examine the predator-prey interactions between bacteria and a protist predator. You will examine the interactive effects of bacterial growth and bacterial defense on protist predators, and the effect of selective protist predation pressures on bacterial diversity.

Procedure

1. To prepare agar plates for bacterial isolation and growth, mix 5 g Proteose Peptone per liter with 15 g agar per liter in spring water. Autoclave (mix well after autoclaving since the agar may sink) and pour into petri dishes (just enough to cover bottom about 0.5 cm deep). After the agar has cooled and solidified, store the dishes in a refrigerator. Per group: 8 dishes Week 1, 48 dishes Week 2, 48 dishes Week 3.

2. Autoclave the following:
   - 16×125 mm screw-capped test tubes with Proteose Peptone and Glucose medium for *Tetrahymena*. Make enough to grow one tube per team, and any necessary to maintain stock cultures
   - 16×125 mm screw-capped test tubes with 9 ml of spring water for dilution blanks (per team: 6 Week 1, 48 Week 2, 48 Week 3)
   - 16×125 mm screw-capped test tubes empty (2–4 per team)
   - pipet tips for digital micropipettor
   - glass graduated pipets (1 and 10 ml)
   - conical bottom 15 ml centrifugation tubes (2 per group)
   - milk dilution bottles (4 per group)

Week 1

1. Make sure to always use sterile equipment when collecting samples. As you collect samples from natural water bodies, such as a stream, pond, or puddle, never touch the part of the pipet that actually goes in the water. Hold the pipet away from you to minimize the bacteria, dust particles, and skin flakes that might fall from your hair.

2. Unwrap a sterile pipet, fix a pipet bulb to the end, and use it to collect 10 ml of water. Carefully draw up the 10 ml sample, and dispense it into a test tube—*don't touch the open end of the tube with your fingers, only the outside of the cap.* If you are collecting samples from soil or sediment, add about 1 ml of material to a sterile dilution blank with a pre-sterilized spatula.

3. Label each sample tube with the location and the date. Also record your group's name, the date, the location, the water and air temperature, and the weather conditions on a data sheet.

4. Back in the laboratory, make 1:10 serial dilutions of sample water. To do this, transfer 1 ml of sample water with a sterile pipet to a 9 ml sterile dilution blank, mix well, then transferring 1 ml of that suspension to a new 9 ml dilution blank. Continue until you have dilutions from 0 (the original sample) to –6 (the sixth dilution tube

4.5 Objective

To understand how protozoan predation pressures affect bacterial abundance and diversity, and how this predator-prey interaction has an impact on the way an ecosystem functions.

✔ Materials

- ❑ Compound microscope
- ❑ Slides and coverslips
- ❑ Autoclave
- ❑ Spectrophotometer and cuvettes
- ❑ Centrifuge
- ❑ Digital micropipetor and tips, 1 and 10 ml graduated and Pasteur pipets, pipet bulbs
- ❑ Sterile, screw-capped test tubes (16×25 mm)
- ❑ Milk dilution bottles (or screw-capped 125 ml flasks)
- ❑ Petri dishes
- ❑ "Hockey stick" spreader
- ❑ 15 ml conical centrifuge tubes
- ❑ Bacto agar
- ❑ Spring water
- ❑ Reagents:
  95 percent ethanol
  Lugol's Iodine
  Proteose Peptone
- ❑ Culture:
  Axenic *Tetrahymena*

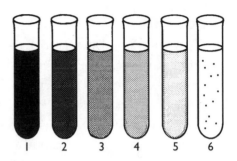

Figure 1
The process of serial dilution.
The density of the bacterial
suspension in each tube is
exaggerated to make the serial
dilution sequence more clear.
One ml of the thoroughly
suspended bacteria in tube 1 is
transferred to 10 ml in tube 2.
This is fully mixed, and 1 ml of
this suspension is transferred to tube 3, etc. At each transfer, the bacterial
concentration is lowered by diluting it into the 10 ml of the next tube.
Finally, the last tube (tube 6) will have a very diluted suspension of the
bacteria serially transferred from the first tube.

in the series). Figure 1 provides an example of this process. If samples are taken from highly-enriched environments, such as sewage or compost, further dilutions may be necessary.

5. With the digital pipettor, remove 50 μl from each dilution, and dispense the sample into the center of an agar plate—one plate per dilution tube. Dip a "hockey stick" spreader in ethanol, and quickly touch the tip to the flame of a bunsen burner to burn off the excess. *Do not hold the spreader in the flame or it will get hot and cook your bacteria!* Use the spreader to spread the sample evenly across the agar.

6. Seal each petri dish with tape, and incubate at room temperature for one week.

7. Repeat Steps 3–4 with one sterile dilution blank. This is called a negative control, and will let you see how contamination occurs due to skin, hair, dust, air currents, sloppy technique, and so forth. If your technique is good, no bacteria will grow.

Week 2
1. Calculate the number of bacteria in the sample. To do this, first count the total number of colonies on a plate with at least 20 colonies that can be easily distinguished from each other. Multiply your colony count by 20 (to get 1 ml from the 50 μl used) and then by the number of the dilution tube (10^1 to 10^6) that particular plate came from. This will give you a calculation of the number of bacteria per ml. Count as many different colony types as possible from all the dilutions. Distinguish the colonies according to morphological type and color.

2. With a sterile spreader, scrape a sample of one colony and transfer it to a new dilution blank. Use the spreader to agitate the sterile water and dislodge attached bacteria. Tighten the cap, and shake the tube vigorously to disperse bacterial cells.

3. Read the bacterial suspension's optical density (OD) in a spectrophotometer at 480 nm. Make the dilution necessary to adjust the suspension to 0.1 OD in a sterile milk dilution bottle (i.e., if OD is 1.57, 1 ml plus 14.7 ml sterile spring water will give a 0.1 OD suspension). If the starting OD is below 1.8, add more bacteria with the inoculation loop. Repeat for each bacteria type.

4. If time permits, examine bacterial suspensions under a microscope with a phase contrast 100x oil immersion objective. Record whether the bacteria you observe are rods, cocci, or filaments on your data sheet. Figure 2 provides examples of the shapes you should look for to make your identification.

5. To set up the experimental cultures, mix equal volumes of each bacterial type to provide a stock solution of mixed bacteria. You will need a minimum of 50 ml, or about 17 ml each.

6. Fill five sterile test tubes with 10 ml of mixed bacterial suspension. Label them: Control, Added Substrate, Added Predator, and Added Substrate and Predator. Perform the following:

   • **Control:** Make serial dilutions of one tube of bacterial suspension out to –6 and plate out 50 µl from each dilution for bacterial counts.

   • **Added Substrate:** To two tubes, add 0.1 ml of a solution of 10 mg Proteose Peptone in 10 ml spring water (can be made fresh or autoclaved in portions for each team and stored in a refrigerator). Make dilutions and plate counts of one tube. The other will be used for the Substrate and Predator treatment.

   • **Added Predator:** Harvest *Tetrahymena* cells by centrifugation of two 5 ml cell suspensions in centrifuge tubes (2 to balance) at a setting of three on a bench top clinical centrifuge (about 300 g) for five minutes. Pour off supernatant and add 10 ml sterile spring water with sterile 10 ml pipet. If necessary, resuspend cell pellets by drawing up fluid in pipet and gently jet water into the bottom of tube. Pellet cells and resuspend once more in 5 ml spring water to wash away the proteose Peptone in which the ciliates were grown. Combine final resuspensions and add 1 ml of cell suspension of washed ciliates to a small vial or tube with 20 µl Lugol's iodine preservative. Dispense 10–20 µl onto a glass slide and count all ciliates in the drop with a 10x objective on the microscope. Calculate the number of ciliates per ml from this count. Calculate how much volume will be needed to add 1,000 ciliates to one treatment tube (100 ciliates per ml). Make dilutions and plate counts of this treatment. Record all calculations on your data sheet.

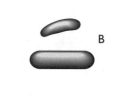

Figure 2
Common bacteria shapes include (A) cocci, (B) rods, and (C) spiral filaments.

• **Added Substrate and Predator:** Add the same volume of ciliate suspension as in Added Predator to one of the two tubes from Added Substrate. Make dilutions and plate counts.

7. Seal the four sets of petri dishes with tape, and incubate them for one week at room temperature.

Week 3

1. Examine the plates from time zero (the previous week), and determine plate counts for each of the three colony types. Take OD readings on all treatment tubes.

2. Fix 1 ml portions from ciliate-added treatments in 20 μl of Lugol's iodine. Determine ciliate densities as before. Larger volumes (up to 100 μl) may be required for these counts.

3. Make serial dilutions of each treatment, and plate out 50 μl portions as before. Incubate the plates at room temperature.

Week 4

1. Count the plates for each colony type from the previous week. Compile and compare data to show changes in the abundance of the three bacteria species due to growth from added substrate, predation effects, and for added substrate providing bacterial growth with predation effects. Record this data on a data sheet.

Discussion and Inquiry

• Graph your data about how the bacterial populations changed in response to predation and substrate treatments. How might predatory activity in other communities influence the species composition in the habitats you examined during this investigation? These impacts may include effects of predators on species composition and abundance for organisms dwelling in the same habitat.

• To take your hypotheses one step further, make theoretical linkages to the effects of changes in diversity and abundance. For example, if the predators are removed by pollution or another disturbance, what might happen to the prey populations? How might the loss of predators affect the way an ecosystem functions? If a prey is eaten by a predator, how does that affect energy flow and nutrient recycling in the ecosystem? If a prey is resistant to predation, what happens to an ecosystem's energy and nutrient cycles?

Predator-Prey Interactions

This is an advanced investigation, suitable for a science fair research project, and it requires some basic microbiology skills. It also involves an elementary understanding of some basic ecological concepts: nutrient cycling, trophic interactions, and predator-prey dynamics. By having students examine a predator-prey interaction at the microscopic level, they can hypothesize about the potential ripple effect that interaction has among macroscopic levels. In this way, students will come to appreciate the ecological impact of predator-prey interactions, and their effects on ecosystem function.

Selective predation affects bacterial communities as well as nutrient recycling and biomass transfer among higher trophic levels. The selective pressures of substrate availability and predation can alter bacterial abundance and species diversity. Bacterial diversity is reflected in the diversity of the chemical substrates the bacteria utilize for growth. Greater bacterial diversity results in more complete mineralization processes, and more efficient transfer of matter and energy to higher trophic levels. Reductions in bacterial diversity will impair these important ecological processes.

This investigation may be used to encourage students to think more creatively about how predator-prey interactions influence species composition among other trophic levels and among other habitats. This may include effects of predation on insect diversity. Further theoretical links may be made to larger organisms such as vertebrate communities. A possible follow up activity might be for students to do field research to investigate the validity of their theories.

This investigation also provides an opportunity to highlight an important aspect of scientific methodology. Conceptually, this investigation links ecological theories about species abundance and diversity, predator-prey interactions, and population dynamics with theories about nutrient production, evolutionary adaptation, and community structuring.

Micro-Macro Link

Interactions between specific predators and specific prey may affect all the other organisms in an ecosystem.

Time Management

This investigation will require between one and two class periods per week for approximately four weeks, depending on the number of students involved, how they are organized, and the degree to which they incorporate adaptations and variations.

4.5
TEACHER SECTION

Preparation Note

Procedures for preparing the "hockey stick" spreader appear in Appendix IV (pages 215–216).

Adaptations and Variations

Separate investigation set ups may be divided between lab teams, or the teams can perform all adaptations and variations. Separate investigations may also use different sample sources for bacteria.

◆

You can make the investigation a week shorter by obtaining bacterial cultures from a supply company. Strains with different pigments are available, such as red, yellow, and white.

◆

Another way to make the investigation shorter is to provide the class with prepared ciliate suspensions for the Added Predator test tube in Week 2, Step 6.

◆

By chance, some teams may have three species of bacteria that the ciliate will not eat, or all three may be equally consumed. Having each team start with material from a different sample type will increase the variation in the results.

◆

An alternative would be to use only primary environmental samples with and without added substrate, and examine bacterial diversity on plate counts. You can vary the substrate type by using simple, single-source substrates such as glucose and individual amino acids, or complex substrates such as yeast extract, proteose Peptone, or starch. This approach cannot control for predators that will appear in both, but these treatments can be examined for species diversity of protozoa (microscopically) as well as bacteria (plate counts).

◆

Make extrapolations to macroscopic communities. For example, sea otters act as a keystone predator that keeps sea urchins in check. Removal of the sea otters allows the sea urchins to proliferate to the point where they eat the bases of kelp that form kelp forests. Thus the presence of the kelp forest community is dependant on the predation activity of the sea otter. Starfish feeding in the rocky intertidal zone also act as keystone predators, limiting the proliferation of blue mussels (Figure 3) which are superior competitors for space and will exclude other species that have different ecological specializations.

Assessment and Evaluation

A full understanding of food webs should go beyond a simple understanding that larger organisms prey on smaller ones, and that this can occur at increasing size ranges up the food chain. Students should recognize that predator-prey relations have an influence on the quality of an environment, and hence may alter the life of all organisms living

Figure 3
Starfish preying on mussels in the rocky intertidal zone limit the size of the mussel population. Without the starfish, mussels would exclude other organisms, such as chitons, barnacles, and limpets.

in a community. Additionally, predators—especially top predators like birds of prey, wolves, and lions—are vulnerable to environmental degradation. Students should be aware that removing predators affects biological diversity and the functioning of an ecosystem.

In the case of microbes, this investigation demonstrates how protozoa may selectively prey on different bacteria. This not only shifts the relative proportions of bacteria in a community, but can change the types and amounts of substances processed by bacteria. The chemical composition of the environment as well as the flow of materials and energy within the ecosystem is consequently altered.

Students should be able to explain what evidence supports the conclusion that some bacteria are not consumed so readily by the protozoa. They should also be able to identify evidence for the balance of bacterial growth and predation pressures. Encourage students to think of additional experiments that could be done to investigate the feeding preferences and behavior of a variety of protozoa.

About the Author

Richard A. Snyder teaches ecology and protist biology at the University of West Florida. He developed this investigation to give students an appreciation of the fundamental mechanisms that affect biodiversity, and the effect of perturbations on the balance between these mechanisms. Many of the biodiversity concepts developed in macro-ecology can be demonstrated in the time scale of lab exercises with bacteria and protist populations.

Resources

Butterfield, C.T., Purdy, W.C., and Theriault, E.J. 1931. "The influence of the plankton on the biochemical oxidation of organic matter." *Publ. Health Rep.* 46: 393.

Fenchel, T. and Harrison, P. 1976. "The significance of bacterial grazing and mineral cycling for the decomposition of particulate detritus." *The Role of Terrestrial and Aquatic Organisms in Decomposition of Particulate Detritus.* pp. 285–299. Anderson, J.M. and MacFadyen, A. (eds.). Oxford: Blackwell Publishers.

Gerhardt, P., Murray, R.G.E., Wood, W.A. and Kreig, N.R. (eds.). 1994. *Methods for General and Molecular Bacteriology.* Washington, DC: American Society for Microbiology.

Guruala and Alexander, M. 1990. "Effect of growth rate and hydrophobicity on bacteria surviving protozoan grazing." *Applied Environmental Microbiology.* 56: 1631–1635.

Javornicky and Prokesová. 1963. "The influence of protozoa and bacteria upon the oxidation of organic substances in water." *Int. Revue ges. Hydrobiol.* 48: 335–350.

Pomroy, A.J. 1984. "Direct count of bacteria preserved with Lugol's iodine solution." *Applied Environmental Microbiology* 47: 1191–1192.

For distributors of biological supplies, such as *Tetrahymena*, see Appendix VI (pages 219–221).

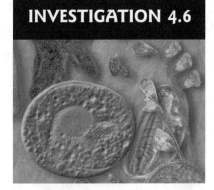

Responding to Gradients

A gradient is a consistent change over distance. In nature there are many kinds of gradients—temperature, rainfall, salinity, light, oxygen, nutrients, and many others. Gradients can be found for all of the features of the environment that determine where living things will survive. Humans recognize chemical gradients with their sense of smell; an odor increases in intensity as you get closer to its source.

The concept of a gradient can be visualized by thinking of a tall mountain. Rainfall and temperature create gradients up the side of the mountain that limit the distribution of plants and animals (Figure 1). If the mountain is high enough, it may be too cold and dry at the top for trees to live. This limit within the gradient is called the tree line. Lower down on the mountain we might find fir trees while, still lower on the mountain, the fir trees are replaced by oaks and other hardwoods. So, within the gradients on the mountainside, species exist within the tolerance of their limits.

For microorganisms, chemical gradients are especially important in determining the distribution and abundance of species. Some species are able to tolerate the absence of oxygen and, in fact, oxygen is poison to them. They are called anaerobes—life without oxygen. Other species require plentiful oxygen. They are called aerobes—life with oxygen.

For many microorganisms, the oxygen and nutrients they require often create opposing gradients, sometimes as a result of the microorganisms themselves using up all the oxygen where nutrients are plentiful. In this investigation, you will examine how microorganisms respond to the gradients of oxygen and nutrients.

So What?

The many different kinds of gradients in nature—such as temperature, rainfall, and salinity—determine where all organisms, large and small, will live.

Figure 1
A mountainside provides a good representation of the concept of a "gradient."

4.6 Objective

To understand how microbial communities respond to chemical gradients.

✔ Materials

- ❑ Microscope
- ❑ Glass slides, coverslips
- ❑ Autoclave
- ❑ Gooseneck dissecting stereoscope lamp, or other light source
- ❑ Magnifying glass
- ❑ Cotton, or synthetic wool
- ❑ Test tubes, 16×25 mm
- ❑ Petri dishes
- ❑ Bunsen burner
- ❑ Agar media
- ❑ Pipets, graduated and Pasteur
- ❑ Ruler
- ❑ Sediment from a natural water body, or soil and sterilized spring water
- ❑ Student Data Sheet

Procedure

Week 1

1. Follow your teacher's instructions for dividing into investigation teams. Each team will prepare two tubes of proteose peptone agar and two tubes of sulfur agar. Cut cubes of the appropriate agar medium from prepared petri plates. Carefully melt the cubes using low heat applied to the tube bottoms. *Use caution when working with flame.*

2. To several test tubes, add small amounts of sediment from a pond, river, lake, estuary, or marsh. Then fill the tubes to within 3–4 cm of the top with water. (Soil and sterilized spring water may also be used.) Plug the tubes with cotton or synthetic wool to allow air exchange, as shown in Figure 2. *Do not get the plugs wet.* Let the plugged tubes stand at room temperature. A cross-gradient will form: oxygen will diffuse downward from the top through the cotton plugs, and nutrients or chemicals will diffuse upward from the agar.

Figure 2
Gradient tube culture with cotton or synthetic wool plug, water sample, and agar nutrient source.

3. Place one set of tubes in the dark and the other underneath a light source. The oxygen gradient can be visualized using methylene blue or other indicator dyes. Follow your teacher's instructions for adding indicator dyes to the tubes, and note that they may be toxic to some of the microorganisms. Incubate some of the tubes in the light and the rest in darkness. Gradients will be established within a few days, and they should last about one week.

Week 2

4. Examine the organisms in your tubes at two magnification levels: naked eye and magnifying glass. Record your observations on a separate data sheet. Pay particular attention to the structure of the gradient and to how organisms are distributed through the gradient. Use side illumination against a black background for easier observation, but be careful not to place the light too close to the tubes. The heat will generate convection currents and destroy the gradient structure.

5. Use a micropipet and very carefully take a subsample from each tube. Make a wet mount slide of your subsample, and observe the

distribution of organisms. Record your observations on your data sheet. Be sure to accurately record the depth from which you removed subsamples from the tubes, which tube your subsample was drawn from, and what magnification you used to make your observations.

Discussion and Inquiry

- Why would microorganisms try to go where they do?

- What limits the downward distribution of organisms in the tubes you observed?

- What would you expect to happen as the nutrients become depleted in the agar at the bottom of the tubes?

- When the tubes were set up, there was oxygen throughout. What happened to create an oxygen gradient?

Responding to Gradients

Microorganisms will proliferate where they can tolerate conditions, and will often establish sharp limits within the diffusion gradients by consuming the diffusing compounds (Figure 3). Often, organisms proliferate not at their optimum conditions, but at the conditions they are able to tolerate where they can escape predators or competition from other organisms. In most cases, macroscopically obvious concentrations of organisms will result. Anaerobes will occur in the bottoms of the tubes, microaerophiles in a sharp band at the oxygen limit, and a protist band (consuming bacteria) may form just above bacterial band (limited more by oxygen than by the bacteria). Some protists will only occur in the aerobic zone.

Before students begin the investigation, make the following agar preparation (prepare 100 ml of each as agar plates):

1. **General heterotrophic media:**
   0.2 percent proteose peptone with 1.5 percent agar.

2. **Anaerobic sulfur bacteria media:**

$Na_2S_2O_3 \cdot 5H_2O$	1.0 g
KH_2PO_4	0.1 g
K_2HPO_4	0.1 g
$MgSO_4 \cdot 7H_2O$	0.08 g
NH_4Cl	0.04 g
yeast extract	0.00001 g
spring water to	100.0 ml
agar	1.5 g

This investigation offers an opportunity to discuss the distribution of species relative to gradients that span the globe across major biomes, or that occur within a few centimeters in a test tube. Encourage students to discuss the responses of microorganisms to the gradients of oxygen and nutrients. Point out that tolerance often is more important than what is physiologically optimum. Provide physiological characteristics of hypothetical organisms, and ask students where in the tubes they might be found. Discuss what limits the occurrence of different examples of organisms in nature.

Adaptations and Variations

Agar media are limited largely by imagination. In addition to nutrients, various antibiotics and inhibitors can be used. For additional media formulations for specific bacteria, see the Gerhardt book listed under Resources at the end of this investigation.

◆

As a supplement, a "Winogradsky column" can be set up by sealing sediment in a glass tube and placing it in a sunny window. Colorful patches of various microorganisms will develop over several weeks.

Assessment and Evaluation

When addressing Discussion and Inquiry questions, students should understand that the microorganisms try to get as far down the tube as possible as they search for more concentrated nutrients. Their downward distribution is limited by oxygen availability. As nutrients become depleted, microorganism growth slows, oxygen consumption decreases, and the bacteria band at the oxygen limit migrates down the tube with the increasing oxygen and decreasing nutrients.

An oxygen gradient is created by the growth of microorganisms on nutrients in the agar consuming oxygen in the bottom of the tubes until the only oxygen available is what diffuses downward from the top. Organisms then become dependent on the rate at which a needed element is supplied. In disturbed habitats, resources are often readily available, everything is mixed and the potential for explosive growth exists on the pool of resources. In stable habitats at equilibrium, resource pools tend to be diminished and organisms are dependent on the rate at which resources are made available.

About the Author

Richard Snyder teaches ecology and protist biology at the University of West Florida. This investigation was developed to stimulate students to think of the environment not as a homogeneous place, but that gradients of resources and limiting factors structure communities in the natural world, even down to the microscale. The opposing gradient factors of oxygen and nutrient availability provide a demonstration of how the balance of limiting factors determines the distribution and abundance of species according to their particular adaptations.

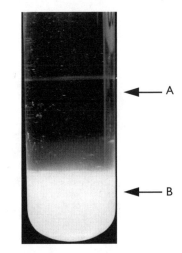

Figure 3
Bacterial and protist concentration at limit of oxygen diffusion. (A) haze of anaerobic bacteria, and (B) agar plug in a gradient tube culture of an estuarine marsh sample.

Resources

Gerhardt, P. et. al. 1994. *Methods for General and Molecular Bacteriology.* Washington, DC: American Society of Microbiology.

Fenchel, T. 1969. "The ecology of marine microbenthos IV." *Ophelia,* 6: 1–187.

Jacob, H.E. 1970. "Redox Potential." *Methods in Microbiology.* Norris, J.R. and Ribbons, D.W. (eds.). New York: Academic Press.

Snyder, R.A. and Small, E.B. 1984. "The response of protists to spatial heterogeneity produced by a gradient culture technique." *Journal of Protozoology,* 31.

Wimpenny, J.W.T., et. al. 1984. "Growth and interactions of microorganisms in spatially heterogenous ecosystems." *Current Perspectives in Microbial Ecology.* Klug, M.J. and Reddy, C.A. (eds.). Washington, DC: American Society for Microbiology.

For distributors of biological supplies, see Appendix VI (pages 219–221).

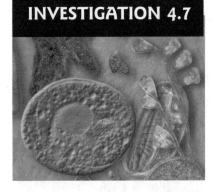

Ecological Effects of Contaminants

Contaminants can alter the structure and function of ecological communities. Usually, contaminants reduce biological diversity and inhibit normal functions. When biological diversity is reduced, several important consequences occur for the environment. The stability of the ecological community may be reduced. With fewer species, any other agitation—such as severe temperature changes, disease, or new predators—may completely eliminate the remaining species. Also, the remaining species may not be good prey for a wide range of organisms. Therefore, the food web (Figure 1) is upset and the productivity of the ecosystem may decline.

In this investigation, you will examine the kinds of changes that occur in ecological communities affected by one or more pollutants.

So What?

Contaminating some organisms in a food web means all the organisms that rely on them for food become contaminated too.

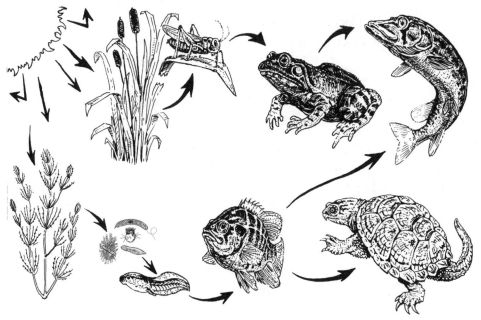

Figure 1
Some of the organisms inhabiting a wetland ecosystem; arrows depict the direction of energy flow. Because of the cyclical nature of energy flow and the interdependence of organisms, contaminants introduced at any point in the cycle eventually affect all the other organisms.

4.7 Objective

To examine how pollutants affect ecological communities.

✔ Materials

- ❏ Compound or video microscope
- ❏ Glass slides, coverslips
- ❏ Serrated knife
- ❏ Polyurethane foam (PF) blocks
- ❏ Distilled or aged tap water
- ❏ 5–10 l aquaria or trays
- ❏ Eyedroppers
- ❏ Collecting jars, beakers, or zipper-locked bags

Procedure

1. Follow your teacher's instructions to make artificial substrates from polyurethane foam. *Be extremely careful when using the knife, and do so only under the supervision of your teacher.* Wet or wash the blocks with water—this step is essential for the organisms' growth.

2. Place several of the cultured PF blocks in a tray or aquarium. You may want to find a way to anchor the blocks to the bottom of the tray. (Try using hooks glued to the bottom with non-toxic silicon caulk.) Place the same number of PF blocks, usually 4–5, in each aquarium or tray, and arrange the blocks so they do not touch each other. Place enough water in the tray to cover the PF blocks. (If you have enough trays or aquaria, try to duplicate the experimental conditions. That is, you should have at least 2 "controls" and 2 of each "polluted" condition.)

3. Take samples from the cultured PF blocks before contaminating them to see what organisms they contain and how they interact. To sample a PF block—both before and after contamination—lift it from the tray or aquarium and squeeze its contents into a collecting receptacle. Let the contents settle for a few minutes; the organisms will concentrate in the bottom. Pipet a 1-2 drop subsample from the bottom of the receptacle, and make a wet mount slide with a cover slip of your subsample.

4. After placing your subsample on the stage of a microscope, examine it by systematically scanning from left to right using 200x or 400x magnification. Pay particular attention to species diversity and ecological interaction, and be sure to observe algae as well as protozoa. The protozoa will usually be moving, but they should settle down after a few minutes.

5. Identify and record the organisms you observe in your subsample in the "before contamination" column of a life list (use Figure 2 as a model). You may want to make rough sketches of the organisms as you enter them in the column. Next to each entry, make a notation about the organism's behavior and physiology. For example: Is it moving quickly or slowly? Is it eating? What color is it? Is it grouped together with other organisms of the same or different species? After you add contaminants, you will perform these same steps and record your observations in the "after contamination" columns of your life list. This will allow you to compare the physiology and behavior of organisms before and after contamination.

6. It can also be useful to assess the ecological function of the micro-environments. After squeezing the contents of a PF block into a

receptacle and before taking subsamples and preparing wet mount slides, illuminate the receptacle using a light whose period can be controlled (12L:12D works well). At the same time each day, measure either the pH or the level of dissolved oxygen in both the controls and contaminated microcosms. Your teacher will instruct you how to obtain these measurements.

7. Following your teacher's instructions add contaminants to each tray or aquarium. Be sure to accurately record what type of contaminant and how much you add to each. Gently stir the water using a glass or plastic rod.

8. Allow the organisms several days to be exposed to the contaminants you have introduced to their environments. Follow the procedures outlined in Steps 3-4 to take subsamples and to observe and identify the organisms they contain. Record your observations about the organisms' physiology and behavior in the "after contamination" columns of your life list. Make additional notations as needed about changes in ecological function by comparing pH and dissolved-oxygen measurements before and after contamination.

Discussion and Inquiry

- How do pollutants influence the abundance, diversity, and productivity of organisms in an ecological community? Why are protozoa likely to be susceptible to pollutants? How can they be used as indicators of environmental pollution? What difference does it make to humans if protozoa are seriously depleted in the environment due to pollution?

- In this investigation, we seek evidence that pollutants have an effect on protozoa. What is the experimental design or arrangement of the treatments that allows you to make a conclusion that a pollutant has an adverse effect? Is there a control in your investigation set up? What is the difference between the control set-up and the experimental treatment?

Figure 2
Sample before-and-after "life list" comparing the potential effects of contaminants on several of the organisms depicted in Figure 1. Ecological assessment notes: pre-contaminant pH = 6.3. Acidic laundry detergent changed pH to 3.7; potato flakes had no effect on pH.

Before Contamination	After Contamination	
Organism	Laundry detergent	Potato flakes
cat o'nine tails green, yellow, and brown sturdy stalks	pale green/yellow stalks wispy	green, yellow, brown sturdy stalks
frog dark green, eyes clear smooth skin, slightly slimy	eyes bloodshot skin mottled, very slimy	sluggish
perch active, seeking food moves from middle to upper portion of water column and back	sluggish/disoriented stays in upper water column	sluggish/disoriented

Ecological Effects of Contaminants

Micro-Macro Link

Protozoa occupy the lower trophic levels of food webs. If contamination alters or destroys their productivity, the entire web's productivity is greatly reduced.

Time Management

The actual student investigation portion may be completed in one class period, followed by several half-hour observation periods over one to three weeks.

Protozoa are intimately associated with their environment. As single-celled organisms, usually lacking appreciable cell coverings and often enclosed only by the plasma membrane, they are highly susceptible to chemical changes in their environment. Some chemicals diffuse across the outer membrane rather easily, and thus can build up to toxic levels very readily within the cell. Also, chemical changes induced by relatively localized deposits of foreign substances can be devastating to the protozoa, since they occupy environmental patches that may be less than a meter in size. Hence, local disturbances can have very significant effects on these patchy communities.

Widespread disturbances of the protozoan communities can have adverse effects further up the food web. Protozoa are important members of the lower trophic levels of food webs. They feed on bacteria and replenish nutrients needed by other microorganisms, some invertebrates, and plants. If these members of the food web are destroyed, the productivity of the entire web can be reduced. Hence, it is very important to clearly examine the effects of pollutants and other contaminants on protozoan communities.

Depending on the time and resources available to you, this investigation may be prepared in several different ways. Setup will require one class period, and the student investigation should run for at least a week, or longer if you incorporate adaptations and variations as suggested below. Sampling the trays or aquaria should take more than one class period. Regular measurements of pH, dissolved O_2, or other variables can be performed on a schedule ranging from daily to once or twice a week.

If you have access to a natural water body, you may want to organize a field trip so students will be able to hone both field and lab skills. The time for colonizing PF blocks in the wild varies from one week in a stream to 2–3 weeks in a pond, lake, or intertidal ecosystem. Tie the PF blocks very tightly with string, so they resemble a bow tie. Then tie the string to a rope, which in turn is tied to a cinder block. Submerge the blocks; you will have to squeeze them underwater to fill them, so they don't float. A standard cinder block will anchor about eight PF blocks in a shallow stream.

PF blocks may also be colonized in the ocean; secure them to a cord attached to a long pole, and anchor the pole to the shoreline with a heavy rock or cinder block. Secure a weight to the cord's other end so the blocks remain submerged. Just make sure you take into account how strong the current is; a brick, for example, will not work in a tidal ecosystem.

Alternatively, you can establish a varied culture of protists in an aquarium by either collecting water from natural habitats several weeks prior to the investigation yourself, or by purchasing mixed cultures from a supply company and adding them to the aquarium. See Appendix III for details.

Adaptations and Variations

Two variations on this investigation are possible. The shorter version is to place the same number of PF blocks in each aquarium. Once the pollutants are added, the investigation can be conducted 1–2 weeks later by removing the PF blocks from each tray or aquaria and examining the species and other variables.

◆

A longer version requires approximately 2–3 weeks, and may be successfully linked to Investigations 4.1 and 4.2 on species colonization and succession. In this variation, 1–2 epicenters colonized in the wild are anchored in the center of each aquarium and surrounded by barren, uncolonized PF blocks, usually 4–6. Upon completing the investigation into species colonization, the same setup may be used for this investigation on contaminants. After introducing contaminants and waiting 2–3 weeks, 1–2 blocks can be removed from each aquarium each week for sampling and analysis, or all the blocks can be removed at the end of the 2–3 week period.

◆

A number of household "pollutants" (Figure 3) can be used to simulate sewage (e.g., blended food scraps resemble the oxygen demanding wastes) or contaminants (e.g., herbicides, pesticides, heavy metals). Certain herbicides have low mammalian toxicity but produce significant ecological effects. Good candidates are atrazine and diquat which each affect photosynthesis directly. Toxic metals such as copper and zinc in concentrations of 0.5–5 mg/l will produce dramatic effects. Similarly "acid rain" can be simulated by adding sulfuric acid to microscopic ecosystems to change pH to levels below about 5.5 (typical rain water). *In all cases, care should be taken to properly dispose of "pollutant" materials. Toxic metals should only be used with great caution since they do not degrade.*

◆

Environmental toxicologists recognize the effects of pollutants as producing dose-related effects—the higher the "dose" or concentration

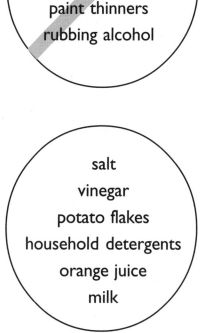

Figure 3
Many household "pollutants" can be used to simulate sewage, but care should be taken if encouraging students to bring any from home. Care should also be taken in disposing of toxic materials.

the greater the effects. An effective procedure is to use several doses that increase by a constant factor, such as 5 or 10. While the most common pollutants are sewage and nutrients—nitrates, ammonia, phosphates—students can also test commercial formulations or herbicides, detergents or soaps, and other substances. Household cleaners may not cause serious environmental problems because they are usually treated in a septic tank or sewage treatment system, so they can represent "new" chemicals whose effects are unknown for the purposes of this investigation.

◆

For assessing ecological function, students can take measurements at the same time each day, as described above. Alternatively, these measures can be made in the morning (before lights on), in the evening (before lights off), and again the following morning. This will reveal the diurnal pattern of change and is analogous to measuring total respiration (in the dark) and net primary production (in the light).

Several alternative measures of function are available, including the activity of enzyme systems (especially phosphatase activity) and the retention of nutrients. Relatively simple procedures for phosphatases are available as kits from biological supply companies. You can visualize the color change or, more precisely, use a spectrophotometer. Concentrations of oxygen and nutrients in the microcosm water can be determined using most standard "limnology" field kits, but the number of samples that can be taken will be limited by the amount of water in the microcosm.

Assessment and Evaluation

Discuss with students why protozoa are so easily affected by pollutants. Help them see that because protozoa are single-celled and often lack protective coverings, they are very dependent on the quality of their environment.

Have them critically assess how pollutants influence the abundance, diversity, and productivity of organisms in a polluted environment. Of what importance are the protozoa in replenishing nutrients, helping to maintain healthy roots of plants that supply our oxygen, and serving in food chains? Protozoa are essential in purifying water either in the natural environment as water percolates through the soil and flows into streams, or especially in our wastewater treatment plants. Pollutants can interfere with all of these essential roles.

Encourage students to generalize about how pollutants may affect larger organisms. Stimulate them to discuss the likely effects on our quality of life if we alter the balance of the planet's living things. Help students to see that we are all interlinked as living organisms into a web of life that has many interdependent relationships.

This investigation uses a standard control-group and experimental-group design. Students should be able to explain why the control preparation is necessary, and how comparisons of results with the pollutant-treated PF blocks and the controls allow us to draw conclusions about the effects of pollutants. They should recognize that the control trays are identical to the treatment trays with the exception that the treatment tray has pollutant added. Thus, any change in the protozoa in the treatment tray should be attributed to the pollutant. If students have used a range of pollutants in their experiments, they should be able to make a judgment about the relative effects of the contaminants.

For example, which ones are most likely to completely destroy a protozoan community, which are most likely to only shift the relative abundances of certain species, and which have only a mild disturbing effect? Students should be able to justify their ranking of the pollutants based on observations they have made from their culture samples. Furthermore, they should be able to make these judgments in the broader context of the importance to the stability and productivity of microbiotic communities within larger ecosystems. Students should be able to generalize their conclusions to larger ecosystems by comparing their results to possible effects of widespread contamination of terrestrial and marine ecosystems.

About the Author

James Pratt is Director of Environmental Sciences and Resources at Portland State University in Oregon. He specializes in protozoology, and his work has ranged from basic studies of the ecology, distribution, and biogeography of protozoa to their use as indicators of contaminant effects in freshwater and estuarine ecosystems. He has developed standardized methods for assessing ecological effects of contaminants in multispecies systems, and has applied his knowledge of protozoan community ecology to using protozoa as water quality monitors of effect and recovery in human-influenced systems.

Resources

For distributors of biological supplies, see Appendix VI (pages 219–221).

5
Adaptive Strategies

Life thrives or perishes depending upon its ability to adapt to changes in the environment. Over time, living organisms develop adaptive strategies that enable them to meet the demands precipitated by those changes. The ground beneath our feet contains the fossilized remains of many organisms that were unable to meet such demands.

In this section, students will explore reproductive and feeding strategies, strategies for avoiding predators, strategies for rising to both short- and long-term environmental challenges, and adaptive behavioral strategies to biotic and abiotic conditions. As they conduct these investigations at the microscopic level, students will acquire an understanding of how organisms at all levels evolve strategies to adapt to environmental changes.

Reproductive Strategies

So What?

The reproductive strategies (how, when, and in what numbers) of all living organisms are a primary way for them to increase their numbers and adapt to environmental changes.

Note

Another reason why protozoa populations remain constant, is that some species are able to form cysts or other dormant stages to persist during adverse conditions.

Every day, astronomical numbers of protozoa die. They are easily killed, most often by changes in acidity, oxygen concentration, temperature, and drying up of their medium. Despite this high death rate, the average number of protozoa in the world remains about the same. Why? Because protozoa are able to reproduce quickly enough to balance this death rate.

Most protozoa reproduce by an asexual form of cell duplication. Binary fission is the most common of these forms, but other possibilities are multiple fission, external budding, and internal budding. Just before asexual division, though, it is not unusual for some protozoa to first reproduce sexually. This combination allows the protozoa to have a "birth rate" that is rapid enough to keep up with their death rate.

Sexual reproduction among flagellated protozoa may occur by fusion of two nearly equal-sized gametes, called isogametes. Isogametes will only fuse together if they are genetically compatible, and—unlike humans—a given species may have more than one compatible pair of mating types. Attracted to each other by pheromones, compatible mating types gather together in a huge mass of cells. They then pair off and fuse. The product of this isogamete fusion is a zygote.

The zygote of *Chlamydomonas reinhardii* is a cell about twice the size of the original. This zygote will eventually divide by meiosis, forming four haploid cells, each with two flagella. These four haploid cells remain inside the cell wall of the original zygote.

The mating solution contains nutrients and chemical compounds in solution to promote the fusion of the compatible pairs of flagellates and support subsequent growth of the progeny. In this investigation, you will examine the various stages of this reproductive strategy using the green-algal flagellate *Chlamydomonas reinhardii*.

Procedure

1. To prepare glass micropipets, follow your teacher's instructions.

2. Use the glass micropipets to combine a drop of mating type positive with an equal-sized drop of mating type negative on a glass slide, as shown in Figure 1. Place a coverslip over the combined drops, and observe under low power with a compound microscope.

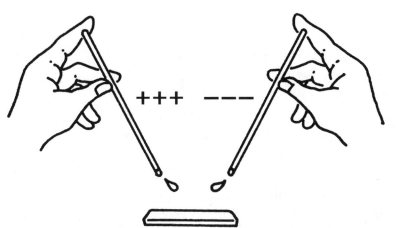

Figure 1
Use the glass micropipets to combine a drop of mating type positive with an equal-sized drop of mating type negative on a glass slide.

3. Immediately draw and label your initial observations of the individual cells. Then, record your observations when the cells begin clumping together. Be sure to note the number of flagella and stigmata (eye spots), as well as the size of their chloroplasts.

4. Remove the slide for a few minutes after completing your observations; this will help avoid rapid evaporation and heating.

5. After a few more minutes, place the slide back on the microscope. By this time, zygotes should have formed. You will be able to easily recognize the new cells, because zygotes are double the size of the mating cells. Draw and label your observations of these zygotes. As in Step 3, note the number of their flagella and stigmata, and the size of their chloroplasts.

Discussion and Inquiry

As you just observed, flagellates form an intermediate zygote. Ciliates, however, exchange motile haploid nuclei that fuse with the immotile haploid gamete in each opposite cell of the pair, before separating and swimming away. They undergo cell division later. What are the advantages of both methods of sexual reproduction? What are the relative merits of asexual versus sexual reproduction?

5.1 Objective

To analyze the reproductive strategy of the flagellate, Chlamydomonas reinhardii.

✔ Materials

- ❑ Compound light microscope, oil immersion objectives
- ❑ Glass slides, coverslips
- ❑ Immersion oil
- ❑ Mating solution
- ❑ Glass micropipets, or eyedroppers
- ❑ Grooved forceps
- ❑ Blank paper, pencil
- ❑ Screw-cap test tube cultures: *Chlamydomonas reinhardii,* mating type + and −
- ❑ Microscope video camera, TV monitor, and cassette recorder (optional)

Reproductive Strategies

Micro-Macro Link

All species of organisms have reproductive strategies that enable them to maintain population levels in changing environments.

Time Management

This investigation may be completed in one class period.

Sexual reproduction requires that the reproductive cells locate and properly combine with cells of the same species. Some form of cell-cell recognition is required to ensure that only two cells of the same species pair and fuse. In the case of *Chlamydomonas reinhardii*, there is also a sex gene that regulates which pair of cells will be attracted to one another. The two forms are designated + and –. In addition, the cells pair and fuse at a particular location, where the flagella attach. The *Chlamydomonas reinhardii* cells exhibit specific behavioral responses in pairing; they do not join at just any point on their surfaces. Figure 2 shows the stages in the reproductive cycle of *Chlamydomonas reinhardii*.

These behavioral responses and cell pairings can be compared to sexual reproduction in plants and animals, as suggested in Assessment and Evaluation. Organisms that have sexual as well as asexual reproductive strategies are more likely to adapt to variable environments. Their populations may be larger and more stable compared to species that exhibit only asexual reproduction. Also, if the species is potential prey for other organisms, sexual reproduction may introduce variations in size of the offspring, chemical composition, or swimming behavior that will make the offspring less appropriate as prey compared to the parents. This may add additional survival potential for the species and further stabilize this population of organisms.

Adaptations and Variations

If a video camera is available students can watch all this activity from a TV monitor. Also, you can record especially good scenarios with a video recorder.

◆

Have students compare the differences between flagellate and ciliate pairing. There are mating strains of ciliates available from major biological supply companies.

◆

If the class has studied genetics, this investigation is an excellent opportunity to apply the principles of Mendelian genetics to

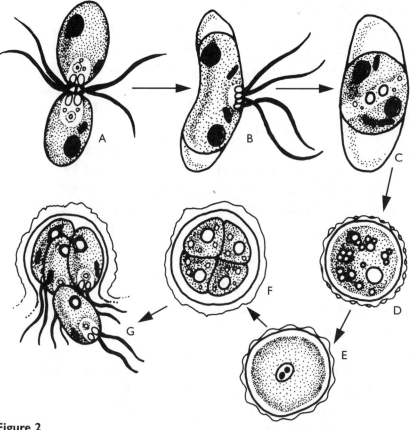

Figure 2
Two haploid cells (with only one set of chromosomes) join at the anterior end (A) and begin fusion leading to a four-flagellated stage (B) as the cytoplasm begins to contract. This leads to a spherical stage lacking flagella (C) still within the elongated cell wall. The two nuclei fuse producing a diploid cell (with two sets of chromosomes) and the spherical cell contracts into a cyst with a thickened wall (D). The cyst may either enter a dormant period (E) or immediately undergo meiosis by repeated nuclear division to produce four haploid daughter cells (F) that are released by rupture of the cyst wall (G). These swim away and later may fuse (A) completing the life cycle.

Chlamydomonas. For example, if a deep-green pigmented *Chlamydomonas* cell mates with a yellow-green pigmented cell and the progeny are all deep-green pigmented, what is the likely genotype of the parents? The deep-green cell could have genotype GG (homozygous dominant) and the yellow-green cell gg (homozygous recessive). Then, all the offspring would have the genotype Gg. Deep green genes would be dominant. How can we check this? By back-crossing the progeny to the yellow-green parent cell, we can find out if indeed, the gene for yellow-green pigmentation is recessive. The hybrid offspring with genotype Gg when crossed with the yellow-green parent (gg), should yield one half progeny with hybrid deep-green pigmentation (Gg) and one half with yellow-green pigmentation (gg).

Assessment and Evaluation

Have students discuss the advantages of ciliate and flagellate sexual reproduction. (Flagellates form an intermediate zygote, while ciliates share motile gametic nuclei before separating.) Since the flagellates form a zygotic stage, this can become a resting spore in some cases and permit the organism to survive during unfavorable growth conditions. Also, this allows the zygote to immediately share all the combined genetic potential from the two parent cells. The new combination of chromosomes and mix of genes may make the zygote and some of the offspring released from the resting spore more adaptive to the environment. The intermediate zygote stage may be able to withstand adverse environmental conditions, thus permitting the flagellate to endure conditions of hardship before the sexually produced daughter cells are released into the environment.

The reproductive strategy of the ciliate, however, allows the fertilized cells to immediately swim away and continue to feed while they undergo preparation for asexual division. The ability of ciliates to swim away before dividing allows the daughter cells to immediately exploit the environment if they are more genetically capable of adapting to it. In this way, sexual reproduction can allow a population to respond quickly to environmental change.

In general, asexual reproduction is favorable when the organism is already well adapted to its environment and the environment does not change very rapidly. Asexual reproduction also takes less time to accomplish. Each of the asexually produced daughter cells is identical to the parent and thus should be well suited to survive in the favorable environment. This allows continuous exploitation of the stable environment. On the other hand, if the environment is changeable, then sexual reproduction may be more advantageous because the offspring will have a genetic makeup that is different from each of the parents. Some of the offspring may therefore be better equipped to adapt to environmental change.

Students should be able to explain what genetic and behavioral factors determine which cells will pair and fuse, and how the process is regulated to ensure the proper orientation of the cells during union. The cells interact first by flagellar contact, then if they are a compatible pair they join at the flagellar end and fuse by union of their cell membranes. Only a + and – strain will unite. This helps to ensure a more likely new combination of genes. If the same strain were to unite, the diversity of the genes available to be united in the daughter cell might be less.

Students should be able to discuss why sexual reproduction is particularly advantageous in an environment that is likely to change dramatically and somewhat frequently. Also, they should be able to compare the process of sexual reproduction in *Chlamydomonas* with sexual reproduction in plants (when a pollen-derived sperm fuses with the "egg" in the ovary of the flower) and when sperm and egg fuse in reproduction of animals.

About the Author

Arthur J. Repak teaches protozoology, environmental microbiology, and freshman biology at Quinnipiac College in Hamden, CT. Survival of species depends upon organisms mating. In natural environments, chemical signals are issued by appropriate mating types to attract the proper mating types and therefore a successful fusion of haploid cells.

Resources

For distributors of *Chlamydomonas reinhardii*, mating type + and –, and mating solution, as well as other biological supplies, see Appendix VI (pages 219–221).

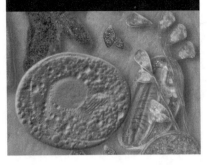

Environmental Challenges

So What?

Adaptations to environmental change don't have to evolve over thousands and thousands of years. Sometimes they consist of a short-term change in behavior.

When they hear the word "adaptation," many people think in terms of physical adaptations that evolve over hundreds, thousands, even millions of years. But organisms can also adapt to shorter-term changes in their environments. They do this by changing their behaviors. Such behavioral strategies include finding a suitable habitat in which to live and reproduce, getting food, avoiding predators, finding suitable mates, and exploring new regions of their environment.

However, environments don't always stay the same for very long. In the macroscopic world, elements such as climate, food sources, and landforms change continually. An animal may encounter a different environment just by moving about! An ant, for example, may walk a few feet down a concrete surface, only to abruptly encounter dust, then mud, then grass. An observer might see that the ant had moved from a curb onto a recently-watered lawn, but from the ant's perspective, it had just faced a series of environments that required it to use a different behavior to successfully keep moving forward.

Because environmental conditions are constantly shifting, organisms must also continually change their behavior to survive. Protozoa exhibit this ability by developing a repertoire of adaptive locomotory responses. To elude a predator, for example, they may first swim forward, then backward, turn left, then spin around. If one behavior works better, the protozoa may continue it until it is safe. Such diverse responses allow animals to find the most suitable behavioral pattern for a particular environment. In this investigation, you will challenge the protozoa with some unusual obstacles, and test their ability to cope with changing environments.

Procedure

1. To analyze ciliate reaction to the surface texture of their environments, you will need a glass slide with one half of the surface roughened (Figure 1). The perfectly smooth area of the slide is the control half and the roughened surface is the experimental half. Use a different grade of sandpaper for each slide. Uniformly scratch the surface to yield a regular pattern of etchings. Be sure to carefully protect the smooth side so that it does not get scratched, and to label each slide with the grade of sandpaper you used.

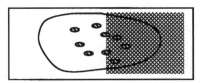 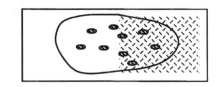

Figure 1
Preparation of two slides, each with one half roughened with sand paper of different coarseness. A drop of culture containing hypotrich ciliates has been added to each slide. By observing the slide over time, you will discover which of the surfaces is most preferred by the ciliates.

2. Place a drop (about 0.5 ml) of a ciliate culture on the surface of the slide so that it covers both the smooth and rough area. Do not use a coverslip! The ciliates must be free to move on the surface of the slide.

3. Use a stereomicroscope to count the number of ciliates in each half of the slide. Count them every five minutes for half an hour. If you notice the culture beginning to evaporate, gently add a small amount of water to the drop's edge.

4. Write a description of how the ciliates on each half of the slide. move. Illustrate your description if it helps explain what you see.

5. Which substrate does the species prefer? Calculate the "preference" as the ratio Nr/Ns, where Nr is the number of ciliates on the rough side of the slide, and Ns is the number on the smooth side of the slide. If the species prefers the rough side, the ratio Nr/Ns will be greater than 1.0. If, however, it prefers the smooth side, the ratio will be less than 1.0. A value very near to 1.0 indicates no clear preference.

6. Repeat this procedure with each of the slides you have prepared.

7. To examine ciliate escape behavior, prepare a thin wisp of cotton that has been teased and pulled to form a very thin network of fibers just large enough to fit on a microscope slide (Figure 2). Place this cotton web on the surface of a slide—the web should be just

5.2 Objective
To examine protozoan responses to environmental challenges.

✔ Materials

- ❏ Compound light microscope
- ❏ Stereoscopic dissecting microscope
- ❏ Slides, coverslips
- ❏ Pasteur pipets
- ❏ Charcoal-filtered pond water (CHPW) or bottled spring water
- ❏ Sandpaper, fine to coarse
- ❏ Fiber optic/cold light illuminator (optional)
- ❏ Cultures:
  Paramecia
  Blepharisma
  Tetrahymena
  Euplotes
  Oxytricha
  Stylonychia

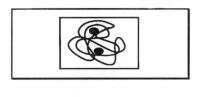

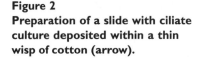

Figure 2
Preparation of a slide with ciliate culture deposited within a thin wisp of cotton (arrow).

thick enough to trap ciliates without completely immobilizing them. Add a droplet of one of the ciliate cultures, and place a coverslip on top of the preparation.

8. Observe the preparation with low power under a compound microscope. Isolate an area where ciliates have become enclosed within the spaces formed by the cotton web, then examine them on high power.

9. Following the movement of a single ciliate, note your observations on the behavior checklist (Figure 1). Each time you observe a particular behavior, enter a number in the space to indicate the step in the sequence where it occurs. For example if the first behavior you see is swimming backward, enter a 1 in the space to the right of swimming backward. If the next behavior is turning right, then enter a 2 in the space next to the category "turning right." When you have finished, count up the total number of entries in each line and put the sum in the box under the heading "Frequency." There are extra spaces for you to enter other behaviors you may see.

Discussion and Inquiry

- Did you detect differences in the movement patterns on the roughened surface compared to the smooth surface? Describe them in writing or make a drawing.

Figure 1
Behavior checklist

Behaviors	Order of Occurrence	Frequency
Forward Swimming		
Backward Swimming		
Turning Right		
Turning Left		
Rotating Around Long Axis		
Spinning Around Short Axis Like a Top		
Body Contraction		
Twisting Body into Spiral		
Burrowing Into Fiber Spaces		

- Contrast the behavior of different species to different surfaces textures. Also, compare the ciliates' behaviors when confronted with an extremely hostile environment (the cotton web) to when they are able to freely move about.

- When a ciliate was trapped in a space among the cotton fibers, how long did it take the protist to escape?

- What behaviors did you observe as the ciliate tried to escape the cotton? Which occurred most frequently?

- Did you notice a change in the protist's behavior pattern as it found better coping mechanisms? Describe what you observed.

- Did obtaining a ratio for ciliate movement assist your observations of the protist's behavior? If so, how?

- Might the protist's behavior be affected by the fact that it moves with cilia, rather than with pseudopods or flagella? If so, how?

- Apply the behaviors you observed to situations a ciliate might encounter in real-life.

- For Steps 1–6, describe the characteristics of the sequence of movements. For example, when the protist changes the direction of movement, what angle is made in relation to the direction of motion? This can be determined by applying a protractor to the tracing of the path of motion and measuring the angle of deviation from the line of motion.

- When and how often does the protist rotate its body (rotate around the long axis of the body)? The ratio of the various kinds of movement categorized above can be used as an index of relative motion. For example what is the ratio of the number of times the ciliate rotates its body (R) to the number of times it changes direction of motion (D) along a given path. If you observed the ciliate for 3 minutes and, during that time it rotated its body 8 times and made a zig-zag change in direction of swimming 24 times, the ratio R/D would be 8/24 which reduces to 1/3.

- Make additional ratios. For example, count the number of times the protozoan moves in a straight path after it has changed direction, symbolized by S. Then, count the number of times the protozoan turned to the right, symbolized by A+, and the number of times it turned to the left symbolized by A–. These numbers can be expressed as a ratio S/A+/A–. As an example, if you observed the ciliate for a given period of time and found that S = 10, that A+ = 4, and that A– = 2, then the ratio is 10:4:2, which reduces to 5:2:1. Ratios like this one can be calculated for movements on the smooth side of the slide and be compared to ratios for movements on the rough side of the slide. This comparison will allow you to make a quantitative estimate to determine if there are differences in the protozoan's behavior on surfaces of different roughness.

Environmental Challenges

Micro-Macro Link

Many species develop adaptive behavioral strategies to suit challenges of the moment because no single response works in all situations.

Time Management

This investigation may be completed in about 45 minutes, if protozoa cultures are prepared in advance. If time allows, students may convert data into ratios during class or as homework.

Studying behavioral biology makes an excellent bridge between animal physiology, evolution, and ecology. This investigation helps link these major areas of biology. Behavioral biology can be subdivided into neuroethology, ethology, and behavioral ecology. You might wish to introduce these areas into a class discussion about behavioral adaptations, then have students discuss where this particular investigation fits in.

Neuroethology focuses on behavioral mechanisms—the sensory apparatus organisms use to monitor themselves and the world, the neural processing that processes that information, and the circuitry that guides their responses.

Ethology tends to look more at how individual animals respond to stimuli. For example, ethology examines such behaviors as hunting/foraging, communication, and learning. Ethologists are concerned with how stimuli trigger behavior, and how behavioral patterns are programmed to respond to the varying situations an organism might encounter. The investigation, because it examines a protist's response patterns to external stimuli, fits into this subdivision.

Lastly, behavioral ecology concentrates on how behavioral sequences evolve. One way they do this is to contrast the different behavior patterns of related species. Behavioral ecologists use these comparisons to examine the selective weighing of a behavior's advantages and disadvantages for different organisms. Behavioral ecology is a good way to introduce students to the concept that selection works on individuals, rather than on groups or species.

One of the most interesting aspects of adaptive behavioral strategies is that species develop alternative strategies because no single response works well in all situations. This investigation demonstrates on a microscale how an organism selects an adaptive strategy to fit a challenge of the moment.

Before the surface texture section, demonstrate how to prepare slides with one half roughened and the other perfectly smooth. Show students how to stroke the slides with sand paper, using a regular set of motions to produce a uniform roughened surface. The quality of their investigations will depend on how carefully they prepare the glass slides. Before beginning the escape behavior section, discuss the movement categories (from the check list) with your students. They need to know exactly what the categories stand for before they observe and record behaviors.

During the escape behavior section, students may inadvertantly observe a ciliate that will not escape within a reasonable time. If this happens, students can examine another area of the slide. They can also create a new set of constraints by lifting the cover slip and replacing it; this usually changes the the cotton web pattern, and the ciliates will be offered a new set of challenges. If this doesn't work, have students create a completely new preparation with a new wisp of cotton and a new wet mount.

Since students will need to keep the same culture viable over a long period of time, it is better to use cold light from a fiber optic illuminator, than a normal light on a microscope. If this device is not available, use a lamp that is placed at some distance from the surface of the stage.

Adaptations and Variations

You can vary the investigation very simply by increasing or reducing the number of hypotrich species students observe. Also, if there is enough time available, you may want to have each group of students perform the experiments on each of the ciliate species. If time is limited, you have each group "track" the behavior of a certain species. You can also have them observe the ciliates for a full hour, rather than a half hour.

◆

Another option is to let students compare movement patterns between species with different methods of motility. For example, are ciliates, flagellates, or amoebae better able to escape from a hostile environment?

◆

Other micro-environments that can be created on a slide include extremes of heat and light. Have students close the microscope condenser to its smallest opening and let it sit for about five minutes. Using an identical microscope set up, students can then compare and contrast this environment with one in which the entire field has been illuminated for five minutes, as well as one in which the light source has been turned off for five minutes. Another variation is to place a drop of vinegar on one edge of the coverslip and allow it to diffuse through the medium.

Teaching Note

If you would like to involve students in preparation, and if time allows, they can help prepare filtered water as a substitute for sodium-free, bottled mineral water. Prepare charcoal-filtered pond water by adding 2 g of activated charcoal to one liter of pond water. Mix for 20 minutes, then filter out the charcoal through a large piece of circular filter paper. Repeat if necessary until no charcoal remains. The result is charcoal-filtered pond water (CHPW).

◆

If possible, make a TV record of the ciliates' behavior over time. To do this, you will need a TV camera, tape recorder and a display screen with attachment to the stereomicroscope. This equipment will also let you create a "map" of the ciliates' movements. Using a tape of the ciliates' movement over a half-hour period, place a piece of transparent acetate plastic over the monitor screen. Advance the videotape frame by frame. Trace the position of the ciliates at each new frame step. (You can follow the position of one specific ciliate, or several.)

◆

You can use this acetate procedure to describe major behavioral characteristics, such as directional patterns and escape responses. You can also determine velocity by dividing the distance the ciliate traveled by the time. To get the exact velocity, convert the distance on the acetate sheet into original distance by dividing the distance by the magnification factor.

Assessment and Evaluation

When all groups have completed the investigation, have them paste their record sheets on the wall in front of the class so they can compare the differences in behavior among the ciliates. In this way, students may assess and evaluate their own and each other's efforts.

Students should understand that ciliates respond to even very slight alterations in the surface texture of their environment. Ask them what other types of environmental variations a ciliate might experience. Would a ciliate be as responsive to the changes they suggest as it was to this investigation's changes in surface texture? Student ability to appreciate how a ciliate might change its behavioral strategies to compensate for a wide variety of environmental challenges provides a mechanism for assessment and evaluation.

When students note that the behavior patterns are not simply random motions, they may be tempted to impose their own views or feelings on the animals' behavior. Explain the meaning of anthropomorphism, and discuss how it hinders the scientific process. Yet, at the same time, it is important for students to recognize that there are similarities between us and the protozoa. Even these simple protozoa respond to their environment in ways that help them survive better, as do humans and other animals. Student appreciation of the connections among these broad concepts, as well as others, provides another mechanism for assessment.

Use the theory of natural selection as a controlling theme in a discussion about how the different protozoan species reacted to barriers and surface textures. What similarities or differences were there? Why might a certain behavioral pattern develop in one species, and not another? Student aptitude for discussing the specifics of this investigation within the context of an organizing scientific principle provides another evaluation mechanism.

About the Author

Nicola Ricci studies the adaptive biology of protozoa at the University of Pisa, in Italy. His specific focus is ciliate behavior. He developed this investigation to help students learn about the ciliates' control of their behavior. It is a good way to show how protozoa can change their electrophysiology, adhesion, body shape, and dimensions in response to their environment.

Resources

Paramecia, large and small species, may be obtained from biological supply companies, as can *Blepharisma*, *Tetrahymena*, *Euplotes*, *Oxytricha*, and *Stylonychia*. For distributors of biological supplies, see Appendix VI (pages 219–221).

Giantism among Ciliates

So What?

Sometimes in nature, bigger is better. Some species have developed adaptive strategies that make them appear larger and more ferocious than they really are.

A unique feature of many protozoa is their ability to form giant cells. It is not unusual for some members of the order Heterotrichida to form giants. *Blepharisma* (Figure 1) and *Fabrea salina* (Figure 2), for example, form giants with twice the normal body size and number of adoral (meaning near the oral) and somatic ciliary organelles. *Blepharisma* form giants when they consume large prey and when they are exposed to certain amounts of vitamin E. In this investigation, you will induce giantism by exposing the organisms to decomposing wheat germ, which adds vitamin E to their environment.

This investigation will enable you to observe and examine this ciliate adaptive strategy. Increased size allows the ciliate to consume larger prey. The mouth region is larger, and there is an increase in the size and number of food vacuoles that are formed. This allows capture of larger numbers of the bigger prey. For example, when *Blepharisma* is feeding on bacteria (about one μm in size) it typically does not form a giant. When, however, it feeds on small ciliates or flagellates it gradually forms a giant. This gives the *Blepharisma* greater advantage in competing for food resources. The giants also sometimes cannibalize smaller *Blepharisma*. Scientists don't know how vitamin E induces giantism in *Blepharisma*. As you conduct this investigation, maybe you'll have some insights about vitamin E. Eventually, your scientific work here may answer questions about how vitamin E functions in higher organisms, including humans.

Figure 1
Blepharisma.

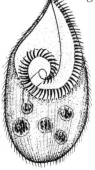

Figure 2
Fabrea salina.

Procedure

1. Prepare glass micropipets by following your teacher's instructions.

2. Prepare charcoal-filtered pond water by adding 2 g of activated charcoal to 1 l pond water. Mix for 20 minutes, then filter out the charcoal through a large piece of circular filter paper. Repeat if necessary until no charcoal remains. The result is charcoal-filtered pond water (CHPW). If you have sodium-free bottled mineral water, you may be able to use it directly without the charcoal treatment.

3. Add 950 ml of CHPW into a 1 l Erlenmeyer flask. Line a funnel with a piece of filter paper. Measure an additional 50 ml of CHPW into a beaker, and add 3 g of Cerophyl. Stirring constantly, heat over a Bunsen burner until just before it boils. Carefully remove the beaker from the flame. Filter the heated solution into the flask that contains 950 ml of CHPW. The result is a 0.3 percent Cerophyl solution. As always, take proper safety precautions when using a Bunsen burner.

4. Measure 200 ml of the 0.3 percent Cerophyl solution into a beaker. Add several drops of concentrated protozoa and four wheat germ kernels to the solution. Be sure to label the beaker with the contents and your group's name.

5. Let stand for about three weeks in an area with indirect light and no drafts. Observe daily, and continue the investigation when there are enough protozoa for the group to make observations.

6. Use the dissection microscope to observe the giants' behavior. If you have a younger culture of *Blepharisma*, transfer several smaller forms near the giant and see if they will cannibalize the vegetative forms.

7. Using dissection scopes and prepared micropipets, capture several giants. Transfer the small drop onto a clean glass slide, and add a drop of protozoan slowing solution. Before covering with a coverslip, break a coverslip square into long thin pieces. Place one piece on either side of the drop containing the giants. This will keep the cells from being squashed.

8. Observe under 400x magnification. Locate the food vacuoles and observe their contents. Do you see any signs of cannibalism? Record your observations.

9. Transfer the giants to fresh Cerophyl culture medium as in Step 4, and observe the reduction through division to a "normal" vegetative size and appetite. Record this process through a step-by-step drawing.

5.3 Objective

To examine giantism as an adaptive strategy among heterotrichous ciliates.

✔ Materials

- ❑ Stereo binocular dissection microscope
- ❑ Compound light microscope
- ❑ Glass slides, coverslips
- ❑ Immersion oil
- ❑ Wheat germ kernels, rinsed with distilled water
- ❑ Cerophyl
- ❑ Activated charcoal
- ❑ Large pieces of circular filter paper
- ❑ Pond or aged tap water
- ❑ Protozoan slowing solution
- ❑ Pasteur pipets
- ❑ Bunsen burner
- ❑ Rubber bulbs
- ❑ Grooved forceps
- ❑ Two finger bowls
- ❑ Blank paper, pencil
- ❑ Culture: *Blepharisma stoltei*

Discussion and Inquiry

- Among the various factors that confer a competitive advantage for living organisms, size can be a decidedly positive feature. Larger individuals within a group can often compete more efficiently for food, often are able to command more life space, and in sexually reproducing populations sometimes are more successful in attracting mates. However, the largest living organisms are not necessarily the most abundant. There is a greater abundance of individual protozoans and a greater diversity of protozoa species than there are of some of the largest animal species on earth.

- Within a species or a particular community, size can be advantageous. Larger individuals may be less likely to be consumed as prey (Figure 3) and they may have an advantage in getting prey (Figure 4), as is demonstrated in this investigation with *Blepharisma*.

- Giantism in ciliates is the exception, not the norm. The rapid response of increase in size of individuals when treated with

Figure 3
Many species, such as cats, have the ability to make themselves appear physically large when threatened by a predator.

Figure 4
Some species, such as schools of fish, make themselves appear physically larger by traveling in groups. This adaptation helps them deter predators, and also gives them an advantage in chasing down prey.

vitamin E illustrates the supple way some protozoa have of quickly adapting to their environments, especially to take advantage of new resources. What are some of the ways giantism favors survival? What are some disadvantages of giantism in ciliates?

- One hypothesis to explain how the vitamin E produces giant forms is that the vitamin retards the rate of cell division. This implies that individuals may grow larger since they do not divide as often. However, this doesn't necessarily explain the larger mouth ciliature. Some change in the basic organization of the cilia-forming bodies in the cell must be taking place. Vitamin E is known to have an important role in maintaining sexual fertility in higher animals and in improving the general physiological vigor of an organism. How it induces giantism in *Blepharisma* is unknown, and invites serious scientific investigation.

Giantism Among Ciliates

Giantism among species of *Blepharisma* is the result of exposure to vitamin E at molar concentrations of about 10^{-4} M. The source of the vitamin is probably the wheat germ decomposition caused by bacteria. Cannibalism is evident more often from viewing the contents of the food vacuoles of giants.

To prepare the vitamin E solution, obtain vitamin E succinate (alpha-tocopheryl succinate) from a pharmacist or chemical supply company. It is very unstable, and must be protected from oxidation. The vitamin E is not water soluble, and must be dissolved in ethanol first. Dissolve 523 mg in 1 ml of 95 percent ethanol/aqueous solution while stirring and warming slightly in a water bath. This is a 1 M solution. The solution produces giantism in a range from 10^{-4} to 10^{-6} M.

To make 10^{-4} M solution, take 0.1 ml of the ethanolic vitamin E solution and place it in 1L of Chalkey's solution (0.1 g NaCl; 0.004 g KCl; 0.006 g CaCl2; 1.0 l distilled water). Prepare solutions immediately before use. Also, before using the solutions test their pH. If it is not 5.5–6.0, adjust it with NaOH.

Adaptations and Variations

An alternative is to subject vegetative forms individually to 10^{-4} M quantities of Vitamin E. If a video camera is available, students can watch from a TV monitor. Also, you can record especially good scenarios with a video recorder.

◆

Freeze-dried cereal leaves distributed by Sigma Chemical Co. may be used as a substitute for Cerophyl. To speed the process, you may wish to prepare the protozoa cultures and micropipets (Steps 1–5) without student involvement.

Assessment and Evaluation

This investigation provides an excellent opportunity for students to evaluate how good the evidence is that vitamin E causes changes in cell size versus some other explanation. For example, challenge students to

Micro-Macro Link

Many species of organisms have the ability to make themselves appear physically larger, whether as individuals or by combining themselves with others of their own species. This may help them compete for food and avoid predators.

Time Management

Preparation and Steps 1–5 take 45–50 minutes. The rest of the investigation may be completed three weeks later in one class period.

devise an investigation to show that it is vitamin E that can cause the change. First, they should note that the use of wheat germ alone is not conclusive. Wheat germ has many other constituents in it besides sources of vitamin E. However, with the ethanolic solution of vitamin E, it is possible to do a rather rigorous experiment. There should be a control and a treatment culture. The two cultures should be set up identically to each other; however, the control treatment receives only an aliquot of Chalkey's solution emended with the ethanol solution used to solubilize the vitamin E. The experimental culture should receive an aliquot of the vitamin E-containing Chalkey's solution as described above. Since everything is identical in the control and experimental culture except addition of vitamin E to the experimental treatment, this is a good controlled experiment. If the vitamin E treatment produces giantism but not the control, there is evidence of the induction of giantism by the vitamin.

Encourage students to discuss how likely it is that giantism may occur in the natural environment. For example, there would have to be a wheat kernel deposited in some restricted part of a pond. Or, the *Blepharisma* might be growing in a patch of microorganisms where it could begin to feed on small ciliates and flagellates and start to form giant stages. If, however, there were water currents, or some forms of competitive pressure that disturbed the feeding pattern of the *Blepharisma*, it may never reach a stage or the proper environmental conditions where giantism can be induced. More advanced students should be encouraged to suggest how the vitamin E may be inducing giantism in *Blepharisma*.

About the Author

Arthur J. Repak teaches protozoology, environmental microbiology, and freshman biology at Quinnipiac College in Hamden, Connecticut. This investigation is part of his curriculum on eukaryotic microorganisms showing the effects of various chemicals on the life cycle of certain ciliated protozoa.

Resources

Pierce, E., Isquith, I.R., and Repak, A.J. 1978. "Quantitative study of cannibal-giantism in *Blepharisma*." *Acta Protozoologica*, 17 (4): 493–501.

Blepharisma stoltei is available from the ATCC and from biological supply companies. Activated charcoal is also available from biological and chemical supply companies, as are protozoan slowing agents. For distributors of biological supplies, see Appendix VI (pages 219–221).

Feeding Strategies

Some protozoa get nourishment through photosynthesis and by ingesting solid food particles. Organisms that have the ability to both photosynthesize (photoautotrophy) and ingest food particles (phagotrophy) are called "mixotrophic." Mixotrophic protozoa can adopt either of these feeding strategies, depending on environmental conditions, or they can use both simultaneously. Some protozoa species are fundamentally phagotrophic but can photosynthesize when food is in short supply. Others are fundamentally photoautotrophic and can ingest food when light levels are low. These adaptations may occur when the protist resides deep in the water column, under ice, or during winter months in polar regions.

Because many flagellates have the ability to adopt multiple feeding strategies, it is important—especially from an ecological point of view—to know when they are behaving as photoautotrophs (primary producers) and when they are behaving as heterotrophs (consumers). An ecologist would use this information to describe the protist's role in a microbial food web. In this investigation, you will study *Ochromonas*, a protozoan species that exhibits mixotrophic feeding strategies in response to changing environmental conditions.

So What?

Some protozoa species can change their feeding strategy when the environment changes. These species either photosynthesize light energy or ingest solid food particles, depending on the availability of each.

5.4 Objective

To understand how mixotrophic protozoa adapt their feeding strategy to environmental changes.

✔ Materials

- ❑ Compound microscope
- ❑ Slides, coverslips
- ❑ Pasteur pipets
- ❑ Culture flasks
- ❑ Small vials with stoppers
- ❑ Aluminum foil
- ❑ Freshwater alga medium
- ❑ A supply of bacteria using:
  Autoclavable bottle
  Autoclave or pressure cooker
  Petri dishes
  Bunsen burner
  Agar (10 g)
  Glucose (0.08 g)
  Yeast extract (2.0 g)
  Distilled water (400 ml)
  Alcohol solution (70 percent)
- ❑ "Hockey stick" spreader
- ❑ Student Data Table
- ❑ Cultures:
  Ochromonas tuberculata
  Poterioochromonas
  Ochromonas malhamensis
- ❑ Incubator (optional)

Procedure

Before carrying out the investigation, bacteria cultures should be maintained in the light for up to seven days. Each experimental treatment can use less than 10 ml of each culture.

1. Divide each culture into three separate vials. Put approximately 2–3 ml of culture per vial depending on the vial size. Label the vials A, B, and C as shown in Figure 1.

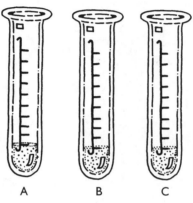

Figure 1
Vials A, B, and C containing 2–3 ml of bacteria culture each.

2. Use a "hockey stick" spreader to add bacteria to vials A and B (approximately 0.5 ml/2 ml culture). Add an equal volume of freshwater medium to vial C.

3. Cover vial A with foil, as shown in Figure 2.

4. Place all vials in an incubator at a light intensity of approximately 50–100 µE /square meter/sec (moderate fluorescent illumination) on an approximate 16:8 h Light/Dark photoperiod and a temperature of between 15–20° C. If you don't have access to an incubator, place the vials in a non-heated, north-facing window.

5. After 3–4 days, add a second amount (approximately 0.5 ml/2 ml of culture) of bacteria to vials A and B. Add an equal volume of freshwater medium to vial C.

6. Incubate cultures for a further 3–4 days.

7. Take a sample from each vial and examine the cells under the microscope. Record your observations on the Student Data Table. In particular, look for color which would indicate the presence of pigment, and the abundance of cells.

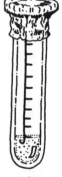

Figure 2
Vial A covered with foil.

Discussion and Inquiry

- Discuss your observations of the three vials. Why does *Ochromonas tuberculata* (vial A, dark treatment) maintain chlorophyll levels when there is no light source? Could energy from the ingestion of prey be used to maintain the chlorophyll/photosynthetic system?

- With *Poterioochromonas (Ochromonas) malhamensis*, if more chlorophyll is produced in the light with an abundance of prey—as opposed to in the light without an abundance of prey—could the protist be gaining something from the bacteria that is essential for the formation of chlorophyll?

- If these protozoa grow so well in the dark with an abundance of prey, why would they produce chlorophyll in the light when prey is still abundant?

- Why is it important for these protozoa to be able to respond quickly to high quality sources of energy, such as light? Does this ability favor the presence of chlorophyll even when grown in the dark with particulate food?

Student Data Table				
Poterioochromonas (Ochromonas) malhamensis				
Vial	Light/Dark	Bacteria	Pigment	Abundance
A				
B				
C				
Ochromonas tuberculata				
Vial	Light/Dark	Bacteria	Pigment	Abundance
A				
B				
C				

Feeding Strategies

Micro-Macro Link

Many species of organisms, such as humans, are able to switch back and forth between various feeding strategies depending on nutrient quality and availability. How an organism feeds usually determines its role in a food web.

Time Management

This investigation may be completed in one class period, if cultures are prepared in advance and placed in the prescribed treatment conditions. Students should be informed, however, of the rationale and procedures used in establishing the various culture regimes. If you wish to involve students in preparation, follow the procedure outlined in Adaptations and Variations.

Feeding strategies are often used to identify an organism's role in the food web. Primary producers are capable of deriving energy through photosynthesis, while consumers are herbivores, carnivores, or both (omnivores). It is important for students to appreciate the variety of feeding strategies used by living organisms, and to understand that some organisms are capable of employing one or all of several different feeding strategies available to them, depending on environmental conditions.

Many mammals, for example, are both herbivorous and carnivorous—able to derive energy by consuming primary producers as well as other consumers—and adopt one or the other strategy (Figure 3) depending on environmental conditions, such as availability. Mixotrophic organisms, such as the *Ochromonas* under study in this investigation, also respond to changing environmental conditions by adopting a particular feeding strategy. As their investigation into the feeding strategies of mixotrophic organisms progresses, encourage students to think about how changing environmental conditions affect

Figure 3
Many species of organisms are able to switch back and forth between various feeding strategies depending on nutrient availability.

the feeding strategies of broad ranges of organisms. For example, what options are available to organisms that have only one strategy? How might they adapt to a severe change in environmental conditions?

Humans are naturally omnivorous, and to some extent mixotrophic. This investigation may be used to highlight for students the necessity of their maintaining a balanced diet. It may also be used to point out that their "diet" consists of more than what they actually ingest. Sunlight, for example, is necessary for the production of vitamin D.

The following are suggested as the expected results (variations may occur depending on where the particular strain was obtained):

Poterioochromonas (Ochromonas) malhamensis

Vial	Light/Dark	Bacteria	Pigment	Abundance
A	Dark	yes	none	++
B	Light	yes	yes (low amount)*	++
C	Light	no	yes	+

* This result may vary between strains

Ochromonas tuberculata

Vial	Light/Dark	Bacteria	Pigment	Abundance
A	Dark	yes	yes	++
B	Light	yes	yes	+++
C	Light	no	yes	++

These results suggest that *Poterioochromonas malhamensis* employs a heterotrophic strategy in the absence of light and a photoautotrophic strategy in the presence of light. However, without an abundant food supply *Poterioochromonas* appears incapable of producing high amounts of chlorophyll. This species has a clear requirement for solid food, with photosynthesis acting as only a secondary feeding strategy. With *Ochromonas tuberculata*, chlorophyll is always present and there is a reasonable abundance of cells in the absence of an abundant source of prey. However, the presence of abundant prey appears to supplement its nutritional requirements. In this case, phagotrophy is the secondary feeding strategy.

Adaptations and Variations

1. To culture food bacteria, first prepare the agar plates by adding agar, glucose, and yeast extract to the distilled water. Autoclave and pour into petri dishes when cool enough to handle. Leave to cool.

Preparation Note
Procedures for preparing the "hockey stick" spreader appear in Appendix IV (pages 215–216).

2. Pipet a small drop of each of the *Ochromonas* species culture, with food bacteria in it, on to an agar plate as prepared in Step 1. If the cultures are axenic (without bacteria), a small drop of pond water can be deposited onto the agar surface as an alternative, so there will be food bacteria available. Gently swirl to spread the culture as much as possible on the surface.

3. Using the short segment of the sterilized "hockey stick" spreader, have students disperse the bacteria deposited in Step 2 on the agar surface.

4. Seal the petri dish with plastic tape or enclose it in aluminum foil, and leave it for 3–5 days at room temperature. After the colonies of bacteria appear, the dish can be stored in the refrigerator as a source of food bacteria for the *Ochromonas* to be cultured as described below.

5. Scrape off a small clump of bacteria and add it to approximately 10 ml of freshwater algal culture medium. Shake vigorously to disperse the bacteria. Add a small amount of glucose using the end of a spatula.

6. Leave for 2–3 days. The *Ochromonas* are then ready to use in the investigation.

Assessment and Evaluation

Sound logic in designing investigations is a cornerstone of discovery in the natural sciences. This investigation provides an opportunity for students to critically explore the logic of scientific inquiry and discovery. They should be able to clearly identify the variables used in any investigation, and this one provides a mechanism for evaluating their ability to do so. The variables in this investigation include light or dark, and presence or absence of bacteria (experimental variables or independent variables). The outcome (dependent) variables are presence of pigments and abundance of the protozoan. Students should be encouraged to become adept in identifying variables carefully. They should describe the variables in terms of the changing quality, not just the name.

This investigation provides an opportunity to engage students in a discussion to determine how clearly they understand the logic of the experimental design. This can be facilitated by making a large diagram of the data table or using an overhead projection. Why are the combinations of variables used in rows A, B, and C? Not all possible combinations of illumination and food bacteria are used. Students should be able to identify all total combinations. If they have difficulty, show them a simple chart with columns labeled light and dark, and rows labeled bacteria yes and bacteria no. The chart contains four squares representing four possible combinations. Only three are used here. Why? The "Dark, No Bacteria" combination is not used. Students should appreciate that its inclusion would be futile, since there is no source of energy for either photosynthesis or heterotrophy to occur. Thus, the protozoa would eventually starve. The remaining combinations are adequate to determine the effects of light and food availability on pigmentation and survival.

About the Author

Harriet Jones works at the NERC Centre for Population Biology researching the physiology and ecology of mixotrophic protists. She has found that observing mixotrophic behaviour can help demonstrate that protists are neither little animals nor little plants, since mixotrophic protists combine characteristics associated with both plant and animal kingdoms.

Resources

In the United States, *Poterioochromonas malhamensis* is often sold as *Ochromonas malhamensis*. Freshwater algal culture medium can be purchased in various forms, including concentrated solutions diluted to the proper concentration with pasteurized or sterile pond water, or non-carbonated spring water purchased at the food store. For distributors of biological supplies, see Appendix VI (pages 219–221).

Life Stages and Responses to Stimuli

So What?

Organisms evolve adaptive strategies far more complex than just sharper teeth or longer legs. Life strategies—how and when they reproduce, how long they live, and so forth—are an example of a complex adaptation.

Histophagous ciliates invade animal tissues as a source of nutrition. These ciliates typically have five distinct life stages, each of which exhibits different size, shape, motility, and sensitivity to external stimuli. The various stages of the life cycle include: 1) theront, free-swimming stages searching for new hosts to invade and feed upon; 2) trophont, the feeding stage; 3) protomont, a large stage at the end of feeding; 4) tomont, a relatively large inactive stage; and 5) tomite, a relatively small stage produced by division of the tomont. Figure 1 shows the life stages of a histophagous ciliate.

In this investigation, you will consider three responses to external stimuli: phototaxis, response to light; chemotaxis, response to chemicals; and gravitaxis, response to gravity. You will contrast how a ciliate's response to different external stimuli changes according to its life stage.

During this investigation, you may also examine an organelle that is found only in *Ophryoglena* and *Ichthyophthirius multifiliis*. Called the organelle of Lieberkühn, it probably plays an important role in light perception.

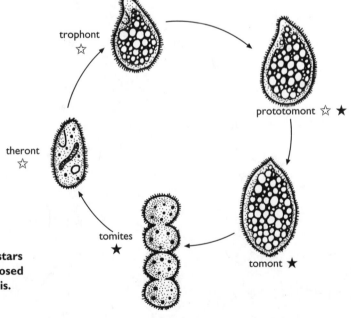

Figure 1
Various stages of the reproductive cycle of the histophagous ciliate, *Ophryoglena caterula*. Open stars represent stages that show positive phototaxis; closed stars represent stages showing negative phototaxis.
© European Journal of Protistology

Procedure

1. To collect histophagous ciliates, collect some *Daphnia*, other crustaceans, or small worms from a freshwater pond, or obtain them from a pet store or biological supply company. Freeze and bind a few *Daphnia* into a small packet within a polyester net. Instead of frozen organisms, small pieces of liver or spleen may be used as bait.

2. Suspend several polyester net packets in a pond using floats made of plastic jars. Suspend them at three or more different places, and immerse them to different depths using the heavy weights.

3. After several hours, place the bait from the polyester net, which by now should contain trophonts of histophagous ciliates, into several of the glass jars filled with filtered or heat-sterilized pond water, or with carbonic-free mineral water.

4. Place the jars in a cool area with indirect sunlight. Add one or two frozen *Daphnia* every third day.

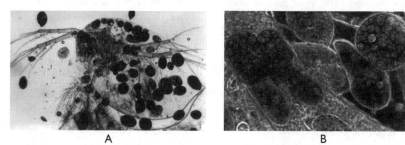

A   B

Figure 2
Trophonts of *Ophryoglena* caterula inside a *Daphnia*. (A) Several dozen feeding ciliates are visible inside the transparent cladoceran. (Bright field illumination) (B) The same image at higher magnification. Observe that the cell form of trophonts is quite flexible. Two ciliates left inside, revolving around their long axes, try to penetrate one of the *Daphnia*'s antennae. (Phase contrast illumination)

5. To isolate and observe histophagous ciliates, culture them for two weeks. During this time, examine their morphology and life's stages. You can examine theronts before they are fed *Daphnia*; trophonts will be visible a few minutes after the feeding (Figure 2). If you find different species in one jar, isolate a few cells of each with a micropipet and culture them separately.

6. After two weeks more than 100 cells of one species (e.g., *Ophryoglena*) should be present in some of the jars. Locate trophonts and pipet them into a new jar filled with the same medium you have used previously. If you have trouble locating trophonts, look inside a *Daphnia* a few minutes after feeding.

7. Wait 2–3 days until theronts have occurred in the new jar. Study their photo-orientation by making the classroom as dark as possible

✔ Materials

❏ Magnifier, or compound light microscope, 1:1 macro-objective

❏ Compound microscope

❏ Slides, coverslips

❏ Micropipets

❏ Large glass petri dish, or light-transparent container

❏ Several glass jars (10–100 ml)

❏ Test tubes (10–20 ml)

❏ Filtered or heat-sterilized pond water, or carbonic-free mineral water

❏ Chemical attractants

❏ Chemical repellants

❏ Polyester net

❏ Three plastic jugs

❏ Three cinder blocks, or other heavy weights

❏ Flashlight, or slide projector

❏ Dark sheet of paper

❏ Aluminum foil

❏ Violet felt marker

❏ Student Worksheets

5.5
INVESTIGATION

and using the slide projector or small flashlight to illuminate the cells on one side of the jar. Figure 3 provides an example of this setup. Create a Student Worksheet such as the one in Figure 4, and record your observations. If you have histophagous ciliates different from *Ophryoglena* you will probably observe no photo-orientation. In this case, proceed to Step 11.

Figure 3
A light-transparent container (aquarium) sitting on a dark sheet (left) is illuminated from one side (arrows). The cover of a large petri dish (right) is marked by angular degrees, and is placed in the center of the light-transparent container.

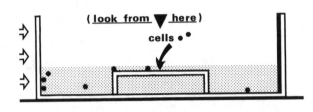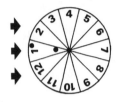

Culture medium in the container reaches a level of about 3 mm above the cover of the petri dish. Cells to be tested for photo-orientation should be placed in the center of the petri dish. Angular degrees of orientation should be determined after the cells have reached the edge of the petri dish. Observe them with a magnifier. To avoid reflections, the side of the container opposite the light source should be covered with a black sheet. (This set up is suitable only for large histophagous ciliates. Smaller species can be placed directly in the middle of a petri dish or other container with a dark sheet of paper underneath.) © *European Journal of Protistology.*

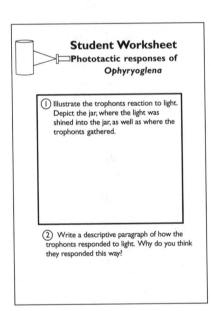

Figure 4
Student Worksheet Sample. Construct your own worksheet using this as a model.

8. Use a micropipet to transfer *Ophryoglena* cells successively into a large petri dish or a light-transparent container. Illuminate the dish from one side before placing a dark sheet of paper so that it lies underneath the dish, allowing you to see the cells. Draw and label your observations on another Student Worksheet, noting the most common angles and direction of swimming.

9. Repeat the investigation using well-fed trophonts. Draw and label your observations on your Student Worksheet.

10. Repeat the investigation after adding frozen *Daphnia*, or fluid of *Daphnia*, to theronts or trophonts. Draw and label your observations on your Student Worksheet.

11. In a glass jar, test the ciliates' chemotactic response to other living or frozen organisms, different chemical agents, or salts. Record the ciliates' response to each item on your Student Worksheet.

12. Transfer a few theronts or trophonts into a test tube. Fill up the test tube to the edge and cover it with a piece of aluminum foil. Be sure that all air bubbles have been removed, as they might attract the cells. Examine their gravitactic response, whether they move towards the bottom or the surface of the tube. Record your observations on your Student Worksheet.

13. Observe theronts of *Ophryoglena* under a compound microscope; press them carefully by partially removing the medium until a

"watchglass organelle"—the organelle of Lieberkühn—becomes visible. Try to stain the organelle of Lieberkühn with the ink from a violet, felt marker by mixing a few living cells with a small drop of ink directly onto a slide. Draw and label the organelle of Lieberkühn on your Student Worksheet.

Discussion and Inquiry

- Explain your data for the photo-orientation experiments with the histophagous ciliates. How did each type of cell react to light? Indicate whether the ciliates' responses exhibited positive or negative phototaxis.

- Discuss your results from Steps 7–8. How and why did the ciliates respond to light? What do you call this type of photo-orientation? What direction characterizes their swimming? Where do they gather in the aquarium?

- Discuss your results from Steps 9–10. Explain the cells' response to light after they have been fed. Why do ciliates in different stages respond differently to light? Do *Daphnia* respond to light?

- Discuss your results for Step 11. Do the cells still show phototactive orientation under these conditions? Did any of the organisms or substances cause a positive chemotactic response? Is there a difference between living and frozen animals? Explain the ciliates' reactions, and why these reactions might be useful in their natural environment.

- Discuss your results for Step 12. Did the ciliates exhibit a positive or negative gravitactic response? Explain the ciliates' reaction, and why those reactions might be useful in the organism's natural environment.

- Explain the importance of phototaxis, chemotaxis, and gravitaxis. How do you think ciliates use these responses in their natural environment? Did you notice that the ciliates swim faster than they did before their taxic response? This is called a positive kinesis.

- Relate your findings from this investigation to larger organisms such as dogs, dolphins, and humans. Do larger creatures also exhibit phototaxis, chemotaxis, or gravitaxis?

- Describe the organelle of Lieberkühn that you observed in Step 13. What is its importance?

Life Stages and Responses to Stimuli

Micro-Macro Link

A species' life strategy—when and how it reproduces, how long individuals survive, and so forth—constitutes an adaptive response to changing environmental conditions.

Time Management

This investigation takes about one hour. If you wish to involve students in advance preparation, begin two to three weeks prior to conducting the classroom investigation.

Taxic responses—behavior characterized by active orientation with respect to a stimulus—and kinetic responses—alterations of an organism's linear velocity with respect to a stimulus—can be observed in many species of *Ophryoglena* (but also in *Ichthyophthirius multifiliis*, *Porpostoma notatum*, etc.). Phototactic, chemotactic, and gravitactic orientation may serve nutritional needs for theronts; in trophonts, protomonts, and tomonts they help the organisms avoid potential predators.

Students should observe that theronts generally move towards a light source (positive phototaxis) and accumulate near the border of the jar. Well-fed trophonts generally move away from the light source (negative phototaxis).

Students should notice that theronts can locate their potential prey by chemical signals (positive chemotaxis). However, the prey can only be located if it is injured or dead. Freezing of the *Daphnia* causes injuries by which the ciliates are attracted. Well-fed trophonts and protomonts do not react chemotactically, but show a remarkable positive gravitaxis.

This investigation provides an opportunity to discuss how a species' life strategy can serve as an adaptive response to changing environmental conditions. The histophagous ciliates under investigation here have evolved a life strategy that enables them to take advantage of certain environmental conditions through specific physiological changes. The ciliates adaptive strategy is to respond to changing environmental conditions by changing both their morphology and behavior. Encourage students to appreciate that organisms can, and often do, evolve adaptive strategies that are far more complex and subtle than sharper teeth or longer legs.

Adaptations and Variations

Students may also observe the histophagous ciliate *Ichthyophthirius multifiliis*, a common fish parasite (Figure 5). *I. multifiliis* has a similar life cycle compared to *Ophryoglena* and shows a precise orientation, including phototaxis. *I. multifiliis* is also the only other species characterized by the organelle of Lieberkühn. If you are unsuccessful in isolating free-living histophagous ciliates from a natural pond, you may use *I. multifiliis* for classroom investigations. This obligate fish parasite is characterized by extremely large trophonts and tomonts, but has quite small tomites ands theronts. *I. multifiliis* can only be grown and harvested from freshwater fish. Ask for infected tropical fish at a pet store; they will have white spots, which are trophonts of *I. multifiliis* lodging within the skin of their host.

◆

Instead of gathering chemicals for the students, have them bring in substances they think will attract or not attract the ciliates. *Be sure to advise them of appropriate and non-appropriate substances before they bring chemicals into class!* Before using the substances in the investigation, lead a class discussion about which substances they think will be most effective in producing positive or negative responses. After the investigation, have students compare the actual data to their original views. They may wish to devise their own Student Worksheets to record any observations. This variation encourages students to feel a greater "ownership" towards their results.

◆

Students may erroneously conclude that the remarkable behaviors are characteristic of only one species that they have observed. It is important to develop the idea that similar behavioral and structural adaptations may occur in very different species as they adapt to similar environments. This additional example of a histophagous ciliate living on a different host (fish), should encourage the students to realize that adaptations of a similar kind can occur when different organisms exploit environments with similar demands.

Assessment and Evaluation

The primary objective of this investigation is to enable students to understand that behavioral responses of organisms may change as they mature to enhance their adaptation and survival in different environments. Students should be able to describe how the chemotactic response of the histophagous ciliates helps them survive.

Not all organisms are so adept at chemotaxis. How does the chemotactic response of the ciliate help it compete for food more effectively? Likewise, at certain stages organisms show phototactic responses but not at others. For example, students should be encouraged to compare the changing patterns of light response of moths during their life cycle to that of the ciliate. Why are the larvae of moths less affected by light than the flying mature stage? Students should be able to discuss the importance of escaping dark places that may enclose the moth and keep it from finding a mate—the major role

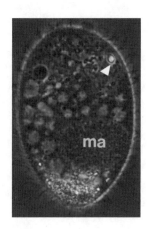

Figure 5
The fish parasite *Ichthyophthirius multifiliis* with small watchglass organelle (arrowhead), and macronucleus (ma). Phase contrast illumination.

of the flying stage being mating and reproduction. Likewise, they should be able to explain why light perception may be important in a ciliate that must seek food by attacking another organism or by swimming away from closed spaces in order to reproduce or mate.

About the Author

Hans-Werner Kuhlmann teaches protozoology at Münster University in Münster Germany, and is affiliated with the Institut für Allgemeine Zoologie and Genetik. The author uses this investigation to demonstrate orientation of unicellular organisms. He uses especially large species of *Ophryoglena* because they are easy to cultivate, and are dramatically better at locating their prey than are predatory ciliates.

Resources

Kuhlmann, H.-W. 1993. "Life cycle dependent phototactic orientation in *Ophryoglena catenula*." *European Journal of Protistology*, 29: 344–352.

Nigrelli, R.F., Pokosny, K.S., and Ruggieri, J.D. 1976. "Notes on Ichthyophthirius multifiliis, a ciliate parasitic on freshwater fishes, with some remarks on possible physiological races and species." *Trans. Micros*. Soc. 95: 607–613.

Some species of *Ophryoglena* can be isolated from brackish water, such as O. macrostoma. *Porpostoma notatum* must be collected from a saltwater marine environment. For distributors of biological supplies, see Appendix VI (pages 219–221).

Chemosensory and Behavioral Adaptation

One reason organisms move is to find food. You're familiar with some ways macroscopic organisms sense that food is nearby. They use their sensory organs to see, smell, hear, taste, or touch a potential source of nutrients. Then they move towards it. But how does a microscopic organism, one that doesn't have eyes or a nose or ears, sense that food is nearby?

The ciliate *Tetrahymena thermophila* (Figure 1), a freshwater phagotroph, is attracted to microenvironments containing peptides and/or proteins. *T. thermophila* senses the presence of these chemicals, is attracted to them, and then moves toward their source. This reaction is called chemo-attraction or a chemosensory mechanism.

In order to stay close enough to consume its prey, *T. thermophila* must be able to adapt. It does this by reducing its swimming speed, which leads to the creation of a cloud of *T. thermophila* cells around a local gradient of the attractant. These cells block each other from moving towards lower concentrations of attractant. The prey cells thus become "trapped" long enough to be ingested. This investigation demonstrates how ciliates locate a food source using chemosensory mechanisms, accumulate as a cloud of cells at a gelified attractant of proteose peptone, and ingest it.

So What?

All living organisms, from the smallest plants to the largest animals, respond to their environments as a means of enhancing their ability to survive.

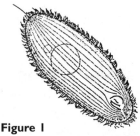

Figure 1
Tetrahymena thermophila.

5.6 Objective

To analyze and describe adaptive chemosensory mechanisms in ciliates.

✔ Materials

❑ Stereoscopic microscope

❑ Aged tap water

❑ Proteose peptone

❑ Powdered gelatin

❑ Petri dish

❑ Beaker

❑ Culture:
  Tetrahymena thermophila

Procedure

1. Add proteose peptone to aged tap water to create a 1.0 percent proteose-peptone solution. If this solution is autoclaved or boiled, you can grow *T. thermophila* in 1–2 cm layers. Be sure to keep everything sterile during their growth period.

2. Prepare a 10 percent gelatin solution by dissolving 1 g of powdered gelatin in 10 ml of water. Gently heat the suspension until the gelatin dissolves. Add 10 mg of proteose peptone powder and swirl to mix. This creates a 10 percent gelatin to 0.1 percent proteose peptone solution

3. Make a second solution containing 10 percent melted gelatin in aged tap water alone.

4. Put a drop of each of the two gelatin solutions 2-5 cm apart from each other in the bottom of a petri dish. Let the two drops solidify in the refrigerator.

5. Make a suspension containing about 100,000 cells/ml, which is equivalent to 1 ml of packed (centrifuged) cells/50 ml of tap water. The suspension should completely cover the gelatin drops. Check the petri dish every 20 minutes or so; within an hour, a cloud of cells should accumulate at the gelatinized proteose peptone. Pour the suspension of *T. thermophila* cells, that have been starved overnight, into the petri dish.

6. Observe *T. thermophila* cells as they settle on the gelatin. Observe the cells trying to move away from the gelified attractant, and note that they are pushed back towards it as they are repelled by the tap water. This process maintains the *T. thermophila* cells in the cloud around the attractant.

7. Observe that cells will burrow into the gelatin if it remains solid. Gelatin melts at 27°–28°C, so the *T. thermophila* cells will enter the gelatin only if the temperature is between 23°–26°C.

Discussion and Inquiry

- All life exhibits sensory responses to the environment. Plants move toward light and many grow upwards, away from gravity. Higher animals make complex responses to environmental stimuli including seeking food, migrating to more suitable habitats, exploring new regions of the environment, and seeking mates. List some of the more common sensory responses that humans make, such as responding to food aromas, listening to music, speaking, writing, playing athletic games, and so forth. Note the responses of ciliates and categorize them as similar or dissimilar to those of humans.

- How does the ciliate's lack of the complex sensory organs of higher animals influence the complexity of stimuli to which they are able to respond? What sorts of stimuli is the ciliate able to respond to? What evidence can you provide to support your conclusions?

- This investigation uses chemical gradients as a source of stimuli. What part of the ciliate is likely to sense the chemical signal?

Chemosensory and Behavioral Adaptation

Micro-Macro Link

Single-celled organisms respond to environmental stimuli for the same reasons complex organisms do. They look for food, migrate to more suitable habitats, and seek mates.

Time Management

This investigation may be completed in one class period. If you wish to involve students in preparation, allow two weeks for culturing T. thermophila.

Encourage students to relate protist food-seeking behavior to that of larger organisms, such as the bat in Figure 2, that use sensory organs to locate prey. The chemosensory responses of ciliates are illustrative of a broader range of behavioral adaptations of living things. It is important for students to embed this learning in a broader context. Responsiveness to the environment is a major characteristic of life, and students should be able to rationalize why responsiveness is important for survival.

Figure 2
There are five types of sensory receptors that respond to environmental stimuli: mechanoreceptors, thermoreceptors, chemoreceptors, photoreceptors, and pain receptors. Bats locate prey through a type of sonar called echolocation. Echolocation helps them detect insect prey and avoid mid-flight collisions. Ask students if they can identify which receptor type helps bats perform echolocation.

Chemosensory response is only one form of response pattern within a much larger set. Plants exhibit responses known as tropisms. These responses include phototropism (response to light), geotropism (response to gravity), thigmotropism (response to touch, as when a climbing plant uses a tendril to attach to a support), and various movements, such as a flower orienting to follow the path of the sun during the day. Even bacteria are capable of a variety of responses, including responses to oxygen gradients, magnetic fields, and so forth.

All of these responses help the organism to adapt to its environment, obtain energy and nutrient sources for growth and reproduction, and inhabit environments that are most suitable for its growth. Some of these broader organizing ideas are developed further in the Discussion and Inquiry portion of the student section.

Adaptations and Variation

Place the attractant (1.0 percent proteose peptone) at one end of a short segment of capillary tubing containing a suspension of the ciliates. A non-heparinized serological capillary tube or melting point capillary tube is suitable. Tilt the culture of ciliates and introduce the end of the capillary tube to take up some of the culture to about 3/4 the length. Then, using an eyedropper or fine capillary pipette with a bulb, introduce the 1.0 percent proteose peptone solution into the end of the capillary containing the ciliate suspension. Have students observe under a microscope and note the movement of the ciliates along the length of the capillary. The ciliates should exhibit a decided orientation toward the food source. Compare with a control capillary containing tap water only.

◆

Mass cultures of *T. thermophila* are easy to grow in the classroom in 1.0 percent proteose peptone solution that has been boiled to sterilize it. Alternatively, axenic (bacteria-free) cultures are available from biological supply companies. You may wish to assist students by preparing a suspension of 100,000 *T. thermophila* cells/ml prior to class, about 1 ml of packed (centrifuged) cells/50 ml of tap water.

Assessment and Evaluation

The surface membrane is the most likely site for the sensory organelle used by the ciliate to respond to chemical stimuli, since there is no specialized organ of taste or smell as there is in humans. Light can be sensed by some ciliates, and this raises the interesting question of how it happens. One suggestion would be that the ciliate has a pigment in the cell that absorbs the light and allows it to detect presence or absence. Students should be able to discuss possible adaptive advantages and disadvantages of ciliates migrating by chemosensory responses toward a food source. Competition and crowding at the food source may be harmful to some individuals. However, this may allow only the most competitive to survive, thus ensuring a more vigorous population of individuals.

If students fully understand the dynamics of this investigation, they should be able to describe how a food attractant establishes a gradient. They should be able to describe how small molecules from the food diffuse outward from the source—concentrated near the source and less concentrated moving away from the source. This gradual decline in concentration with distance from the source creates the gradient that the ciliate follows (i.e., moving along a line from the least concentration to most concentration of the diffusing substance). Furthermore, students should be able to understand that, when the cell positions itself along the gradient, the anterior end of the cell will encounter a higher concentration of the attracting molecule than the posterior end, due to the gradient distribution.

This investigation provides an opportunity to evaluate how creative students can be in designing additional investigations to study chemosensory behavior. For example, can students identify a range of substances to be tested, and establish some hypotheses about which substances will be most attractive and which least? How do they propose to test the hypotheses? Can students suggest additional experiments on stimulus-seeking behavior by the ciliate? For example, if the ciliates are placed in one side of a dish separated from the food source by a partition with a small hole in it, do the ciliates find their way through the barrier to the opposite side? Are there differences among species of ciliates? Larger ciliates, such as *Blepharisma*, *Stentor*, or *Spirostomum*, might be more easily visualized in these experiments and can be seen with a good hand lens. What other kinds of complex barriers or challenges can the students suggest to assess the ciliates' adaptability in seeking a food source?

About the Author

Vagn Leick teaches biochemistry and molecular biology at the University of Copenhagen in Denmark. He developed this investigation during his research on studies on chemically induced behavioral responses in the ciliated protozoan *T. thermophila*. He continues these investigations by studying the biochemistry of signal transduction over the cell membrane induced by signal chemicals that induce chemoattraction and growth.

Resources

Leick, V., Koppelhus, U. and Rosenberg, J. 1994. "Cilia-mediated oriented chemokinesis in *Tetrahymena thermophila.*" *Journal of Eukaryotic Microbiology*, 41: 546–553.

For distributors of biological supplies, see Appendix VI (pages 219–221).

Microscope Skills

Byron wrote, "My way is to begin at the beginning." Likewise, you may wish to spend some time reviewing compound microscope skills with your students before starting an investigation. The suggestions below are intended to help students learn how to use the microscope carefully, while still having fun. The procedures follow a three or four day schedule of consecutive lab periods—during which students work in groups with at least one other person—but can easily be adapted according to your particular needs.

Day One:
Setting up the microscope

Before students work with the microscopes, take a few minutes for an introduction. Tell them to care for the microscope like they would a young infant or baby. Carry it with two hands—one on the body, or arm, and the other under the base, as if it were a baby's bottom. Keep the baby close to your body, don't even think about dropping it! Place it on top of the table, not too close to the edge where it might fall. Never leave it alone, or it might "crawl" off the edge! Use soft tissue (lens tissue) to clean its nose (objectives) and eyes (eyepiece) when needed. Remember, the microscope is "priceless," just like a baby!

Then have students familiarize themselves with their "baby." Have them draw the microscope as best they can. Students should label the instrument's parts—but do not supply them with commonly used names just yet. Have the groups discover what the parts do, then report their findings to the class. On their own, groups of students can generally learn the functions of nearly all the microscope's parts.

Once the groups have drawn and labeled their microscopes, discussed in groups what the parts probably do, and attached written descriptions to their pictures, display a large, properly labeled chart of the compound microscope (see Figure 1). Have students "upgrade" their original drawings. Make certain the groups know the correct names of the microscope's parts and understand their functions. Students should then work together to set up their group's microscope.

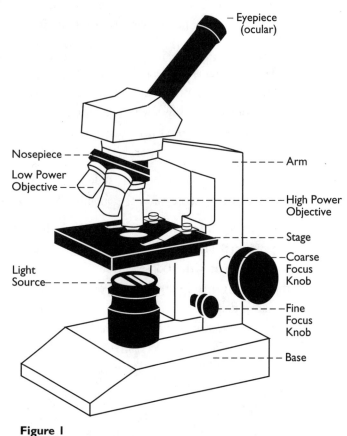

Figure 1
Discovering on their own the functions of the microscope's parts encourages student interest and excitement.

Procedure

1. Once students have successfully set up their microscopes, they can immediately begin using them. A good way to aquaint students with their microscope is to have them work with the letter "e" before they work with protozoa. Students enjoy working with the familiar before they venture into the unfamiliar. In addition, the "e" gives students a sense of direction and scale. It lets them learn about the quality of the tool they are using, as well as its mechanics.

2. Have them cut an "e" from a newspaper, and prepare it as an (unstained) wet mount slide. Students should notice the letter is upside down and backwards when they view it through the microscope. As they view the letter, have them pull the slide towards their bodies. They should notice that all directions are indeed reversed—as the slide moves toward them, it appears to move in the opposite direction.

3. Before locating specimens through the microscope, students should center them in the middle of the tiny window in the center of the stage. Stage clips aren't necessary if microscopes are flat on the desk and not moved around.

4. Have students scan around the slide by moving the mechanical stage—not the slide itself.

5. Students should then learn to focus using their wet mounts. They should first focus under low power, and draw their observations. They can then (very gently) put a higher power objective in place. *Remind them to use only fine focus with their high power objective, so that the lens does not touch the coverslip! If it does, students will ruin their lenses and flatten their specimen.*

6. Have students record their observations through drawings and brief written descriptions. Remind them to always note the lens power.

Tips for Setting Up the Microscope

1. *The microscope should be placed flat on the table, about six inches from the edge. Once set up, it should not be moved.*

2. *All the parts should be cleaned and dusted with lens paper.*

3. *The mirror should be angled so light reflects up through the stage.*

4. *The diaphragm should be set up to allow the maximum amount of light to pass through the stage for mirrored scopes. Optimal light should be adjusted with electric light source scopes.*

5. *The 10x, or low power objective, should be turned into position so it can be used first.*

6. *Use flat slides rather than depression slides. Most protozoa are small enough that a wet mount slide will provide enough space between coverslip and slide.*

7. *Whenever possible, students should complete investigations using only one prepared slide. There are two reasons for this practice. Placing a wide variety and high density of protists on one slide gives students more time for viewing, scanning, focusing, describing, and drawing. Using one slide also decreases movement around the classroom, thereby reducing vibrations.*

Day Two: Working with slides and stains

On the second lab day, students should feel comfortable setting up their microscopes. They can now learn to make wet mount slides, stain their slides, and calculate magnifications using living cells. Specimens that work well include protozoa, epidermal cells, yeast, spirogyra, and students' own cheek cells. While you can use any stain, methylene blue and iodine are easily obtained from biological supply companies, and work especially well with protozoa. Supply companies also offer protozoa slowing and quieting solutions, which give students time to observe and draw their specimens. Apply the solution using the same procedure you would use when working with stains.

Procedure

1. Have students set up their microscopes as they did on Day One.

2. Working in groups, have them clean their slides and coverslips, and place these on a clean paper towel or tissue (rather than on the top of the table).

3. When they are ready to begin, students can use either an eyedropper or a micropipet to draw up protozoa specimens from their culture dishes. Have them try to remove specimens from areas in the dish that have a high concentration of protozoa.

4. Holding the tip of the dropper about one centimeter above the slide, students should allow a large hanging drop to form. They can then slowly squeeze out the drop onto the center of the slide. (During this part of the procedure the slide should still be flat on the paper towel.) Each wet mount slide should hold two or three of these drops.

5. Have one student from each group place a coverslip on their group's slide. One edge should be placed on the slide first; the coverslip can then slowly be lowered with the tip of a dissecting needle or pen tip so that it gently falls on top of the pool of culture. This process helps prevent little air bubbles from sticking to the underside of the coverslip.

6. Students may then pick up the wet mount slide and place it flat onto the stage. They should hold the slide only by the edges, not touching the top or bottom of the glass. The slide should be centered in the stage window so that the specimen is well lit.

7. To use a stain or slowing solution, students should apply a hanging drop by the same method they used when adding protozoa culture to the wet mount slide. They should add one drop of stain/slowing solution to one side of the little pool of protozoa culture, without mixing them together.

8. Students should then learn to focus using their wet mounts. They should first focus under low power, and draw their observations. They can then (very gently) put a higher power objective in place.

9. Because higher power objectives are longer, there is almost no distance between it and the top of the coverslip. Students should therefore use only the fine focus knob when using the high power objective. They should take little peeks from the side to ensure the lens does not touch the coverslip.

10. To calculate magnifications, students should multiply the magnification of their eyepiece by the magnification of the objective they're using. Students should learn to always write down the total magnification next to every drawing they make.

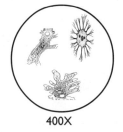

400X

Figure 2
Drawing cells in a circle like this can help students make all their drawings to the same scale.

11. Drawing a ring or circle (about as big as a silver dollar) can be helpful. Students can then draw the cells they find in this ring, at the approximate size they see them (see Figure 2).

12. By the end of the laboratory, students should have several "e" and cell drawings at increasing magnification. Their drawings should be made to about the same scale, and labeled with their respective magnifications.

Day Three: Measuring protist size

By this time, after four to six laboratory hours of practice, students should be familiar with the compund microscope. They should be able to prepare wet mount slides, stain them, center specimens, change objectives, calculate magnifications, and draw what they have seen to scale. They should now be more or less ready to perform microscopic measurement—measuring the diameter of the field of view in millimeters, converting the diameter to micrometers, and then calculating cell cize.

Procedure

1. Have students set up their microscopes as they did on Days One and Two.

2. Provide students with clear metric rulers, and have them note that there are 10 millimeters (mm) in 1 centimeter (cm).

3. Using the 10x objective, students should place the edge of the ruler with measurement markings onto the stage. The edge should be placed across the center of the glass window that lets light up through the bottom.

4. Looking through the eyepiece, move the ruler so the edge is horizontal; line up the 1 mm line so that it is on the left of the circle of the field of view.

5. Students should now be able to record how many millimeters are in their field of view. They should find this measurement for each objective. (If the low power is 100x and high power is 400x, students' high-power diameter should be 1/4 of their low-power diameter.)

6. Explain to students that most cells are much smaller than one millimeter, so scientists use micrometers (µm), or microns, to measure cell sizes. One millimeter is equal to 1,000 micrometers. Pose the problem: If one meter has 1,000 millimeters, how many micrometers are in one meter? Likewise, if a field of view is two millimeters, how many micrometers is this? Students should show the steps they took to arrive at their final calculations.

7. Next, have students draw their low power field of view, showing the millimeter marks.

8. Using this drawing, ask students to calculate the diameter of their field of view in micrometers. (The field of view under 100x is about 1,200 micrometers in diameter; at 400x it is about 300 micrometers in diameter.) Explain that these values will help the groups estimate the length of the protists they will observe.

9. For further practice, have students use their neighbor's microscope. They can check each other's work, and find out if other microscopes have the same field of view as theirs does.

10. Ask students: Does the measurement of the field of view for your microscope ever change, if you use the same microscope? (The answer is no, the same microscope will always have the same field of view.)

11. Have students prepare a wet mount slide of yeast, spirogyra, onion epidermal cells, or a dense population of protists. They should stain the slide, then locate the specimen under high power. (Most cells are too small to estimate their size under low power.)

12. Have students estimate how many cells it would take, if the cells were placed end-to-end, to strech all the way across their high power field of view.

13. Students should divide the diameter of this field of view (in microns) by this estimated number

of cells. This will give them the approximate length of each cell in microns. Have students draw the cells they observe, and record the approximate length of each cell in microns.

For further study

If time allows, it may be helpful to have students practice calculating a protist's rate of speed. Once students have located a protist in their field of view, one student should measure how far the organism moves in one minute. A second student should act as a "timer" so the first student doesn't have to look up from the microscope. A third student can record the final calculations. (It may be helpful to have the first student calculate the distance in millimeters; the group can convert the distance to microns after the minute has elapsed.)

Homework

1. Have students take their rough sketches home with them, and "finalize" them so that the drawings are clean and well-drawn. Each drawing should give as much detail as possible given the magnification level.

2. Different groups can work on different projects, which they can present to the entire class. Some suggestions: Have students use a reference and write a brief report on the history of microscopes; have students draw a large compound microscope—or several types of microscopes—for the classroom walls; have musically-inclined students write a song that describes all the parts of the microscope and what they do.

How to Make a Classroom Aquarium

Begin by choosing an aquarium. The size of the tank depends on how much space to have. Also, you will need a larger aquarium depending on the number and type of fish you may choose to add. Place the empty tank in dim natural light; avoid putting it in direct sunlight. The aquarium should be aerated with a standard pump and filter, which you can obtain at nearly any pet store. You can also purchase the plants and fish from a pet store; or you can have your class collect them from a nearby pond or lake.

Fill the tank almost full with tap water. Wait 24 hours before adding plants and fish. To acclimate fish to the temperature of the water, place them in a small plastic bag in their original water. Let the bag float on the top of the aquarium's water until the bag's water is about the same temperature as the aquarium; then slowly let the fish swim from their bag into the aquarium.

Add small amounts of fish food and water to the aquarium once a day. Take out some water and replace it with aged tap water every few months to reduce mineral build-up. *Do not add chemical clearing agents at any time to the tank.*

Once the basic aquarium has been set up, you can concentrate on its protozoa population. A healthy aquarium is all you need to initiate protist growth; organic material from the food, nitrates from the fish, and the dim light all aid growth. The process is successive—bacteria will be the first organisms to colonize the tank. They will cloud the water a few days after you set up the tank, then the water will naturally clear. After several weeks, thin films of algae will begin to coat the inner glass surfaces of the

Figure 1
Maintaining an aquarium increases student ownership, educates, and motivates.

balanced aquarium. Other planktonic autotrophic protists, including filamentous green algae, will follow. (For viewing purposes, you may want to keep the inner glass surface facing the students clean.) You will see a succession of protist communities until the tank reaches stability.

Although protozoa will naturally grow in the aquarium, there are several ways to speed the process. For example, some biological supply companies sell protozoan pellets that can be added to the water to aid and sustain protozoan growth in an aquarium. Another way to get rapid protozoa growth is to first grow bacteria. Crush and powder about 1/10th of a malted milk tablet, and sprinkle it on the water's surface. (You can also use a pinch of milk solids, sold commercially, or a pinch of proteose-peptone powder from a biological supply company.) The result is a sharp increase in bacterial population, followed by rapid growth of *Paramecium* and other ciliates.

Another way to encourage bacteria is a hay infusion. Alfalfa and timothy hay both work well, or you can use the alfalfa pellets sold in pet stores as rabbit food. Boil the hay in water, then add the infusion to the aquarium. The infusion should produce a color like a light green or brown tea. A few days later the aquarium should have a fair-sized population of *Paramecium*, many hypotrichs, and smaller ciliates such as *Cyclidium*, *Tetrahymena*, and *Glaucoma*.

Lastly, protozoa can be collected from nature just like fish and plants. If your class finds a good source of protozoans on a field trip (see Appendix III, pages 212–214), the creatures may also be added to the aquarium.

Culturing amoebae

You can produce a good growth of amoebae in a shallow glass dish. Start by adding a suspension of pond sediment in pond water to the dish. Add dried hay or a small amount of yeast extract as a nutrient source, as you would for protozoa. Add only enough nutrients to create a light growth of bacteria.

Loosely cover the dishes to prevent evaporation. Keep them in a cool location, away from direct sunlight. Add pond water as needed to compensate for evaporation. About two weeks later there should be a fairly large amoeba population growing on the bottom of the dishes.

Collecting Protozoa

Where to find protozoa

Protozoa live almost everywhere there is moisture—
in ditches, temporary pools, ponds, lakes, salt water,
dam soil, mud, hot springs, snow drifts, glaciers,
brine pools, and sluggish streams. Even the thin
film of water surrounding soil particles contains
protozoa. The table on page 213 lists the habitats of
many of the protozoa listed in this book.

Most vegetation debris collected from outdoor
habitats will contain some resting stages or spores of
protozoa. The best collecting sources are natural
places, such as ditches, shallow ponds, and
temporary pools, that contain plant remains in
various stages of decomposition.

Flagellates and ciliates are found in open surface
water, on or among floating and submerged
vegetation, on rocks and other bottom debris. You
can find amoeboid forms on bottom sediments and
debris and on submerged vegetation, including the
undersides of leaves. You can find stalked ciliates
attached to dead sticks and submerged material, on
the undersides of duckweed and floating plants, and
on bodies of water insects, snails and crustaceans.
During winter, protozoa may still be found on debris
and bottom sediments of bodies of water.

Field trips to collect protozoa

Visit the site before taking the class to get a better
idea of specific collecting tools that will be helpful.
A plastic tote bag with a handle, usually available
in variety stores or supermarkets, makes a handy
field collecting bag. Give each student group their
own bag stocked with baby food jars and lids, plastic
bags, a pocket knife, a long pipet, a fine
mesh-dip net, hand lens, labels, and a pencil.

Small jars with tight-fitting lids, such as baby

food jars, are good containers for collecting water
samples of protozoa. Plastic buckets with lids are
useful for carrying large samples of protists and
water. Don't fill buckets of water samples more than
half full, and seal them tightly only when traveling
back to the classroom.

You can collect floating vegetation by gently
lowering a container below the water's surface and
letting the material flow into the container. A jar
lid makes a handy scoop for gathering surface scum
and floating material. A small fine-mesh dip net is
useful for scooping up material from pools and
around the water's edge.

How you collect protozoa depends on where you
take your samples from. For example, you can
scrape samples from rocks or other submerged
objects with a knife or spatula, and transfer the
sample into a collection jar. To collect protozoa
from open surface water, use a No. 20 mesh
plankton net. Bottom sediments may be gathered
by scraping the surface with a small can attached to
a long pole.

A baster or glass tube 30 to 40 cm long, attached
to a soft rubber bulb, makes a useful device for
collecting on and above soft substrates. To use a
baster, squeeze the air out of the bulb. Slowly draw
the sample into the tube by relaxing your grip on
the bulb as you move the tube over the bottom.
Transfer the contents to a collecting jar.

Put each sample in a separate container and label
with the location the sample was taken. This
information will be helpful in the classroom when
you identify the protozoa. Open the containers as
soon as possible after you return to the classroom—
this will allow aeration, and prevent decay. You can
keep aquatic collections of protozoa near a window,

Common Protozoa Habitats

Protozoa are commonly found in a variety of natural habitats. If you will be collecting your own protozoa before an investigation, this list can serve as a guide when planning a field trip.

Source	Description	Typical Protozoa Species
Freshwater Ponds, Lakes and Streams	May be clear, cool, and spring-fed, or warm, stagnant and rich in decaying organic matter. Includes shallow, semi-permanent farmyard ponds.	*Paramecium caudatum, Blepharisma, spirostomum, Stentor, Vorticella, Euglena, Peranema, Phacus, Distigma, Colpidium*, and many other flagellates, amoebae, and ciliates.
Mud or Sand	Includes wet sand and gravel. Try to find a location where tidal movements keep the mud permanently moist.	*Euglena, Colpidium, Peranema, Vorticella, Oxytricha, Stylonichia*, and a wide variety of flagellates, amoebae, and ciliates.
Sewage and Sewage-Treatment Plants	Includes Imhoff tanks, trickling filters, settling basins, and biodegrading sewage.	*Acanthamoeba polyphaga, Naegleria gruberi, Vorticella, Distigma, Euplotes, Chilomonas*, and other ciliates.
Marine Waters	Includes all types of salt water areas—coastal tide pools, attached or floating vegetation, tidal backwaters, brackish pools, estuaries, bays, inlets, and washed up vegetation.	Two major groups of protozoa, *Foraminifera* and *Radiolaria*, are found only in salt water. Other salt water protozoa include, *Vorticella, Euplotes vanus, Dunaliella salina*, and other ciliates and flagellates.
Brine Pools	Very salty pools or lakes, such as Utah's Great Salt Lake.	Several species of flagellates, ciliates, and amoebae have only been found in this type of location.
Hot Springs	Located in several national parks.	Several species of flagellates, ciliates, and amoebae have only been found in this type of location.
Snowdrifts and Glacial Pools	Includes mountain snowdrifts and the cold waters of pools on or at the foot of glaciers.	*Haematococcus*, and many other species.
Other Organisms	Protozoa may be found in symbiotic relationships on, in, or near other organisms.	Gregarines are easy to study in the classroom because they are commonly found in invertebrates. Two likely sources: insects' digestive tracts and the seminal vesicles of earthworms.

but out of direct sunlight where they may become overheated. A northern exposure is best. (See Appendix II, pages 210–211.)

You can also start cultures of protozoa from dry material. Collect dry culture materials such as leaves, grass, twigs, rocks, and soil. Put them in any type of container—cans, jars, or paper or plastic bags work well. Place the dry materials in jars or flat enamelware pans, and cover them with pond, lake, spring, rain, or aged tap water. Let the flooded material stand undisturbed in a warm place out of direct sunlight for 24 hours before you examine the sample.

Figure 1
A field trip using PF blocks is a good way for students to hone both their field and lab skills.

Using PF Blocks

Polyurethane foam (PF) blocks are an advanced, yet fairly easy, tool for collecting protozoa. Obtaining their own protozoa increases student ownership of their findings, since they will be involved in the investigation from beginning to end.

PF foam can be purchased as cushion or pillow material at fabric stores, or as sheets of foam in variety and department stores. The easiest material to work with is medium-density foam about 5 cm thick—it is the most common kind sold in stores. To make the foam into substrates, use a serrated knife to cut it into blocks about 4×5×6 cm. While still in the lab, rinse the blocks with distilled or aged tap water.

Tie the PF blocks very tightly with string, so that they look like a bow tie. Tie the strings (Figure 1) to a rope, and tie the rope onto a cinder block or a brick. A regular cinder block will typically weight

eight PF blocks in a shallow stream; a brick will weight several blocks in fairly slow-moving currents.

Locate a nearby stream or river. Before submerging the blocks, squeeze them under water to fill the pores with water. This will keep the blocks from floating in the surface. Then place the cinder block close to shore and submerge the blocks. If you place them in a stream, the PF blocks will be colonized in about a week; in a pond or lake, colonization takes two to three weeks.

If you live by the seashore, you can also place the PF blocks in the ocean. Secure the blocks to a cord attached to a long pole, and at low tide anchor the pole to the shoreline with a heavy rock or cinder block. Secure a second cinder block to the other end of the cord so the blocks remain submerged. As with the river-submerged blocks, soak the blocks before submerging them into the tide. PF blocks placed in the ocean will be colonized after only a few days.

National Science Teachers Association

Making Labware

Micropipets

A micropipet is a standard tool for transferring small protozoans. It will even let you capture and move single organisms, if you use it with a dissecting mcroscope. To make a micropipet, you will need a pair of forceps, a pipet, and a Bunsen burner.

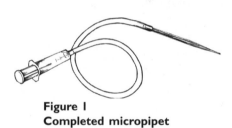

Figure 1
Completed micropipet

Use your fingers or the forceps to hold the tip of the pipet just above the blue cone of a Bunsen burner flame. When the tip begins to melt, quickly remove pipet from the flame. Pull it straight out until it has a thin diameter. Allow pipet to cool before using.

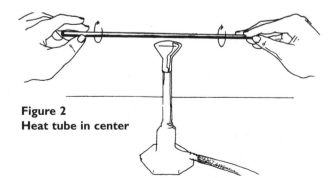

Figure 2
Heat tube in center

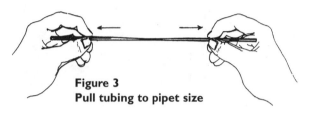

Figure 3
Pull tubing to pipet size

If you have to make a number of micropipets, it may be more efficient to use a 20-cm-long piece of a 4 mm (outside diameter) glass tube. Rather than heating the tip, as you would with a pipet, heat the center of the tubing until it begins to melt. Quickly pull both ends away from each other with the forceps, using a steady pressure. When the glass breaks, you will have two micropipets. For safety, fire polish the large ends to make sure students will not cut their hands.

Then, attach a syringe (minus the needle) to a piece of flexible, plastic aquarium tubing. Attach the other end of the tubing to the large end of the micropipet. Have students practice using the instrument before transferring organisms.

Teaching Notes

Check with your school safety officer before using syringes in your classroom. Micropipets can also be purchased from a biological supply company, or eyedroppers can be used as a substitute for micropipets.

Create a "hockey stick" spreader

"Hockey stick" culture spreaders are handy for evenly distributing substances across an agar culture.

To make a spreader, begin with a standard laboratory glass rod. Using forceps, hold the end of the rod over (not directly in) the blue cone of a Bunsen burner flame. When it begins to melt, pull the rod from the flame and bend it into a 90° angle, at a point about 4/5 from the end of the rod (Another example of how to bend the spreader is shown in Figure 4). Allow the spreader to cool before using it.

Figure 4
"Hockey stick" culture spreader made from a solid glass rod.

Student Evaluation of Investigations

Name:

Class:

Teacher:

Name of Investigation:

Investigation Objective:

Please take a few minutes to complete this evaluation. It will show your teacher what you thought of the investigation you just completed. It will also help your teacher find the best way to teach you. Thanks!

1. Did you enjoy this investigation?   yes   no   (Circle one)

2. How well do you think you met the investigation's objective? Explain:

3. What did you like most about the investigation?

4. What was the most interesting part of this investigation?

5. What are the three most important things you will remember from this investigation?

    a.

    b.

    c.

6. Do you feel like you learned a lot from this investigation? Why or why not?

7. Is there anything you wish you could have learned from this investigation? If so, what?

8. If you worked in a group, how many people were in your group?

9. How well did your group interact with each other to complete the procedure?
   Explain:

10. During labs, do you generally prefer to work in groups or by yourself?
    Explain:

11. Do you think you can work   faster   or   slower   in a group? (Circle one)

12. Do you learn more when you work in groups or by yourself? Explain:

National Science Teachers Association

Resources

BOOKS

Belcher, H., and Swale, E. 1982. *Culturing Algae: A Guide for Schools and Colleges.* Cumbria, United Kingdom: Cambridge Institute of Terrestrial Ecology.

Coombs, G., and North, M. 1991. *Biochemical Protozoology as a Basis for Drug Design.* Washington, DC: Taylor & Frances.

Finlay, Rogerson, and Cowling. 1988. *A Beginners Guide to the Collection, Isolation, Cultivation and Identification of Freshwater Protozoa.*

Harrison, F.W., and Corliss, J.O. eds. 1991. *Microscopic Anatomy of Invertebrates: Vol. 1: Protozoa.* New York: John Wiley & Sons.

Hausmann, K., Hulsmann, N., MacHemer, H Mulisch, M. 1996. *Protozoology. 2nd ed.* Theime Verlag, Stuttgart & New York.

Jahn, T., Bovee, E.C., and Jahn, F.F. 1979. *How to Know the Protozoa.* Dubuque, IA: Wm. C. Brown.

Jones, R.I., and Ilmavirta, V., eds. 1988. *Developments in Hydrobiology: Flagellates in Freshwater Ecosystems.* Boston: Klumer Academic Publishers.

Katsarca, P. 1989. *Illustrated Guide to Common Slime Molds.* Eureka, CA: Eureka Printing Co.

Kreier, J.P., and Baker, J.R. 1995. *Parasitic Protozoa. 2nd ed., vol.10.* San Diego: Academic Press.

Margulis, L., McKhann, H., and Olendzenski L. 1993. *Illustrated Glossary of Protoctista.* Boston: Jones & Bartlett, Publishers.

Margulis, L., and Schwartz, K. 1988. *Five Kingdoms: An Illustrated Guide to the Phyla of Life on Earth. 3rd ed.* New York: Harper Collins.

Patterson, D.J. 1995. *Free-living Freshwater Protozoa. A Colour Guide.* London: Wolfe Publishing, Ltd.

Round, F.E., Crawford, R.M., and Mann, D.G. 1990. *The Diatoms. Research Technical Paper #19.* Cambridge, UK: Cambridge University Press.

Sleigh, M.A. 2000. *Protozoa & Other Protists. 3rd ed.* London: Edward Arnold.

MAGAZINES

Carol, D. and Hampton, C.H. 1979. "Collecting and Observing Protozoa," *Science and Children.* pp. 30-32, 50-52.

RESOURCES

Society of Protozoologists
The Society of Protozoologists is a professional organization. The society is a valuable source of information and educational materials for those interested in protozoology. The society publishes a newsletter three times annually and maintains a World Wide Web home page at: http://www.uga.edu/~protozoa/

MULTIMEDIA: MOVIES, COMPUTER SOFTWARE, AND CD-ROMS

The following multimedia classroom resources are available. Addresses and phone numbers for suppliers are listed at the end of this section.

Videos

Creatures of the Pond. Nebraska Scientific.

Hidden Kingdoms: The World of Microbes. 11 minutes. Carolina Biological Supply Co.

Introduction to the Protozoa. 20 minutes. Carolina Biological Supply Co.

The Microlife Resource: Vol. I, Flagellates & Amoebae. 26 minutes. Ward's Natural Science Establishment, Inc.

The Microlife Resource: Vol. II, Ciliates & Algae. 26 minutes. Ward's Natural Science Establishment, Inc.

A New Look at Algae. 15 minutes. Ward's Natural Science Establishment, Inc.

A New Look at Leewenhoek's "Wee Beasties." 12 minutes. Ward's Natural Science Establishment, Inc.

Microbial Engines: Algae & Protozoa. Ecology to Biotechnology. 36 minutes. Carolina Biological Supply Co.

Primitive Plants: The Algae. Nebraska Scientific.

Protist Ecology. 12 minutes. Ward's Natural Science Establishment, Inc.

The Protist Kingdom. 16 minutes. Ward's Natural Science Establishment, Inc.

Protist Physiology. 13 minutes. Ward's Natural Science Establishment, Inc.

Protist Reproduction. 10 minutes. Ward's Natural Science Establishment, Inc.

Protozoa in Action. Short Highlights. 29 minutes. W.A. Hatch.

Protozoa Through a Microscope. 90 minutes. W.A. Hatch.

Protozoans I: Water Circus. 17 minutes. Nebraska Scientific.

Protozoans II: In the Eye of a Needle. 24 minutes. Nebraska Scientific.

Protozoans III: Wonder Down Under. 24 minutes. Nebraska Scientific.

Science Screen Report. This is an on-going series of elementary and secondary videotapes which focus on the most recent developments in science. Science Screen Report.

Smaller than the Eye Can See. 14 minutes. Nebraska Scientific.

The World of Protozoa. 30 minutes. Ward's Natural Science Establishment, Inc.

Software

Five Kingdoms—Smart Slides. Macintosh or Windows. Ward's Natural Science Establishment, Inc.

Dichotomous Key to Pond Microlife. Macintosh only. Ward's Natural Science Establishment, Inc.

Microlife Clip Art. Macintosh or Windows. Ward's Natural Science Establishment, Inc.

Protista Study Set—Smart Slides. Macintosh or Windows. Ward's Natural Science Establishment, Inc.

Protist Culture Database. Macintosh or IBM. Ward's Natural Science Establishment, Inc.

CD-ROMs

Biological Classification and the Five Kingdoms of Life Photo CD. Macintosh or Windows. Ward's Natural Science Establishment, Inc.

Five Kingdoms. Margulis, L. and Schwartz, K. Macintosh or Windows. Ward's Natural Science Establishment, Inc.

Protoctista: A Comprehensive Encyclopedia of Protists.
Macintosh or Windows. Ward's Natural Science
Establishment, Inc.

TRANSPARANCIES

The Five Kingdoms of Life: The Protoctists. 20
transparencies with printed guide. Carolina
Biological Supply Co.

MICROSCOPE SLIDES

*Explano-slides - Protists (Euglena, Amoeba &
Paramecium).* Ward's Natural Science
Establishment, Inc.

Ward's microscope slides of preserved stained
organisms: Actinopoda, Amoebae (parasitic and
free living), Brown algae, Ciliates, Cryptomonads,
Diatoms, Dinoflagellates, Foraminiferia, Euglenoids,
Golden Algae, Green Algae, Plasmodiophorans,
Red Algae, Slime Molds, Sporozoans,
Zooflagellates.

PROTOZOA SLOWING AGENTS

Detain™, available from Ward's Natural Science
Establishment, Inc.

Protoslo™, available from Carolina Biological
Supply Co.

LIVE PROTISTS

American Type Culture Collection, Carolina
Biological Supply Co.

Connecticut Valley Biological Supply Co.

Fisher Scientific

Nasco

Nebraska Scientific

Ward's Natural Science Establishment, Inc.

MODELS

Carolina Biological Supply Co.

Ward's Natural Science Establishment, Inc.

NASCO Science

Fisher Scientific

SUPPLIER ADDRESSES

Carolina Biological Supply Co., 2700 York Rd.,
Burlington, NC 27215. Tel.: 1-800-334-5551.

Connecticut Valley Biological Supply Co.,
82 Valley Rd., P.O. Box 326, Southhampton,
MA 01073. Tel.: 1-800-628-7748.

Fisher Scientific, 485 S. Frontage Rd., Burr Ridge,
IL 60521. Tel.: 1-800-955-1177. www.fishersci.com

W.A. Hatch, 1330 SW Third Ave., #703, Portland,
OR 97201-6636. Fax: 503-221-7154.
whatch@hevanet.com

Nasco, 901 Janesville Ave., Ft. Atkinson, WI
53538-0901. Tel.: 1-800-558-9595.
www.nascofa.com

Nebraska Scientific, 3823 Leavenworth St.,
Omaha, NE 68105-1180. Tel.: 1-800-228-7117.
www.nebraskascientific.com

Science Screen Report, 1000 Clint Moore Rd.,
Suite 211, Boca Raton, FL 33487-2806.
Tel.: 1-800-275-4636. www.ssrvideo.com

Sigma Chemical Co., P.O. Box 14508, St. Louis,
MO 63178. Tel. 1-800-325-8070. www.sigma-
aldrich.com

Ward's Natural Science Establishment, Inc., P.O.
Box 92912, Rochester, NY 14692-9012. Tel. 1-800-
982-2660. www.wardsci.com